Religion at the Edge

Edited by Paul Bramadat,
Patricia O'Connell Killen, and
Sarah Wilkins-Laflamme

Religion
at the Edge

Nature, Spirituality, and Secularity
in the Pacific Northwest

UBC Press · Vancouver · Toronto

31 30 29 28 27 26 25 24 23 22   5 4 3 2 1

Printed in Canada on FSC-certified ancient-forest-free paper (100% post-consumer recycled) that is processed chlorine- and acid-free.

Library and Archives Canada Cataloguing in Publication

Title: Religion at the edge : nature, spirituality, and secularity in the Pacific Northwest / edited by Paul Bramadat, Patricia O'Connell Killen, and Sarah Wilkins-Laflamme.

Names: Bramadat, Paul, editor. | Killen, Patricia O'Connell, editor. | Wilkins-Laflamme, Sarah, editor.

Identifiers: Canadiana (print) 20210364815 | Canadiana (ebook) 20210364947 | ISBN 9780774867627 (hardcover) | ISBN 9780774867634 (paperback) | ISBN 9780774867641 (PDF) | ISBN 9780774867658 (EPUB)

Subjects: LCSH: Northwest, Pacific – Religion. | LCSH: Spirituality – Northwest, Pacific. | LCSH: Irreligion – Northwest, Pacific.

Classification: LCC BL2527.P3 R45 2022 | DDC 200.9795 – dc23

Canadä

UBC Press gratefully acknowledges the financial support for our publishing program of the Government of Canada (through the Canada Book Fund), the Canada Council for the Arts, and the British Columbia Arts Council.

This book has been published with the help of a grant from the Canadian Federation for the Humanities and Social Sciences, through the Awards to Scholarly Publications Program, using funds provided by the Social Sciences and Humanities Research Council of Canada, and with the help of the University of British Columbia through the K.D. Srivastava Fund.

Printed and bound in Canada by Friesens
Set in Aladdin and Garamond by Artegraphica Design Co.
Copy editor: Lesley Erickson
Proofreader: Judith Earnshaw
Cartographer: Eric Leinberger
Cover designer: George Kirkpatrick

UBC Press
The University of British Columbia
2029 West Mall
Vancouver, BC V6T 1Z2
www.ubcpress.ca

Contents

Acknowledgments

This project followed the process commonly used at the Centre for Studies in Religion and Society (CSRS) at the University of Victoria when putting together an edited volume: authors meet twice, engage seriously with colleagues' draft chapters, and submit final versions that evidence a significant amount of interaction with other contributors' ideas. This process can be a difficult one, but it ideally results in a volume that readers experience not as a collection of disparate essays but as the product of an organic conversation among peers who approach an important intellectual phenomenon in a coherent manner. We would like to thank our authors – from both sides of the national border and from several disciplines – for their willingness to engage in this long but rewarding process.

We would also like to thank Rachel Brown and Noriko Prezeau of the CSRS. Both provided invaluable assistance in keeping our project on track, our authors in communication, and our drafts in order.

Chelsea Horton served as the project's research coordinator as well as a close collaborator on interviews, fieldwork, survey research, data management, and ethics protocols. She and Paul Bramadat travelled quite a long road together – both literally and figuratively – for this project, and she never ceased to impress with her good humour, professionalism, sound judgement, and intellectual acumen. Her organization of the data made it easily accessible to our authors. Thanks, also, to James Wellman of the University of Washington for hosting our second team meeting in Seattle in 2019.

We would also like to express our gratitude to the Survey Research Centre at the University of Waterloo (https://uwaterloo.ca/survey-research-centre/) for its key role in the Pacific Northwest Social Survey (PNSS) data collection and cleaning in 2017. More broadly, we offer a big thank you to all of the research teams that made their survey data available and open access over the years – survey data that we used in this book to complement our own. They include notably the teams at American National Election Studies, Canadian Election Studies, Canadian National Household Survey, Pew Religious Landscape Survey, as well as American and Canadian General Social Surveys and Census.

At the UBC Press, we would like to thank James MacNevin, Megan Brand, and Brit Schottelius for guiding us so capably through the proposal, contract, and editing processes. We benefitted as well from the feedback of peer reviewers and senior colleagues at UBC Press; the volume in your hands is better for their labours.

Our participants – in the survey, interviews, focus groups, and oral histories – were most generous with their insights into this fascinating region. The data we collected from them will be used by other scholars and students for decades to come and for that we are very grateful.

We submitted this manuscript a scant number of days after the murder of George Floyd, amid an energized racial justice movement, a global pandemic, and an accelerating climate crisis. In interpreting the relationships among nature, spirituality, and secularity in the Pacific Northwest, *Religion at the Edge* endeavours to shed light on the region and to contribute to a much larger conversation about how "things religious" relate to the many challenges facing all living things on this planet. Finally, then, we want to thank you, our readers. As interlocutors, your constructive criticisms and extended insights will advance a consequential conversation.

Religion at the Edge

Introduction: Religion, Spirituality, and Irreligion in The Best Place on Earth

PAUL BRAMADAT

The BC government used "Beautiful British Columbia" and "Super, Natural British Columbia" on licence plates, T-shirts, and letterhead for years. However, in 2007, the government registered a new logo and announced that the province would be known as "The Best Place on Earth."

Although the phrase might strike some readers as an example of hubris, it did nonetheless capture a common impression among many residents of Oregon, Washington, and British Columbia, a region sometimes called the "Pacific Northwest" or "Cascadia." The region's dense forests, abundant wildlife, rugged coast, soaring mountains, and mild climate seem to call for superlatives. Its urban environments are also well known for their robust economies, cosmopolitanism, and quirky "you do you" openness.[1] When the "Best Place on Earth" slogan began to appear on licence plates in British Columbia, one could almost hear the sighs from people across the country and even from more modest

FIGURE I.I   BC licence plate. *The License Plate Shack (plateshack.com)*

residents. Not everyone thought the branding exercise was in poor taste: between 2007 and 2011, almost 200,000 of my neighbours paid an additional fee to trumpet our province's pre-eminence.[2]

The relaxed ethos, beauty, and verdant environment of Cascadia also drew my small family to "the garden city" of Victoria on Vancouver Island (a ninety-minute ferry trip southwest of the city of Vancouver) in 2008. We drove 2,400 kilometres (about 1,500 miles) from virtually the centre of the continent to a large island off the far west coast of the continent, from one of the most in-hospitable climates on the planet (Winnipeg, Manitoba) to one of the most enviable. When we arrived, we understood that we had entered a very distinctive terrain. While I had visited the region many times and had read about the society and culture that had emerged out of two centuries of contact between Indigenous peoples, European settlers, and more recent newcomers from all over the world, there was something strange about this place that I could not quite name. Over more than a decade, as I travelled throughout Cascadia and immersed myself in the academic literature on its character, some of its mysteries remained, even as I have felt more and more at home.[3]

The configuration of religion, spirituality, and secularity characteristic of the Cascadian landscape struck me as peculiar. In particular, the states and the province that make up the Pacific Northwest are associated with very low levels of religiosity (measured in a range of ways discussed by Sarah Wilkins-Laflamme and Mark Silk in this volume) when compared to the other states and provinces in the United States and Canada. So, although the region is home to rapidly expanding Sikh, Buddhist, and Hindu communities, thriving yoga and New Age subcultures, evangelical "megachurches," and a resurgence in Indigenous culture and spirituality, one might nonetheless say that the region is also "The Most Secular Place on Earth," or at least in North America. As my colleagues and I demonstrate in this book, the truth is that the region's secularity, spiritual-ity, and openness are complicated and sometimes counterintuitive.

***

Cascadia has been imagined as distinct for a long time by settlers and deeply rooted Indigenous peoples. Consider the following two passages, separated by about 125 years. As the foundations of the new campus of the University of Washington were being built in the 1890s, Adella Parker, president of the alumni association, intoned:

> That the West should unfalteringly follow the East [of North America] in fashions and ideals would be as false and fatal as that America should obey the standards of Europe. Let the West, daring and unprejudiced, discover its own ideals and follow them. The American standard in literature and philosophy

has long been fixed by the remote East. Something wild and free, something robust and full will come out of the West and be recognized in the final American type. Under the shadow of those great mountains a distinct personality shall arise, it shall adopt other fashions, create new ideals, and generations shall justify them.[4]

Parker articulates a regional identity for elite members of settler society in late nineteenth-century Washington. In it, one can detect both the familiar trope of the region's uniqueness and the notion that the land was *terra nullius* – as though Indigenous peoples and societies were not already well established when large numbers of European settlers began to arrive in the early nineteenth century.

The second passage is a more recent effort by the Cascadia Institute to define the region using the words and images of David McCloskey, the founder of the institute and the creator of the widely circulated map of the bioregion (see Figure I.2):

> The purpose of this map is to help ground people more deeply in the life of the wider place. McCloskey's new *Master Map of Cascadia* shows the natural integrity of Cascadia as a whole bioregion. Cascadia is named for the whitewaters [sic] pouring down the slopes of her mountains. Home of salmon & rivers, mountains & forests, Cascadia rises as a Great Green Land from the NE Pacific Rim. Cascadia curves from coast to crest – from the Pacific Ocean on the west, to the Rocky Mountains and Continental Divide on the east. On the seafloor Cascadia ranges from the Mendocino Fracture Zone on the south, to the Aleutian Trench in the corner of the Gulf of Alaska on the north ...
>
> This new small blue and green map of Cascadia ... shows *a real place, not an abstract nor ideal space.* The life of our bioregion has been obscured, split up by boundaries and separated into categories, the matrix disremembered. *This map reveals something important that has long remained invisible – namely, the integrality of the bioregion we are calling "Cascadia." This map provides a portrait of home.* (Cascadia Institute, n.d., emphasis added)

In both passages, observe the passionate, wistful rhetoric, meant not merely to situate the region on an existing map but also to convey what one might call the *geist,* the spirit of the place that exists in time and space but also, perhaps most profoundly, in shared stories. The emphasis in the second passage on water – both cascading down mountains and covering ancient, submerged topographies – evokes the scale and majesty of the region.

Cascadia is sometimes identified with the political borders of states, provinces, and countries; others imagine the region in utopian or dystopian ways;

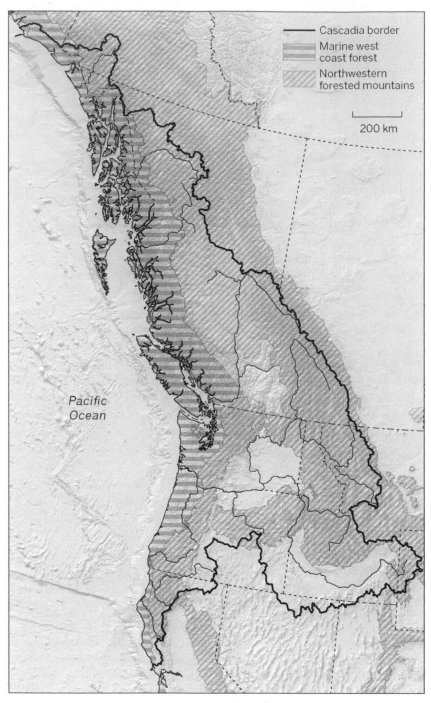

FIGURE I.2   Cascadia, 2014. *By David McCloskey and adapted by Eric Leinberger*

some visions of the Pacific Northwest emerge from traditional Indigenous resource use and kinship systems; and some perspectives are characterized by industrial-scale resource extraction and trade patterns. The Pacific Northwest is a palimpsest: simultaneously material, imaginary, political, metaphorical, and mysterious, often resisting human efforts to control or contain it. This was expressed well during our fieldwork in the summer of 2018 when focus-group participants in Seattle were asked to define what (or where) Cascadia was. Alluding to the way sockeye salmon shape the region's environmental history, Andrew replied to our question: "I will defer to the fish." His modest definition simultaneously expressed an *empirical* reality, since fish cannot travel upstream beyond the mountains that mark the boundary of the watershed; a *cultural* reality, one that reflects the importance of salmon within the region (Crawford O'Brien 2014); and even, perhaps, a *spiritual* reality or attitude I think of as "reverential naturalism" (see Chapter 1). These multiple ways of delineating and thinking about the region are in tension but not mutually exclusive and are also indicative of broader discourses of power, nationalism, capitalism, secularism, and the meaning of land. Our task is to look seriously at the way these forces interact in this region.

At the outset, I should reflect on the common English names for the region. For the sake of convenience, in this book we sometimes use "Pacific Northwest" and "Cascadia" as though they are synonymous, although, in fact, the two terms have slightly different connotations. In practice, the term "Pacific Northwest" tends to be used more descriptively and dispassionately, while "Cascadia" is generally invoked in reference to what we might consider the affective and imaginative "project" associated with the region. However, it is valuable to note that although "Pacific Northwest" is by far the most widely used term in academic and public conversations about and within the region, it is technically inaccurate. After all, most Canadians in the region live in what is, for them, the Pacific *Southwest*. Moreover, the American component of the watershed system includes most of Idaho and very small parts of California, Alaska, Montana, Nevada, and Wyoming that are separated from the Pacific Ocean by areas that are not obviously influenced by what many people would think of as the culture, aesthetics, and ecology of the Pacific Northwest. The terms "Pacific Northwest" and "Cascadia" are often associated simply with the entire states of Oregon and Washington and the province of British Columbia; that practice itself is also somewhat arbitrary since parts of southern Oregon and most of northeastern British Columbia are not part of the larger watershed that most commentators associate with the bioregion. Nonetheless, while we acknowledge the ambiguities of these terms, we generally use as our analytical frame of reference for the region the areas of the watershed that fall within the borders of these two states and one province.

Maps, of course, do not tell the whole story. It is by now virtually a truism that "the map is not the territory it represents" (Korzybski 1933); the land to which people and stories become attached is rarely captured definitively by national, state, county, or city borders. Cascadia exemplifies what Edward Said (1978) called an imagined geography and what Benedict Anderson (1983) would have described as an imagined community, a place and a people not simply discovered as distinct but constructed as distinct by its residents and visitors. For Said, territories and regions emerge discursively as products of political and cultural forces. For Anderson, nations (and other human communities) arise when individuals who would otherwise appreciate their heterogeneity come to feel as though they are members of an indivisible group. The feeling is crucial; even though, obviously, not every Russian, African American, Muslim, or Pacific Northwesterner is equally attached to or defined by their respective imagined communities and the geographies to which these acts of imagination are attached, these human communities are well defined by affectively rich narratives of belonging.

To the extent that we can consider people in the Pacific Northwest as belonging to something like a Cascadian imagined community, its members are bound not by common class, ethnic, or even national narratives, but rather a common story about their relationship to one another and – perhaps principally – to the natural environment in which they are embedded. However, geography is not destiny; all acts of geographical imagination occur against the backdrop of political and historical factors. In this book, we are interested in the ways religion, irreligion, and spirituality are imagined within a region that is both a particular space (i.e., with certain objective physical features) and a storied place (i.e., with the memories, meanings, and values individuals and communities inscribe into spaces as they inhabit them).

In what remains, I discuss the project's methodology, the social processes readers might bear in mind when thinking about Cascadia, and the key claims in the chapters that follow.

Project Design

I am grateful that after over a decade of reflecting on the particularities of this place, I have encountered peers who share my appetite for a consideration of the region's religious, spiritual, and secular landscape that updates and extends existing studies (see Killen and Silk 2004; Todd 2008). In this book, an interdisciplinary team of US and Canadian scholars approach three key research themes: the social implications of secularization in the region; the differences between the Canadian and US "sides" of this bioregion; and the barriers that might exist for traditional and usually conservative believers living in a postinstitutional liberal environment. While these three considerations inform the project as a whole, each author also deals with empirical and theoretical issues related to their own academic interests and with matters (such as the concerns of Indigenous people in the US and Canada) that became more central considerations during fieldwork.

The whole team met in Victoria in 2017 and roughly a year and a half later in Seattle to discuss a broad set of themes and also to share and critique draft chapters, data sources, and approaches. To address our three fundamental and many emergent questions, we combined research methods commonly found in the fields of religious studies, sociology, history, and anthropology. We began by conducting a major literature review of the existing theoretical and empirical research on religion, irreligion, and spirituality in the region. This review was augmented throughout the project. Related to this, we also compiled an archive of historical materials (studies from and about religious groups, newspaper reports about religion and also by religious groups, public policies related to immigration and diversity, etc.).[5]

These forms of data helped to shape the Pacific Northwest Social Survey (PNSS), led by Sarah Wilkins-Laflamme and the University of Waterloo's Survey Research Centre. The PNSS was administered online from mid-September to mid-October 2017 and included fifty-four questions on respondent's sociodemographic characteristics; religious, irreligious, and spiritual affiliations; beliefs and practices; friendship networks; and social and inclusivity attitudes (Wilkins-Laflamme 2018). This data was collected from 1,510 adult respondents nineteen years or older residing in British Columbia, Washington, or Oregon at the time of the survey. Respondents completed a web questionnaire and were recruited through Léger's professional online panel of registered members (leger360.com). Age, gender, and regional quotas were applied during the selection of respondents, and poststratification weights were used during the statistical analyses to make this sample representative of the adult Pacific Northwest population in general.

In addition, we also benefitted from a convenience sample consisting of 841 additional respondents, most of whom were associated with the personal and professional networks of the scholars in the research team. These respondents were contacted through email, social media, posters, and personal interactions, and they were asked to complete the same survey.[6] We then created two focus groups for each of the four featured cities (Victoria, Vancouver, Seattle, and Portland). Groups ranged from five to nine participants. In each city, one group consisted of regular religious adherents (most of whom had no formal training in religion), and the other group consisted specifically of religious, spiritual, or irreligious millennials (defined in this study as individuals born between 1987 and 1996). Each of these two-hour-long focus-group discussions occurred in non-religious public spaces (libraries, credit unions, the Centre for Studies in Religion and Society [CSRS], and a coworking facility).

In these four cities, the principal investigator (myself) and research coordinator (Chelsea Horton) conducted semistructured interviews with religious and community leaders. One coinvestigator (Lynne Marks) and the research coordinator and research assistant (Horton and Taylor Antoniazzi) conducted semistructured oral-history interviews with families and individuals with relatively long histories in the region. Transcripts from our focus groups, leader interviews, and oral histories reveal strong thematic commonalities that both confirm and expand on the existing literature, the PNSS, the archive we created, and the personal experiences of many of the team members who are also residents.

Our data combines the scientific rigour of a professional survey, the benefits of careful archival research, and the unique insights that emerge out of often intimate conversations with individuals and groups. The authors of the chapters that follow were free to use this large and novel data pool in their own ways; this common research resource links the chapters in a way that is uncommon in books involving scholars from a variety of academic backgrounds. In the interest of simplicity, when referring to a comment from our interviews and focus groups, we identify the speakers (pseudonyms in all cases) and the context in which they were speaking (i.e., focus groups with millennials or nonclergy religious adherents, interviews with religious leaders, or oral-history interviews). All interviews took place in the first six months of 2018. To stimulate further research and discussion, anonymized transcripts of these interviews and focus groups will be made available to the public two years after the publication of this book.[7]

I should observe that our archival work, literature reviews, survey, and other forms of data concern all of Oregon, Washington, and British Columbia. However, for practical reasons, we decided to conduct our interviews and focus groups in the region's four major metropolitan areas – Victoria, Vancouver, Seattle, and Portland – where roughly 85 percent of the region's residents live.[8] We anticipate that future field research will provide useful insights into the differences between residents of the densely populated corridor on the "western slope" of Cascadia, roughly between Eugene (Oregon) and North Vancouver (British Columbia) and those relatively understudied groups and individuals in other parts of Cascadia. Moreover, because of their small numbers in the region as a whole, African Americans did not feature prominently in our professionally weighted survey or our interviews, but their real and symbolic importance in the region – especially in Cascadia South – became more obvious in the wake of Black Lives Matter protests in and around Seattle and Portland in 2020.

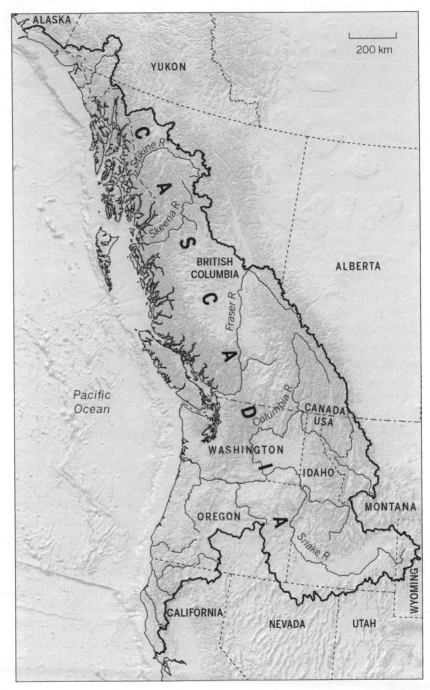

FIGURE I.3   Cascadia, with borders. *By Lauren Tierney, adapted by Eric Leinberger from original on Wikipedia*

Cascadia: Context and Categories

Although our research and previous work demonstrate that the border does make a significant difference in the ways the region is imagined, a fairly identifiable mood, attitude, or orientation has emerged out of 150 years of colonial settlement, economic development, political contestation, and the physical and psychological distance between the Pacific Northwest and the main urban centres of the continent (Albanese 1990; Bunting 1997; Crawford O'Brien 2014; Dunlap 2004; Ferguson and Tamburello 2015; Goodenough 1998; O'Connell 2003; Robbins 2001; Shibley 2011; Wolf, Mitchell, and Schoonmaker 1995). As Andrew Engelson, the Seattle-based editor of *Cascadia Magazine* put it in 2019: "Cascadia really does have a sense of identity you don't find anywhere else in North America ... You don't find much cross-border identity between, say, New England and Quebec. Here, there's a sense of shared culture that I think is unique and worth investigating" (Cheung 2019).

Generally, one can observe four main trajectories of religious development in Cascadia. While these four paths are evident in other regions and societies (Killen and Silk 2004; Bramadat and Koenig 2009; Beaman and Beyer 2008; Beyer and Ramji 2013; Levitt 2007; Diana Eck's Pluralism Project, pluralism. org), they interact in distinctive ways in the Pacific Northwest. These four trajectories tell us a great deal about what I think of as the Cascadia consensus, the almost taken-for-granted culture of the region.

First, although religious monopolies and oligarchies have existed in a number of places in North America, the Pacific Northwest region may have been "born secular" (Marks 2007, 371; see also Clarke and Macdonald 2017; Thiessen 2015) at least in the sense that the nineteenth-century Anglican, Presbyterian, Lutheran, and Catholic churches never achieved as strong a foothold in the region as elsewhere in Canada and the United States. This might help to explain the relative prominence of Cascadia's religious Nones (i.e., people who tell pollsters they have "no religion") when compared with other regions in Canada and the United States. To be clear, very few of these people are atheists in the formal sense of believing firmly that there is no God; they are generally, and rather more amorphously, people who, for a variety of reasons, are not comfortable associating with any formal religious identity or institution.[9]

As readers will observe in Sarah Wilkins-Laflamme's chapter and the two reports she produced for our study, according to the 2011 Canadian National Household Survey, 44 percent of British Columbians do not identify with any religious tradition, compared with only 20 percent in the rest of Canada. South of the border, in the relatively more religious United States, 32 percent of residents in Washington and Oregon identified as religious Nones in the 2014 Pew Religious Landscape Study, compared with 23 percent for the country as a whole.[10]

In our project's 2017 PNSS, 49 percent of British Columbians indicated they had no religious affiliation, whereas 44 percent of the US sample made the same claim. While the "no religion" cohort is growing rapidly throughout Europe and North America, the preponderance of this option in the Cascadia bioregion is quite significant. Although scholars continue to ask questions about exactly what it means for someone to report on a survey that they have no religion (Thiessen 2015; Zuckerman 2015), as the saying goes, these numbers do not mean nothing. The popularity of the "no religion" self-description in the Pacific Northwest is certainly an important indicator of the distinctiveness of the region (Barman 1996; Block 2016; Killen 2004; Marks 2016; Todd 2008; Wellman 2002; Zuckerman 2015).[11]

The second trajectory consists of the small and shrinking number of liberal or mainline Christian communities in the region. Although Christianity was never formally established in Cascadia, until the middle of the twentieth century its leaders could nonetheless have confidence that they could speak to and be heard by the dominant society or at the very least by their own stable congregations (Block 2010, 2016; Burkinshaw 1995; Clarke and Macdonald 2017; Killen and Silk 2004; Marks 2016; Wellman 2002; Wellman and Corcoran 2013). The decline in these conventional forms of Christianity in this region – especially in the last several decades – is, in fact, one of the more remarkable transitions in North American religious history and one that continues to intrigue scholars (Block 2016; Killen and Silk 2004; Klassen 2018; Marks 2016; Wellman 2008). Although the declines evident in membership, identification, and participation in most liberal Christian groups on both sides of the border in the past fifty years have produced a discernible "discourse of loss" (Bramadat and Seljak 2009; Clarke and Macdonald 2017) in these groups, some of the questions that remain regarding the specific ways the communities have responded to their new position in the region will be explored by Patricia O'Connell Killen (Chapter 7), James K. Wellman Jr. and Katie Corcoran (Chapter 8), and Michael Wilkinson (Chapter 9) in this volume.

While the relatively high number of Nones and the declining strength of mainline Christian denominations in Cascadia have attracted some media and academic attention, an equally interesting feature of this region is the third trajectory, which is the growth of relatively conservative communities of Christian and non-Christian backgrounds. This is the trajectory about which the least has been written (Block 2016, 172; Thiessen and Wilkins-Laflamme 2017; Wellman 2008; Wellman, Corcoran, and Stockly 2020). On the one hand, both new and traditional forms of Protestantism ranging from evangelicalism to Pentecostalism to fundamentalism have had success at responding to the needs of those for whom conventional denominational settings are not appealing. Several of these groups are oriented toward millennial Cascadians, which makes the phenomenon quite intriguing since that is also the group among whom "no religion" is such a common selection on surveys (Burkinshaw 1995; Pressnell and Henderson 2008; Wellman, Corcoran, and Stockly 2020; Wilkins-Laflamme 2017, 2018; PNSS 2017). On the other hand, non-Christian groups – especially Muslims, Buddhists, Sikhs, and Hindus – have grown markedly (most obviously in the Vancouver and Seattle areas), largely due to immigration, and their average age is lower than the surrounding society. When compared with the dominant ethos of Cascadia, many non-Christian (and nonliberal Christian) religious communities embrace more traditional views on gender roles and sexual ethics, recreational drug use, generational hierarchies, scripture, and individualism. The tensions that sometimes emerge between their own youth and the broader and increasingly liberal culture that typifies the region is discussed by Rachel Brown in this volume (Chapter 10) (Beyer and Ramji 2013; Smith and Snell 2009).

Finally, Cascadia has long been and continues to be home to a fascinating and dynamic array of religious and spiritual forms, which people have arguably been freer to adopt, adapt, or ignore than possibly anywhere else. In the fourth trajectory, we see an openness to experimentation, usually without any significant concern about the social, personal, familial, or occupational costs of such efforts. As I suggested earlier, in the Pacific Northwest we can see ongoing interest in what we might call religious or spiritual seeking in activities ranging from mindfulness groups in Seattle, to evangelical churches in Vancouver, to gurdwaras in Victoria, to Buddhist temples in Portland, to roughly twenty places of worship on the specially zoned "highway to heaven" in Richmond, British Columbia, to yoga centres in virtually every city and town.[12] The point is that it is probably fair to speculate (see chapters by Killen, Bramadat, Wilkins-Laflamme, and Block and Marks) that the social costs one might have to pay to adopt an unfamiliar or eclectic religious or spiritual path have probably never been lower – or none at all – than they are now in Cascadia. Indeed, there is a pervasive "you do you" ethos in the region, and residents, in general, enjoy tacit permission to seek meaning and purpose from a myriad of sources.

A Complex Consensus
Although these four trajectories are probably the most common way to organize the religious, spiritual, and irreligious phenomena of the region, three important additional observations must be made. First, throughout this book, it will become clear why commentators and residents alike point to the centrality of the natural world in the available data about religion and spirituality in the region (Crawford O'Brien 2014; Killen and Silk 2004; Todd 2008) and muse about the relationship between an increasing attachment to nature and a general

loosening of ties to conventional religious forms.[13] Regarding the second possibility, some studies situate the dominant story about contemporary religious change (especially secularization) within the context of attitudes toward the natural world and that provides context for the rise of what I call "reverential naturalism" in Chapter 1 of this volume. The sociologists Todd Fergusson and Jeffrey Tamburello (2015, 296), for example, argue that "the resources of an area's land and climate are its natural amenities. Mountains, hills, lakes, beaches, and pleasant weather all contribute to the look and feel of a region. Although they are a part of the physical landscape, natural amenities have profound social impacts on a region. They attract population growth, generate tourism, and increase economic development" (see also Wellman and Corcoran 2013).

In an interesting exercise, these scholars assign different "natural amenities" scores to all American counties. They find that if you map this scale onto a conventional map, with a few exceptions, the counties with the most favourable scores are mostly on the West Coast. Then they determine how natural-amenities scores seem to be correlated with each county's level of religiosity, as measured in all of the standard ways. It turns out that the lovelier your county's natural environment, the lower the likelihood that religion will be a strong feature of your community. This is not to suggest simply that residents of these counties have better things to do than to be involved in religious institutions. The other possibility is that in a place and time in which conventional religious institutions are less and less salient or more and more problematized, the natural world itself may be experienced and storied as a site for being religious or spiritual, whatever those categories might mean to people. The approach to the natural world – and spirituality – that seems characteristic of the region will be addressed in Chapter 1, where I suggest that scholars interested in religion in this part of North America may need to account for reverential naturalism.

Second, this region was categorically not *terra nullius* when settlers arrived. Indigenous communities have lived here for millennia and have well-established political, legal, aesthetic, cultural, and spiritual traditions that have survived centuries of catastrophic epidemics (such as smallpox, which in places killed up to 90 percent of Indigenous populations) and mistreatment and misrecognition from the dominant settler societies on both sides of the border (Harris 1997; Diamond 1997; Lutz 2007; Taylor 2007). Among the large number of Indigenous communities in the Pacific Northwest, one often sees creative tension among the forces of syncretism, revitalization, and assimilationist orientations. The "Indigenous fact" of the region is more apparent and politically salient in Canada, where, for a variety of reasons (discussed by Chelsea Horton in this volume), these communities now have an unprecedented opportunity to address historical mistreatment and seek a new way forward.

Third, it is also important to note that non-Indigenous ethnic and religious minorities contribute to the success of the region in ways that are rarely acknowledged. In particular, the growth in populations of Asian, African American, African, Latino, and Middle Eastern minority communities is a harbinger of the future in the region's urban spaces (with Seattle and Victoria and, finally, Portland eventually demonstrating this type of diversification).[14] According to 2016 Canadian census data, this diversity is dramatically evident in Vancouver, where over half the city's inhabitants belong to what the Canadian government calls the "visible minority" category, with some large suburbs – such as Richmond – consisting of roughly two-thirds visible-minority populations (Carman 2017).[15]

Today's rich and generally peaceable expressions of diversity in cities such as Vancouver and Seattle might be featured prominently in branding exercises, but they should not distract us from a dark history. Until the latter part of the twentieth century in Canada and the United States, Asian and other racialized citizens faced bitter discrimination. Consider the *Komogata Maru* incident in 1914 (named after the ship of the same name) that forced Hindu and Sikh migrants to sail back to Asia even though they had not contravened any laws or policies in their voyage to British Columbia; or the clause in Oregon's constitution that simply banned "negros" and "mulattos" from living in the state altogether until 1926, which is, of course, one of the reasons for the relatively low number of African Americans (and the forms of Protestantism with which they are often associated) in the state and region today and perhaps one of the reasons for the dramatic Black Lives Matter protests in Portland, Oregon, in 2020; or the internment of Canadian and American citizens of Japanese descent living near the Pacific Coast during the Second World War (Stanger-Ross and Sugiman 2017); or the expulsion of the Chinese from Seattle and Tacoma in the wake of the United States passing the Chinese Exclusion Act of 1882; or the discrimination faced by Victoria's Chinese community, who had to purchase a separate plot of land to bury their dead (Lai 2005); or widespread anxieties about the health threat posed by South Asian newcomers across the region (Wallace 2016). These minority communities suffered flagrant racism at the hands of many white neighbours, even though the often-exploited labour of the former was indispensable for the economic success of the latter.

The point is not simply that people suffered to facilitate the affluence, stability, and liberalism many identify with the region. Of course, this did happen, but other social and political orders (e.g., the so-called Washington Consensus, the European Union, the post-1947 partitioned South Asian subcontinent, the North American Free Trade zone, the United Nations, etc.) also created deep and unresolved grievances. The broader point I would make is that the generally common – not homogenous, of course, but familiar – perspective one finds especially in the urban centres on the western side of Cascadia is and has always been part of a *political* project. To put it another way, there is nothing natural about the way people speak about the natural and social spheres of the Pacific Northwest. Indigenous, settler, African American, and newcomer Cascadians live within long-term political projects. This is not to say that the outcomes of these politics have been entirely negative but rather, more simply, that the consensus we do find here is as much a social construction and artifice of history, politics, and economics as any other well-established narrative (e.g., those related to the emergence of "Christendom," the Muslim "ummah," or the "Middle Ages"). For these reasons, it is understandable that racialized minorities sometimes resent the sepia hue cast on the region's history and epitomized by branding efforts such as the "Best Place on Earth" licence-plate campaign. They may well ask: "Best place for whom, and since when?"

***

On the western slope of the Pacific Northwest region, the temperate climate, stunning natural environment, cosmopolitanism, and robust economy make for an unusual region, or at least a region different from many other imagined geographies. The Pacific Northwest is almost famously secular or postinstitutional in the simple sense that conventional religion has less and less public presence and taken-for-granted influence in the lives of people. Indeed, those of us who have taught in the region as well as elsewhere on the continent can attest to the relatively high number of undergraduate and graduate students in our programs who identify as Nones or perhaps "spiritual but not religious" and who have parents and in some cases grandparents who were also raised outside of formal religious communities. This is relatively rare elsewhere in North America. It is therefore not surprising that Cascadia is sometimes framed not only as the best place on earth but also as the most secular, or postinstitutional, place on earth. The superlatives do not tell the whole story, of course. While empirical evidence from the last several decades demonstrates a shift away from institutional religiosity, our data also suggest that only critical treatment of claims about Cascadia's secularity will lead to a full understanding of the complexity of the social changes in the region.

Although it is always dangerous to offer predictions, our qualitative and quantitative research suggests that Cascadia may be at the leading edge of what is arguably an epoch-making change in the roles of religion and spirituality in contemporary society (see Mark Silk's chapter in this volume; Brown 2012; Casanova 2006; Chandler 2008; Davie 1994; Heelas and Woodhead 2005; Hervieu-Léger 2006; Meyer et al. 1997; Taylor 2007). As Arthur, one of our oral-history participants, put it, "Somebody told [my family] that the Pacific Northwest was the land of tomorrow," a reflection that says something both about the past and perhaps the future of the region. While the prospects do not look very promising for many of the larger Christian denominations, there are signs of innovation in other communities and movements in Cascadia that will benefit from additional scrutiny. As well, as I contend in Chapter 1, there is evidence here of a reverential approach to the natural world that is not unique to Cascadia but can be seen quite distinctly here perhaps precisely because the dominant ethos has become so definitively identified with postinstitutionalism. In the chapters that follow, the focus is on the current state of religion, spirituality, and irreligion in the Pacific Northwest, but there are clear implications in our volume for our broader understanding of the nature and future of religion in a secular era.

Notes

1   This consensus is clearly conveyed in the popular TV comedy *Portlandia* (2011–18), which plays on stereotypes about the hipsters, hippies, hackers, and slackers who help to "keep Portland weird" (Samson 2011, 98); the nickname "Vansterdam," which is used to connote Vancouver's relatively open approach to sex and drugs; the nickname "Emerald City," that refers not only to Seattle's forests and waterways but also to its kinship with the mythical land of Oz; and the "best coast" and "Left Coast" catchphrases, which are used to capture the spirit of the region.

2   The provincial population is approximately 4.8 million. According to a representative of the British Columbia Insurance Corporation, the plates were available between 2007–11 and cost 35 dollars to purchase and an additional 25 dollars a year to retain. A driver who chose these plates and licensed a vehicle for ten years would spend 285 dollars (Mackin 2011).

3   It is also important to observe that Cascadia is home to dark portents such as the Oregon militia, the wide-spread practices of fish farming and clear-cutting forests, devastating forest fires during most summers, pockets of vaccine rejection and hesitancy, extremely expensive housing in the two largest cities (Seattle and Vancouver), a long history of racism in housing and labour, and entrenched drug and homelessness crises in several of the cities (most alarmingly in the Downtown Eastside of Vancouver).

4   "With Due Formality," *Seattle Telegraph*, July 5, 1894.

5   See https://www.uvic.ca/research/centres/csrs/.

6   There were minor alterations to the wording of some of the questions to accommodate the different samples. Most of the statistical analyses in this book exclude this second convenience sample of 841 respondents to make the sample more representative of the general adult population. However, when minority groups in Cascadia are explored in more detail with the survey data, the Léger sample is sometimes complemented with more respondents from the convenience sample.

7   See the website of the Centre for Studies in Religion and Society at the University of Victoria: https://www.uvic.ca/research/centres/csrs/.

8   The exception to this pattern is a small number of oral-history interviews conducted outside of these four cities.

9   In the PNSS, only 7 percent of Canadian participants and 8 percent of US participants identified as atheists, humanists, or secularists, whereas the vast majority of the "no religion" cohorts indicated they were agnostics, spiritual but not religious, or nothing in particular.

10 See Killen and Silk (2004), Block (2016), and Marks (2016). See also chapters in this volume by Tina Block and Lynne Marks (Chapter 4), Mark Silk (Chapter 6), Patricia O'Connell

Killen (Chapter 7), James Wellman and Katie Corcoran (Chapter 8), and Michael Wilkinson (Chapter 9), in which these statistics are engaged directly.

11 I would like to thank Sarah Wilkins-Laflamme for help with the statistics that appear in this chapter.

12 Of course, scholars and lay people alike sometimes cast aspersions on the ways in which people on the West Coast adopt – in highly selective and often essentializing manners – aspects of Asian religions, such as mindfulness and the many variants of yoga on offer in the spiritual marketplace (Bramadat 2019; Jain 2014). However, in this book we are not seeking to determine the "authenticity" of religious or spiritual practices.

13 A great many books have been written on the role of the natural world in the broader Canadian national narrative. One of the classic observations on this interaction was made by W.L. Morton (1961, 5), who noted that the "alternative penetration of the wilderness and return to civilization is the basic rhythm of Canadian life."

14 Throughout this book, we strive for consistency in the language we use to name the communities we discuss. We are, nonetheless, aware both that US and Canadian societies often use different categories (e.g., "visible minority" in Canada as opposed to "racial minority" in the United States) and that all these categories are subject to flux and may be replaced by new terms (e.g., LatinX, LGBTQI).

15 In Canada, a "visible minority" is a non-Indigenous person who is "non-Caucasian" in race and "nonwhite" in colour. It is important to note that each country uses its own categories to determine visible minority (in Canada) or racial (in the United States) identification. The differences make it difficult to compare and contrast the data.

References

Albanese, C.L. 1990. *Nature Religion in America: From the Algonkian Indians to the New Age.* Chicago: University of Chicago Press.

Anderson, Benedict. 1983. *Imagined Communities: Reflections on the Origin and Spread of Nationalism.* London: Verso.

Beaman, Lori, and Peter Beyer, eds. 2008. *Religion and Diversity in Canada.* Leiden: Brill.

Barman, Jean. 1996. *The West beyond the West: A History of British Columbia.* Toronto: University of Toronto Press.

Beyer, Peter, and Rubina Ramji, eds. 2013. *Growing up Canadian: Muslims, Hindus, Buddhists.* Montreal/Kingston: McGill-Queen's University Press.

Block, Tina. 2010. "Religion, Irreligion, and the Difference Place Makes: The Case of the Postwar Pacific Northwest." *Social History* 43 (85): 1–30.

–. 2016. *The Secular Northwest: Religion and Irreligion in Everyday Postwar Life.* Vancouver: UBC Press.

Bramadat, Paul. 2019. "A Bridge Too Far: Yoga, Spirituality, and Contested Space in the Pacific Northwest." *Religion, State and Society* 47 (4): 491–507.

Bramadat, Paul, and Matthias Koenig, eds. 2009. *International Migration and the Governance of Religious Diversity.* Kingston: School of Policy Studies, Queen's University/McGill-Queen's University Press.

Bramadat, Paul, and David Seljak, eds. 2005. *Religion and Ethnicity in Canada.* Toronto: Pearson.

–, eds. 2008. *Christianity and Ethnicity in Canada.* Toronto: University of Toronto Press.

Brown, Callum G. 2012. *Religion and the Demographic Revolution: Women and Secularisation in Canada, Ireland, UK and USA since the 1960s.* Studies in Modern British Religious History, 29. Woodbridge: Boydell Press.

Bunting, Robert. 1997. *The Pacific Raincoast: Environment and Culture in an American Eden, 1778–1900.* Lawrence: University Press of Kansas.

Burkinshaw, Robert. 1995. *Pilgrims in Lotusland: Conservative Protestantism in British Columbia 1917–1981.* Montreal: McGill-Queen's University Press.

Carman, Tara. 2017. "Visible Minorities Now the Majority in 5 B.C. Cities." *CBC News,* October 27. https://www.cbc.ca/news/canada/british-columbia/visible-minorities-now -the-majority-in-5-b-c-cities-1.4375858.

Casanova, J. 2006. "Rethinking Secularization: A Global Comparative Perspective." *Hedgehog Review* 8 (1/2): 7–22.

Cascadia Institute. n.d. "Purpose and Invitation." *Cascadia: Land of Falling Waters.* https://cascadia-institute.org.

Chandler, Siobhan. 2008. "The Social Ethic of Religiously Unaffiliated Spirituality." *Religion Compass* 2 (2): 240–56.

Cheung, Christopher. 2019. "A Magazine to Capture the 'Shared Culture' of Cascadia: Seattle's Andrew Engelson Is Curating Stories That Make the Region Unique, Warts and All." *The Tyee,* March 26.

Clarke, Brian, and Stuart Macdonald. 2017. *Leaving Christianity: Changing Alliances in Canada since 1945.* Montreal/Kingston: McGill-Queen's University Press.

Crawford O'Brien, Suzanne. 2014. "Salmon as Sacrament: First Salmon Ceremonies in the Pacific Northwest." In *Religion, Food and Eating in North America,* edited by Benjamin E. Zeller, Marie W. Dallam, Reid L. Neilson, and Nora L. Rubel, 114–33. New York: Columbia University Press.

Davie, Grace. 1994. *Religion in Britain since 1945.* London: Blackwell.

Diamond, Jared. 1997. *Guns, Germs, and Steel: The Fates of Human Societies.* New York: W.W. Norton.

Dunlap, Thomas R. 2004. *Faith in Nature: Environmentalism as Religious Quest.* Seattle: University of Washington Press.

Ferguson, Todd W., and Jeffrey A. Tamburello. 2015. "The Natural Environment as a Spiritual Resource: A Theory of Regional Variation in Religious Adherence." *Sociology of Religion* 76 (3): 295–314.

Goodenough, Ursula. 1998. *The Sacred Depths of Nature.* New York: Oxford University Press.

Harris, Cole. 1997. *The Resettlement of British Columbia: Essays on Colonialism and Geographical Change.* Vancouver: UBC Press.

Heelas, Paul, and Linda Woodhead. 2005. *The Spiritual Revolution: Why Religion Is Giving Way to Spirituality.* Oxford: Blackwell.

Hervieu-Léger, Danièle. 2006. "The Role of Religion in Establishing Social Cohesion." *Eurozine,* August 17. https://www.eurozine.com/the-role-of-religion-in-establishing-social -cohesion/.

Jain, Andrea. 2014. *Selling Yoga: From Counterculture to Pop Culture.* New York: Oxford University Press.

Killen, Patricia O'Connell. 2004. "The Religious Geography of the Pacific Northwest." *Word and World* 24 (3): 269–78.

Killen, Patricia O'Connell, and Mark Silk, eds. 2004. *Religion and Public Life in the Pacific Northwest: The None Zone.* Walnut Creek, CA: AltaMira Press.

Klassen, Pamela E. 2018. *The Story of Radio Mind: A Missionary's Journey on Indigenous Land.* Chicago: University of Chicago Press.

Korzybski, Alfred. 1933. *Science and Sanity: An Introduction to Non-Aristotelian Systems and General Semantics.* Englewood, NJ: International Non-Aristotelian Library.

Lai, David Chuenyuan, Jordan Paper, and Li Chuang Paper. 2005. "The Chinese in Canada: Their Unrecognized Religion." In *Religion and Ethnicity in Canada,* edited by P. Bramadat and D. Seljak, 89–110.

Levitt, Peggy. 2007. *God Needs No Passport: Immigrants and the Changing American Religious Landscape.* New York: New Press.

Lutz, John, ed. 2007. *Myth and Memory: Stories of Indigenous-European Contact.* Vancouver: UBC Press.

Mackin, Bob. 2011. "BC No Longer Calls Self 'Best Place on Earth.'" *The Tyee,* October 4. https://thetyee.ca/Mediacheck/2011/10/04/BC-Best-Place-On-Earth/.

Marks, Lynne. 2007. "'Leaving God behind When They Crossed the Rocky Mountains': Exploring Unbelief in Turn-of-the-Century British Columbia." In *Household Counts: Canadian Households and Families in 1901,* edited by Peter Baskerville and Eric Sager, 371–404. Toronto: University of Toronto Press.

—. 2016. *Infidels and the Damn Churches: Irreligion and Religion in Settler British Columbia.* Vancouver: UBC Press.

Meyer, John W., John Boli, George M. Thomas, and Francisco O. Ramirez. 1997. "World Society and the Nation-State." *American Journal of Sociology* 103 (1): 144–81.

Morton, W.L. 1961. *The Canadian Identity.* Madison: University of Wisconsin Press.

O'Connell, Nicholas. 2003. *On Sacred Ground: The Spirit of Place in Pacific Northwest Literature.* Seattle: University of Washington Press.

Pressnell, Jim, and Steve Henderson. 2008. "A Center for Applied Leadership: Need and Vision with the Pacific Northwest." *Missio Apostolica* 16: 169–80.

Robbins, William G., ed. 2001. *The Great Northwest: The Search for Regional Identity.* Corvallis: Oregon State University Press.

Said, Edward. 1978. *Orientalism.* New York: Penguin Books.

Samson, Karl. 2011. *Frommer's Oregon.* Hoboken, NJ: Wiley.

Shibley, Mark A. 2011. "Sacred Nature: Earth-Based Spirituality as Popular Religion in the Pacific Northwest." *Journal for the Study of Religion, Nature and Culture* 5 (2): 164–85.

Silk, Mark, and Andrew Walsh, eds. 2004–11. Religion by Region Series. Walnut Creek, CA: AltaMira Press.

Smith, Christian, and Patricia Snell. 2009. *Souls in Transition: The Religious and Spiritual Lives of Emerging Adults.* New York: Oxford University Press.

Stanger-Ross, Jordan, and Pamela Sugiman, eds. 2017. *Witness to Loss: Race, Culpability, and Memory in the Dispossession of Japanese Canadians.* Montreal/Kingston: McGill-Queen's University Press.

Taylor, Charles. 2007. *A Secular Age.* Cambridge, MA: Belknap Press, Harvard University Press.

Thiessen, Joel. 2015. *The Meaning of Sunday: The Practice of Belief in a Secular Age.* Kingston/Montreal: McGill-Queen's University Press.

Thiessen, Joel, and Sarah Wilkins-Laflamme. 2017. "Becoming a Religious None: Irreligious Socialization and Disaffiliation." *Journal for the Scientific Study of Religion* 56 (1): 64–82.

Todd, Douglas, ed. 2008. *Cascadia: The Elusive Utopia – Exploring the Spirit of the Pacific Northwest.* Vancouver: Ronsdale Press.

Wallace, Sarah. 2016. *Not Fit to Stay: Public Health Panics and South Asian Exclusion.* Vancouver: UBC Press.

Wellman, James, and Katie Corcoran. 2013. "Religion and Regional Culture: Embedding Religious Commitment within Place." *Sociology of Religion* 74 (4): 496–520.

Wellman, James, Katie Corcoran, and Kate Stockly. 2020. *High on God: How Megachurches Won the Heart of America.* New York: Oxford University Press.

Wellman, James K. Jr. 2002. "Religion without a Net: Strictness in the Religious Practices of West Coast Urban Liberal Christian Congregations." *Review of Religious Research* 42 (2): 184–99.

—. 2008. *Evangelical vs. Liberal: The Clash of Christian Cultures in the Pacific Northwest.* New York: Oxford University Press.

Wilkins-Laflamme, Sarah. 2017. "The Religious, Spiritual, Secular and Social Landscapes of the Pacific Northwest: Part 1." *UWSpace.* http://hdl.handle.net/10012/12218.

–. 2018. "The Religious, Spiritual, Secular and Social Landscapes of the Pacific Northwest: Part 2." *UWSpace*. http://hdl.handle.net/10012/13406.

Wolf, Edward C., Andrew P. Mitchell, and Peter K. Schoonmaker. 1995. *The Rain Forests of Home: An Atlas of People and Place*. Portland, OR: Ecotrust/Pacific GIS/Conservation International. https://ecotrust.org/wp-content/uploads/Rainforests_of_Home.pdf.

Zuckerman, Phil. 2015. *Faith No More: Why People Reject Religion*. New York: Oxford University Press.

Reverential Naturalism in Cascadia: From the Fancy to the Sublime

PAUL BRAMADAT

Most people will worship God by hiking Mount Hood on a Sunday morning. That's kind of the public narrative. This is a place where nature-based spirituality tends to be our native language.

– Reverend Olsen

Sophie: No one will say, "Uh, you believe in Mother Earth and the beauty of nature? You're totally off your rocker," or "Oh, that's so quaint." You don't get that response so much.
Muhammad: Yeah, you're right. You wouldn't.

Sociology, history, religious studies, anthropology, and political science help define the questions we address in this book and the debates we have as peers. We arrive at our conclusions by using conventional methods (such as surveys, interviews, archival work, and focus groups) and concepts (such as religion, spirituality, irreligion, secularization, and secularity) that are bequeathed to us by previous generations of scholars. These concepts inspire ongoing debates, with some critics contending that even the concept of religion is not an obviously meaningful category (Fitzgerald 2007; McCutcheon 1997, 2003). In the interest of our broader objectives, we have generally pursued our research as though the conventional methods and concepts are adequate for our purposes. Although I am convinced that my colleagues and I provide a fair and useful account of the communities, individuals, ideas, documents, and discourses we encountered in the region, it is also true that scholars tend to "look where the light is." Therefore, it is useful to ask whether the tools we have inherited from our scholarly forebears are entirely adequate for describing and interpreting complex phenomena, especially when these events, people, discourses, and politics are situated in a region that appears to be at the leading edge of major social changes, some of which might not have been anticipated by the major figures in our fields.

While some readers might contend that the conventional questions and categories we use to measure and interpret religion, irreligion, and spirituality in this book are quite sufficient, it strikes me that the concept of reverential naturalism might help explain what makes this region unusual. In this chapter, I define "reverential naturalism" as a broad and naturalized schema that helps to explain the ways Cascadians think and talk about religion, spirituality, and nature. We see evidence of the ubiquity of this organizing schema in Canadian and US stereotypes of the region, branding campaigns, survey and archival data, and the personal stories we heard in our research. Nonetheless, although this metanarrative arguably permeates what we might call the dominant cultural rhetoric of the region, it is as yet so inchoate or subliminal that it is not easy to articulate. In the remainder of this chapter, I use our data to provide both an operational definition of reverential naturalism as well as an evidence-based thematization of its main features.

I then return to the fundamental question: What difference does drawing attention to such a story make to our understanding of the region? I outline how this metanarrative generates additional questions that will enrich future reflections on the region (and perhaps elsewhere). I hope that future research will measure (or, for that matter, dispute) the importance of this shared narrative in the interpretation of the region.

Operationalizing "Reverential Naturalism"

Although a common feature of most forms of naturalism would be the assertion or assumption that this-worldly, materialist explanations are sufficient to account for all observable phenomena (Papineau 2021), the variant that seems to be common in Cascadia is neither generally antagonistic nor indifferent toward experience, discourse, or phenomena related to spirituality. Instead, reverential naturalism favours an orientation that is both accepting of scientific approaches to nature and inclined to perceive and imagine the natural world in ways that are redolent (from the Latin *olere,* "to smell") of mysticism, panentheism, animism, pantheism, and inclusive forms of theism. Reverential naturalism may be considered a metanarrative – with concomitant attitudes, assumptions, habits, and practices with respect to a breathtaking natural world – that animated the individual stories and perspectives of almost all the people we met during our research.

To be clear, reverential naturalism is not unique to the Pacific Northwest (Barman 1991; Dunlap 2004; Schwantes 1989).[1] It is similar to what other scholars have called "nature religion" (Albanese 1990), "religious naturalism" (Goodenough 1998), and "dark green religion" (Taylor 2010), both in that there is no antipathy toward a naturalistic orientation and there is an interest in themes and values that emerge from or echo conventional religion. Nevertheless, it is important to note that for many (but certainly not all) people in Cascadia, "religion" and "religious" are increasingly problematic and sometimes even inert terms that fail not only to capture what is occurring in the region but also to resonate with many residents (Kleeb 2013).

Interestingly, the rhetoric associated with reverential naturalism – regardless of who used it – occasioned virtually no resistance during our research. When the metaphors associated with this variant of naturalism (see below) arose in our discussions, there was no eye rolling, no sarcasm or irony, and no condemnations from orthodox religionists (who might be expected to be irritated by the naturalistic perspective) or elderly participants (who might be expected to see this perspective as a threat to conventional religious institutions). Of course, there must be individuals for whom the natural world is entirely comprehensible in materialist terms and thus for whom any talk of reverence or the sublime would be anathema, but in truth, I have never met such a person here. Moreover, there must be others for whom a "maximalist" religious consciousness (Lincoln 2003) is normative and thus for whom the privileged place of naturalistic orientations in the region would be deeply misguided. Nonetheless, I want to argue that reverential naturalism is by far the most common, but typically tacit, feature of Pacific Northwest approaches to the natural world and our relationship to it.[2]

Reverential naturalism is not a new form of religion, which one might expect to become institutionalized or perhaps in some sense to compensate for the losses occasioned by secularization; nor is it merely a type of spirituality, which one might expect to be idiosyncratic and salient mainly to individuals or specific subcultures; nor is it simply an expression of implicit (or nascent) irreligion.[3] Although, as I mentioned above, further research will be required to address the future of this form of naturalism, I doubt that it names a transient mode of approaching the natural world and religious or spiritual matters.[4] Instead, this attitude toward nature appears to be the common language used to converse across differences. I use the word "attitude" in its ordinary sense of mood, perspective, or dispositional orientation but also in the way it is used in dance vernaculars to describe a bodily posture. Reverential naturalism is an embodied perspective, a way of physically being, or being physical, in a particular geography. Whether Pacific Northwesterners are more likely than other Canadians or Americans to spend time in the natural environment is beside the point; our research points to the presence of an overarching meaning-conveying narrative according to which deference to and, for many, veneration of nature is framed as a distinctive, even definitive, feature of what it means to live well here.

Elements of our project's transcripts, field notes, and supplementary sources help flesh out the presence and meaning of this variant of naturalism in Cascadia.

In addition to what people explicitly told us in our interviews, focus groups, and surveys, I would argue that we can also find evidence of reverential naturalism in previous studies (e.g., Killen 2004; Killen and Silk 2004; Todd 2008; Dunlap 2004; Bunting 1997; O'Connell 2003; Lutz 2007; Pressnell and Henderson 2008; Robbins 2001; Taylor 2010; Wolf, Mitchell, and Schoonmaker 1995) and our own experiences as residents of the region.[5] I have grouped the data into what seemed to be the common themes evident among our participants; together, they reflect a pervasive regional narrative.

The Land of Tomorrow

During an oral-history interview, Arthur spoke about his family's arrival in the region from Kentucky several generations ago. "Somebody told them that the Pacific Northwest was the land of tomorrow," he said. The phrase is pregnant with meaning. Cascadians consistently story their region in a manner that underlines the ways it allows not just residents but all people to imagine individual lives and whole societies that are unencumbered by the traditions and social constraints that stultify human life elsewhere on the continent, militating against novel creative ventures. This enthusiasm for the region's utopian potential animates the popular 1975 novel *Ecotopia: The Notebooks and Reports of William Weston,* by Ernest Callenbach. Set in a geography roughly approximating what my colleagues and I call Cascadia South, in what was then a futuristic 1999, the book describes a society that has broken away from the United States. Although a work of fiction, the novel captures the broadly circulating consensus in the region that Cascadia is not simply different than other regions (and not just a place of refuge for free thinkers) but rather, in some sense, is the spatialization of possibilities that may exist in nascent form elsewhere.

In our project data, recent arrivals and members of long-settled families shared a clear sense of the marked difference between the region and an actual or imagined elsewhere. As Dustin, a Victoria millennial put it, when he visits other provinces, he realizes of his own region, "Oh, wow, this is a very different culture and conversation happening." This consensus is also evident in what I think of as the "escape stories" that circulate among relative newcomers to the region. When meeting for the first time, urban (settler) Cascadians often tell stories of how they or their families, as it were, escaped *the other place.* In British Columbia (especially the Lower Mainland and Vancouver Island), that other place is inevitably one that is storied as colder, more conventional, or more fast-paced; in the United States, the other place is often framed as too polluted, crowded, tradition-bound, or materialistic (Marks 2007, 2016; Block 2010, 2016; Todd 2008). For example, we met Jane, a Christian whose family has lived in Cascadia South for three generations. In an oral history, she noted:

So we consider, not to be arrogant, but there was a time when we considered ourselves the real Northwesterners. Real Northwesterners live outdoors, they don't even have an umbrella, they are friendly, they don't lock their doors. But the people who are, who are transplants, I would not say those, I don't know very many that have really become Northwest, you know, Northwesterners. So as you're studying Cascadia, what you're really studying is people who have come here from California, and there's a different culture. People are ... attracted by the invisible God and the things we see in creation. But they are running away from all kinds of other things. Hopefully, they'll find something that works up here.

Kamal, one of the millennial participants in our focus group in Vancouver, was a more recent arrival in the region, but he also understood its distinctive features:

When I lived in Toronto, I was like, "It's a city. No one goes away over there." For the weekend, you're just, like, in the city and doing city things. [In Ontario there is] just a lot more social contact, a lot more people contact, a lot more ideas and culture, whereas over here it's a lot more nature and hikes.

Beyond the lifestyles the region allows, Cascadia is a place where old forms of solidarity may be shed and new futures imagined. The diminished presence of religious communities and attachments interests us in this project, of course. Pastor Novak, an evangelical from Oregon, noted that "Portland represents and Cascadia represents the beginning of post-Christian America. So, it's just the front end of the post-Christian story in America. America in fifty years is gonna be completely different than it is now, and whatever you're seeing here now will be in Kansas in ten years." However, it is also the case that new forms of spiritual life are arguably easier to identify when conventional religiosity occupies less and less social space. Cascadia as the "land of tomorrow" represents a promise of reconciliation of conflicting forces. Beyond the opportunity to observe syncretic expressions of existing religious practices and traditions (e.g., yoga, Buddhism(s), reiki, Christianity(ies), traditional Chinese medicine, Ayurveda, agnosticism, mindfulness), I suggest that reverential naturalism captures characteristic aspects of the region's emerging zeitgeist.

Immanent Spirituality, the Church of Hiking, and "Fancy Nature"
A compilation of references in our interviews to the spiritual value of hiking, camping, running, kayaking, skiing, sailing, paddle boarding, surfing, cycling, or gardening would fill dozens of pages. These comments came in response to questions we posed about the ways that participants framed their outdoor

activities and to broader discussion themes in our semistructured interviews and focus groups. A few emblematic selections should capture the common themes we encountered. I should note that there was a remarkable consonance between these stories, regardless of the age, gender, ethnic or racial background, formal religious identity, education, or national location of the participant in question.

The Church of Hiking, and Fancy Nature

I asked one liberal religious minister (who had lived in Portland for a decade) how he would explain the disproportionate number of religious Nones in the region, and he immediately drew attention to the ways institutional religion – as it is practised in the rest of North America – struggles in Cascadia. Reverend Richards said that whereas in most of the United States people would be assumed to have some loyalty to one or another conventional religious identity, in Cascadia,

> the default assumption is that you go walk in the woods ... The message of the culture is that where you find your spirituality is out in the pines. Or at the coast, right? Or up Mount Hood, or wherever your particular piece of nature is. That's the cultural message, rather than the cultural message being that you go to Vancouver Avenue Baptist ...
>
> They come to church regularly, but their spiritual practice, rather than prayer or meditation in some organized fashion, is walking in nature. So, that's almost a ubiquitous feeling here ... And living in Portland, it's very real.[6]

Benjamin, a millennial from Victoria with a professional interest in Christian ministry, also reflected on the tension between the liberal institutional church and reverential naturalism. Speaking during a focus group about a moving lecture he had heard about the way all of existence is "imbued with the sacred" but the way humans now live is in an "immanent frame," he noted that "there's something very transcendent and *beyond* about [the natural world in the region], if we're willing to see it in that way. And, again, I think our religious systems sometimes miss that opportunity to do that, and it doesn't happen ... So that's what I see when I think of the outdoors."[7]

Caitlin, an agnostic millennial from Portland, captured the way many speak about hiking:

> I have *lots of friends here who talk about hiking being their church, or whatever* ... I think that really is, in my anecdotal experience, tied to people's spirituality because it's – *this feels obvious for me to say because I've lived here my whole life,* but maybe it's not. But because we're so close at any time, wherever you are in

the Pacific Northwest, to getting to, like, nature, I think that that really seems to have impacted a lot of people I know.

Pastor Rodrigues, the leader of a new religious movement in Tacoma, Washington, said, "Nature is a big factor in this area ... I mean that's in our spiritual DNA, so to speak." In response to a question regarding whether his congregants link the natural world and their spirituality, Reverend Olsen, a liberal Protestant minister in Portland, commented:

> Most people will worship God by hiking Mount Hood on a Sunday morning. *That's kind of the public narrative* ... This is a place where *nature-based spirituality tends to be our native language.* And the church is sort of secondary to that ... I have core families who think nothing of saying, "Oh, you won't see us next Sunday. We're going for a hike." Right? There's no embarrassment. There's actually a little bit of pride around it. Like, "We're going to make the good choice next week. You won't see us. We'll be in nature." And that's interesting to me, that not only is there broad permission for that but even a little bit of a, like, I feel like *they think they're getting brownie points for it.*

Rabbi Levi, also from Portland, remarked that in this region, "On a certain level, *everybody's an environmentalist ... I think that many people find their spirituality, you know, outside,* in one form or another, and that that's a very meaningful spirituality to people." A Buddhist abbot in Portland echoed this sentiment by saying that the approach to nature among her community could best be described as "cherishing. One of the *things that I hear from people is that they don't feel quite right unless they make regular trips to the beach or mountains.*" Similarly, Linda, a Protestant woman with deep roots in the region, noted during an oral-history interview: "Yeah, I think that's an, that's an important thing that we still take walks in the park as often as we can, and try to do hikes. And get out in God's work, in creation, or whatever. That's an important part of our, of helping us stay sane, you know."

Kamal, a millennial Vancouver Muslim who grew up in Toronto, recalls a conversation with an academic mentor in British Columbia with whom he was discussing mosque design:

> And [the mentor] was like, "What are you talking about mosques for? Spirituality is in the forest." My mind was blown. I'm like, "Oh, okay." And that's when I had this ... realization that spirituality is probably not in the city. It's not at the mosque, it's not in the temple or church but in nature, and *I suspect that might be like a very West Coast way of thinking because I hadn't heard that articulated in other parts of the world.*

We met Margaret, a woman in her seventies from Victoria, in a focus group. She compared the kind of nature found in Cascadia to what one finds elsewhere in the country:

> I think the Pacific Northwest, particularly, *we have such fancy nature.* [Laughter.] Compared to other [places]. It's hard to ignore it. *I mean, it's right there ...* I have a friend who's an archaeologist ... He calls people that do archaeology in Greece "fancy archaeologists," because, of course, there's so much amazing stuff that you can dig up there ... But the Pacific Northwest, it's so spectacular – the natural environment.

From the Easy to the Sublime

It is worth noting that people raised (as I was) in the relatively harsh climate of the northern prairies are often struck by the tameness of the wilderness on the West Coast. The Pacific Ocean currents guarantee that, at least for the coastal areas of Cascadia (where, again, over four-fifths of the region's residents live), the climate is generally moderate. Because of this, the membrane between indoors and outdoors is far more permeable than in other parts of North America. Father Travis, a Roman Catholic leader in British Columbia (with roots in Manitoba), noted that the history of human habitation in most places in Canada has been quite difficult, whereas "everything about living here in Cascadia is, like, so easy. We have the easy life. Everywhere you go, everything is easy ... You don't have to have five cords of wood stacked up to stay warm. So, everything about *the environment here is conducive to ease.*"

Nonetheless, there is more to the story and experience of reverential naturalism than ease and pleasure. It is also important to observe that when people wax poetic about the region's grand natural qualities, they are sometimes alluding to a *sublime* dimension. The philosophical notion of the sublime can be traced to ancient Greece, where it was initially related to prose and poetry of profound beauty. The concept was later rediscovered by European philosophers (e.g., Burke, Kant, Hegel, Schopenhauer) and came to be associated with scenes in nature that humans experienced as beautiful (in the conventional sense of being harmonious, well-balanced, pleasing, picturesque, attractive) but also mystical and terrifying (Shaw 2006).

The very nature of academic prose and the experience being described may limit my ability to convey the terrifying or dread-full aspects of the sublime. Nonetheless, I can approach the task elliptically, by noting that many readers will have had the experience of standing at the edge of an ocean, appreciating the beauty (again, in the conventional sense above) of large waves crashing against the shore. This is an impression one might have *at the same time as* experiencing the visceral sense that the ocean is overwhelming and utterly indifferent to you. To be in the backcountry just as the weather shifts, to be in a kayak in the middle of an ocean swell, to cross paths with a cougar in a park, to stand at the foot of a volcano such as Mount St. Helens that just a few decades ago wreaked havoc on the region, or to have a relatively small (five- to seven-metre) orca or massive (twenty- to twenty-seven-metre) fin whale swim beneath one's small vessel: these are moments when one may be struck by the beauty of the natural world *and* by an anxiety-provoking sense of one's own evanescence. The implications of this kind of dual and vertiginous perception are profound.

One can intuit this sort of experience just below the surface of many of our participants' comments. Jeremy, a millennial from Vancouver, questioned the idea that reverential naturalism might be apparent here in a distinctive way. He noted, "It feels weird to think that, like, there is something special about this land that makes people extra-reverential. That seems ridiculous, actually. Like what, like other land isn't amazing?" However, he immediately added that there was something distinctive and ineffable about his experiences here:

> But ... at the same time, there does seem to be something, that when I meet people from the West Coast and other places, that we connect a lot of times on that subject, around a certain type of reverence or a certain way of speaking about it. I don't know what it is ... I have lots of reverential experiences in [Cascadia]. Something hard to quite pin down. I'm afraid to pin it down, because it's going to be inaccurate when I do.

As Samuel, a millennial surfer from Victoria, put it during a focus group when talking about what it is like to wait for a wave in the deep, frigid, turbulent waters off Tofino, knowing that he shares the space with porpoises, whales, seals, otters, sea lions, and jagged rocks: "I feel like being kind of immersed in nature in that way, physically being in the ocean, being present there, like, witnessing all of these natural powers, whether or not it's animals or waves coming at you, or whatever, and just like seeing the landscape from out there has a very kind of awe-inspiring effect on you."

Public Discourse and Personal Anguish

Two stories covered extensively in the media offer additional evidence of the metanarrative I am tracing. For several weeks in 2018, Cascadians were reminded almost daily of a tragedy unfolding in the Salish Sea, as the inland sea between Puget Sound (near Seattle) and the northern reach of the Strait of Georgia (north of Vancouver) has recently been renamed in honour of Coast Salish peoples. As dozens of news outlets reported, on August 13, a female orca finally released a dead calf she had been balancing on her nose for seventeen days. The orca mother in question is J35, or Tahlequah, a twenty-year-old member of the "J Pod" of "southern resident" killer whales that live in the Salish Sea. Tahlequah had been engaged in what journalists and biologists throughout the region described as uncharacteristic "grieving" and "mourning" behaviour that would certainly jeopardize her own life if it continued.[7] The orcas are threatened because their food supply – mostly coho salmon – has been diminished by (among other possible factors) changes in ocean and river patterns related to climate change, overfishing, fish farming, vessel traffic, and seals and sea lions (which also eat coho). As well, public concern has been expressed about the plans (of the Canadian federal government as well as international oil companies) to increase massively the capacity of existing pipelines to bring diluted bitumen from the Alberta tar sands thousands of kilometres southwest to a harbour in Burnaby (part of the Greater Vancouver Area), bound mostly for Asia.[8] The consequences of a virtually inevitable oil spill have become a central concern in the region.

The popularity of J Pod might be explained by the fact that orcas are aesthetically striking, live near humans, live in hierarchical and intimate family units (like humans), and have a provocative name (actually, there is no record of orcas attacking humans in the wild). But the actual cause of J Pod's general plight and Tahlequah's particular grief are less interesting for my purposes than the fact that the drama was framed as a symptom of an imbalance between the region's untamed, reverence-inducing natural splendour and the powerful turn toward corporate priorities.[9] More to the point, campaigns meant to prevent us from destroying animals that are framed as pristine, innocent, and noble arguably come to symbolize the larger threat to survival of life on the planet.

The second story, the cost of living in the region, has become one of the galvanizing concerns animating younger urban residents. These worries are by far the most acute in Vancouver and Seattle, where, for a variety of reasons, it is difficult for many young people – even educated professionals – to imagine ever owning a home. It might seem strange to include this-worldly troubles regarding rents, mortgages, down payments, and basement suites in an essay that traces the contours of reverential naturalism. However, throughout our study, residents routinely framed the natural environment as a site of some inextinguishable, ineffable, and reverence-worthy spiritual presence. As often unforgiving modern neoliberal priorities come more and more to define these urban spaces, the easily accessible woods, mountains, and oceans (in "fancy" nature) regularly become storied as both besieged (subject, for example, to the depredations of oil companies) and spiritually restorative. A relatively tame and spiritualized nature may thus compensate for the unforgiving realities of a certain kind of capitalism. In this land of tomorrow, the land and sea are framed as extremely vulnerable and imbued with an indefatigable capacity to humble, nurture, and inspire humans.

Exceptions, and the Rule

According to what I call the "Cascadia consensus," the natural world in the region is fancy, conducive to ease, within easy reach of urbanites, a site of restoration and renewal, and imbued with spiritual meaning. Furthermore, treating the natural world as set apart, sacred, sublime, or spiritual is integral to our native language, part of our spiritual DNA, taken for granted by people born here, part of a ubiquitous feeling, and the default orientation of residents regardless of age, ethnicity, nationality, or formal religious identity.

Nevertheless, it is important to identify themes that challenge the dominant account. For example, however appealing the environment seems to those who might perceive the region as pristine, the broader and more critical environmental movement troubles this notion. While Reverend Richards articulated his own and his community's commitment to reverential naturalism, he also noted that people of colour and other members of lower socioeconomic strata often pay a high price:

> For a long time, this congregation bought into the notion that environmentalism meant saving the pristine wilderness ... And now I think most of the people in this congregation have heard enough. They've learned enough to know that that's not the be all and the end all, although that may be a part of it. You know, it's also about where the sludge and the trash is deposited and whose communities are adjacent to it.

The Cascadian consensus and its characteristic approach to nature are also somewhat socially hegemonic. Some people have therefore become fatigued by both its ubiquity and its tendency to obscure some of the harder truths of the region. In fact, the concentration of most of the region's population in four western liberal cities can create, in the words of Dustin, a Victoria millennial, "an echo chamber. Like, even in classrooms, it's very difficult to approach a different side [of environmental issues], out of curiosity, without being very ostracized by fellow students."

As well, this approach to both nature and institutions in the region may threaten religious institutions. Reverend Olsen colourfully articulated some misgivings about the dominant narrative:

> Like, it's one of the places where I feel like my inner asshole, like, "Come on, you guys." Yeah, I feel good when I look at a pretty view, too, but that's, is that

God? There's a piece of me that really kind of wants to unsettle that a little bit. 'Cause sometimes it feels really thin to me. Yeah ... I feel like in some ways [the natural world] gets pitted against more traditional forms of Christianity. Like, you can do that weird Nicene Creed thing, but we're all going to go here and pray to an earth goddess. And I think, Bullshit ... So, there are ways in which I'm a little suspicious of that narrative. I recognize that it has a lot of cultural valence, and there's a lot of people for whom that is an important thing. It is certainly a phenomenon in this neck of the world, and I sometimes feel like I kinda wanna push back on it ... Like, I'm a church guy ... Music is probably for me a native spiritual language. Nature, I can speak that language. I'm maybe a little bilingual in it, but it's not my native tongue.

Reverend Olsen's concerns about the impact of reverential naturalism on the viability of traditional organizations were shared by Rabbi Bauman, from Seattle, who noted:

I think there are a lot of people who still feel that this is kind of the frontier ... [characterized by] *rugged individualism, but in a spiritual kind of vein.* People here just, they want meaning, but they want it with fewer obligations and commitment ... Because I think they feel like they come out here and, you know, they find God in nature, or spirituality in nature, or in yoga, or in their co-op and whatever.

While the default approach in the region is one according to which virtually everyone we met, from atheists to Anglicans, imagined the natural world to be integrally reflective of beauty, mystery, and awe, there are also discourses and subcultures in which one can find a more conventional perspective on the location of spiritual energy and what it might mean to spend time outside. Even in the dissenting voices, though, there is a clear recognition that this distinctive approach to spirituality is ubiquitous.

Survey Data

In the Pacific Northwest Social Survey (PNSS; Wilkins-Laflamme 2017; 2018), participants were asked how often they engage in outdoor and environmental activities and to what extent these activities were experienced or construed as spiritual.[10] The results were interesting and have a bearing on the themes that concern me here. An estimated 62 percent of residents of Cascadia North (British Columbia) and 54 percent of people from Cascadia South (Washington and Oregon) indicated that they participated in outdoor activities at least once a month. Among those respondents who took part in outdoor activities at least once in the year before the survey, 52 percent of Canadians and 48 percent of

Americans described their experiences as either definitely or probably spiritual. These figures are parallel in that Canadians seem slightly more active and more likely than Americans to associate these activities with spiritual meaning. This pattern is echoed in the data related to environmental activities: 40 percent of British Columbians and 41 percent of residents of Washington and Oregon indicated that they participated in such activities at least once a month, and 53 percent of the Canadian participants and 48 percent of the US residents who took part in such activities at least once a year attributed a spiritual meaning to them (either definitely or probably).

Although we would need to conduct this study in other regions in North America to draw strong conclusions about whether Cascadia is unusual in this regard, the quantitative data indicates high levels of both engagement in and support for activities in the natural world and fairly high levels of attribution of spiritual significance to those activities. As our interviews demonstrate, this way of engaging and storying experiences in the natural world is a deeply embedded part of what Reverend Olsen referred to as the "native language" of the bioregion.

***

Our qualitative and quantitative data confirm previous studies showing the decline of dominant, conventional forms of religiosity. The declines are real, and, it appears, more or less unidirectional for the main Protestant and Catholic communities. So it is quite understandable that when scholars think and write about the region, we spend most of our energy trying to understand and explain how so many forms of conventional religiosity seem to mean less – both socially and individually – in the Pacific Northwest than elsewhere in Canada and the United States. Of course, it is also common among scholars to observe some exceptions to (or peculiarities of) this general trend: the growth of mostly Asian religious-minority communities; the relative strength of fairly new urban evangelical congregations; revitalization movements among Indigenous peoples; and the popularity of something akin to spiritual bricolage or syncretism. It seems unlikely that these phenomena will alter the general trends in the region with regard to organized religion.

However, I suggest that it may be worthwhile to consider adding one more concept to our analytical toolbox. Reverential naturalism is a metanarrative that helps to inform individual stories in and about the region. This is evident, though often *sotto voce,* in our project data, the growing academic literature on the region, and both informal popular cultural narratives and formal branding of the region. It is important to underline that while this is a form of naturalism, it is not generally an adversarial variant. Moreover, even for religiously identified individuals (as with the young architect, Kamal, above), it seems to be fairly unproblematic, and even predictable, that the natural world might sometimes supplant the built environment of formal religious institutions as the *sanctum sanctorum* of spiritual life in the Pacific Northwest. Furthermore, integral to this grand narrative is the trope that even for people with no interest in religious or spiritual rhetoric, the Cascadian natural environment is distinctively sublime, arresting, majestic, restorative, and humbling. This reverence-worthy force is not *only* located in the natural world; but it is reliably, conveniently, and distinctively *there*. In fact, this is such a commonsensical notion that Reverend Olsen realized that to question it out loud was itself rather scandalous.[11] Olsen's reticence speaks both to the decline of conventional religiosity and the ubiquity of this metanarrative.

Relations between the religious, spiritual, and irreligious populations in the region strike me as remarkably congenial. As mentioned elsewhere in this volume, there is a strong "you do you" orientation in the region. Sophie, a Vancouver millennial, contrasted Cascadia with the rest of the country: "No one will say 'Uh, you believe in mother Earth and the beauty of nature? You're totally off your rocker,' or 'Oh, that's so quaint.' You don't get that response so much." Muhammad, her fellow focus-group member and a Muslim, said, "Yeah, you're right. You wouldn't."

What this "land of tomorrow" portends for the rest of the continent is difficult to predict, but it is arguably the case that what we see clearly in Cascadia are exemplary (though not unproblematic) responses to fault lines that run through other places. For example, the region is home to a range of environmental movements that transcend borders (and other limitations) and may offer us insights into how to respond to climate change and pollution. In addition, as our colleague Chelsea Horton observes in this volume, Cascadia North is the site of a dramatic resurgence in Indigenous pride and political activism, largely because most of British Columbia is "unceded," and Indigenous communities represent a larger proportion of the provincial population when compared with their counterparts in Washington and Oregon. British Columbia may thus offer some lessons about how reconciliation might work elsewhere in the continent. Moreover, the Pacific Northwest is also the location of some of the continent's largest and most powerful corporations (Starbucks, Boeing, Amazon, Costco, and Microsoft), a fact that has laid bare some of the environmental and social consequences of late capitalism.

Reverential naturalism is not a new religion, an ersatz personal spirituality, or a stepping stone from religious identification to complete "irreligion." It might function like this for certain individuals, but it is more helpful to see it as constituting a deep narrative that coexists with and complicates the concepts and categories we normally use to analyze religion (religious, spiritual, irreligious,

None, spiritual but not religious, etc.). Reverential naturalism is so ubiquitous in the data we collected and in the existing writing on the region that it is arguably worthwhile to, first, identify it as a coherent metanarrative and, second, consider it as a part of the broader social reality against which we might read existing and emerging data.

What name we give to this narrative is of less importance than the new questions we might ask about its origins and uses:

- How is the story instrumentalized in corporate or governmental branding exercises (such as the "Best Place on Earth" campaign in British Columbia)?[12]
- Does this popular variant of naturalism explain why the conventional "religion versus science" dichotomy that is such a prominent feature of the so-called culture wars seems to be less salient in Cascadia than in other regions in North America?
- How might reverential naturalism resonate differently for people of different social classes (i.e., would people with less access to expensive camping, kayaking, or hiking equipment, not to mention transportation and vacation opportunities, be less inclined to embrace it)?
- How might the story be of use to Indigenous peoples with an interest in problematizing the role of Christianity in their communities?
- Do mainline religious communities respond to this schema as a threat or an opportunity?
- Are ethnoreligious minority communities as likely to accept the rhetoric of reverential naturalism as members of the more settled and even nominally Christian communities? In particular, how might African American Christians relate to this default orientation, and are African Americans in the United States likely to engage differently than their counterparts in Canada with the common values and tropes of reverential naturalism?
- Do Cascadian millennials use or approach this narrative in the same way as older residents?
- Does the narrative take different forms in Cascadia North and South?

These questions might take us deeper into the elusive utopia (Todd 2008) that is Cascadia. It is certainly clear that many residents see this imagined geography (Said 1978) as the land of tomorrow. What we can also observe is that reverential naturalism seems to be implicit in the stories told by people who are formally aligned with institutional religions and by those who would never darken the door of a religious building. This shared story seems to orient the region's residents on a map that is both real and imaginary. It is difficult to say whether the approach to the natural world, religion, irreligion, and spirituality that we

see in Cascadia is a harbinger of changes to come in other places, but the up-
heavals occasioned by climate change and secularization (among other things)
might well lead people in other regions in a similar direction.

NOTES

1　After I wrote this chapter, I discovered that an American Thomist high school teacher, James
   Chastek (2017), had used "reverential naturalism" in a blog post in 2017 to refer to "a version
   of methodological naturalism, stating that we should not expect divine causality to be appropriate until the inquiry into secondary causes has been more or less completely exhausted,
   and that it is unreasonable to assume that we are anywhere close to this point yet." Chastek
   is interested in the possibilities of grounding a conventional form of theism, and so I take
   him to be pointing in a different direction than I am. I also recently discovered that the late
   Unitarian Universalist pastor William D. Hammond had used the term in a collection of
   sermons titled *Ecology of the Human Spirit: Fourteen Discourses in Reverential Naturalism,*
   published by the now defunct Rising Press in 1996. "Reverential naturalism" is used only a
   few times in his collection, and Hammond's interests in the sermons were – naturally – pastoral
   rather than scholarly. Consequently, he does not delineate the meaning(s) of the term clearly.

2　Our survey and archival work covered the region as a whole, but it would certainly be the
   case that the account I am providing mostly emerges from our encounters with urban dwell-
   ers. I suspect that people (roughly 20 percent of the region's residents) who live outside of
   these four urban centres would share this perspective on the natural world, but we would
   need a separate study to confirm this.

3　"Reverential naturalism" better describes this core story than "ecospirituality" because, in
   the latter approach, "eco[logical]" is a modifier of the core fact of "spirituality," whereas in
   the former approach, an enriched and open naturalism is the starting point. While "spirituality" remains an important analytical term, it now refers to so many movements, claims,
   and contexts (from mindfulness practices to tarot cards to mystical Christian practices) that
   its meaning has become somewhat unclear. Naturalism itself has a long history (Papineau
   2021), but in my view it is less encumbered and easier to operationalize than spirituality.
   Moreover, when I informally field test "reverential naturalism" in a wide range of Cascadian public and private spaces, it often has immediate resonance for people, apparently regardless of their level of interest in religion and spirituality. Conversely, I can say that when
   I field test "ecospirituality," some people wince because it is associated with pagan and
   New-Age connotations.

4　The two passages discussed in the first few pages of the Introduction span roughly one
   hundred years, and so the narrative seems quite deeply rooted.

5　For archival and interview data, see https://www.uvic.ca/research/centres/csrs/.

6　I have added italics to emphasize certain features of these claims.

7　Orcas have been called "charismatic mega-fauna" (Kaufman and Franz 2000, 342), large
   iconic animals with broad appeal that galvanize public opinion around environmental
   concerns or tourism campaigns (see also Colby 2018).

8　For background, see https://thenarwhal.ca/topics/trans-mountain-pipeline/; https://
   vancouversun.com/news/local-news/no-less-controversial-trans-mountain-continues-on
   -with-expansion-project; https://www.nytimes.com/2019/06/18/world/canada/trudeau-trans
   -mountain-pipeline.html.

9　These concerns are certainly captured in the way J35's grief and J Pod's future are framed by
   groups such as the Wilderness Committee and the Sierra Club. A week before the end of
   J35's apparent refusal to accept her calf's death, Sierra Club BC penned a press release. In it,
   Simon Pidcock, head captain of Ocean Ecoventures, is quoted as saying: "We have been

following the story of J-35's grief with broken hearts. It is an overwhelming tragedy on our coast that should be a watershed moment where the plight of the orcas solidifies in the public consciousness as at a crisis point" (Sierra Club BC 2018).

10 In the survey, we provided the following definition of "spiritual experience": a profound and usually positive experience that helps individuals find their authentic self as well as connects them to a mysterious, universal, and overarching reality. We defined "environmental activities" as "activities to help the environment/the natural world." There are limitations to using such broadly defined terms, but if all participants answer the same question in the same context, it is still useful to compare and contrast responses.

11 Indeed, he said to question such an assumption would be to reveal his "inner asshole."

12 Travel Oregon's website proclaims: "Welcome to Oregon: a 100% real place. But when you're here, you might swear otherwise."

REFERENCES

Albanese, C.L. 1990. *Nature Religion in America: From the Algonkian Indians to the New Age.* Chicago: University of Chicago Press.

Barman, Jean. 1991. *The West beyond the West: A History of British Columbia.* Toronto: University of Toronto Press.

Block, Tina. 2010. "Religion, Irreligion, and the Difference Place Makes: The Case of the Postwar Pacific Northwest." *Social History* 43 (85): 1–30.

—. 2016. *The Secular Northwest: Religion and Irreligion in Everyday Postwar Life.* Vancouver: UBC Press.

Bunting, Robert. 1997. *The Pacific Raincoast: Environment and Culture in an American Eden, 1778–1900.* Lawrence: University Press of Kansas.

Chastek, James. 2017. "Reverential Naturalism." *Just Thomism* (blog), August 24. https://thomism.wordpress.com/?s=reverential+naturalism.

Colby, Jason. 2018. *Orca.* New York: Oxford University Press.

Dunlap, Thomas R. 2004. *Faith in Nature: Environmentalism as Religious Quest.* Seattle: University of Washington Press.

Fitzgerald, Timothy. 2007. *Discourse on Civility and Barbarity: A Critical History of Religion and Related Categories.* New York: Oxford University Press.

Goodenough, Ursula. 1998. *The Sacred Depths of Nature.* New York: Oxford University Press.

Hammond, William D. 1996. *Ecology of the Human Spirit: Fourteen Discourses in Reverential Naturalism.* Minneapolis: Rising Press.

Kaufman, Donald G., and Cecilia M. Franz. 2000. *Biosphere 2000: Protecting Our Global Environment.* Dubuque, IA: Kendall Hunt.

Killen, Patricia O'Connell. 2004. "The Religious Geography of the Pacific Northwest." *Word and World* 24 (3): 269–78.

Killen, Patricia O'Connell, and Mark Silk, eds. 2004. *Religion and Public Life in the Pacific Northwest: The None Zone.* Walnut Creek, CA: AltaMira Press.

Kleeb, Sarah Lynn. 2013. "Anonymous Believers in Bron Taylor's *Dark Green Religion.*" *Studies in Religion* 42 (3): 309–14.

Lincoln, Bruce. 2003. *Holy Terrors: Thinking about Religion after September 11.* Chicago: University of Chicago Press.

Lutz, John, ed. 2007. *Myth and Memory: Stories of Indigenous-European Contact.* Vancouver: UBC Press.

Marks, Lynne. 2007. "'Leaving God behind When They Crossed the Rocky Mountains': Exploring Unbelief in Turn-of-the-Century British Columbia." In *Household Counts: Canadian Households and Families in 1901,* edited by Peter Baskerville and Eric Sager, 371–404. Toronto: University of Toronto Press.

–. 2016. *Infidels and the Damn Churches: Irreligion and Religion in Settler British Columbia.* Vancouver: UBC Press.

McCutcheon, Russell. 1997. *Manufacturing Religion: The Discourse on Sui Generis Religion and the Politics of Nostalgia.* New York: Oxford University Press.

–. 2003. *The Discipline of Religion: Structure, Meaning, Rhetoric.* London: New York.

O'Connell, Nicholas. 2003. *On Sacred Ground: The Spirit of Place in Pacific Northwest Literature.* Seattle: University of Washington Press.

Papineau, David. 2021. "Naturalism." *The Stanford Encyclopedia of Philosophy,* Summer 2021 ed., edited by Edward N. Zalta. https://plato.stanford.edu/archives/win2016/entries/naturalism/.

Pressnell, Jim, and Steve Henderson. 2008. "A Center for Applied Leadership: Need and Vision with the Pacific Northwest." *Missio Apostolica* 16: 169–80.

Robbins, William G., ed. 2001. *The Great Northwest: The Search for Regional Identity.* Corvallis: Oregon State University Press.

Said, Edward. 1978. *Orientalism.* New York: Penguin Books.

Schwantes, Carlos. 1989. *The Pacific Northwest: An Interpretive History.* Lincoln, NE: University of Nebraska Press.

Shaw, Phillip. 2006. *The Sublime.* New York: Routledge.

Sierra Club BC. 2018. "Victoria Ecotourism Outfitter and Environmental Advocates Invite Trudeaus to Bear Witness to Orcas' Wake." Press release, August 3. https://sierraclub.bc.ca/tag/whales/.

Taylor, Bron. 2010. *Dark Green Religion: Nature, Spirituality and the Planetary Future.* Berkeley: University of California Press.

Todd, Douglas, ed. 2008. *Cascadia: The Elusive Utopia – Exploring the Spirit of the Pacific Northwest.* Vancouver: Ronsdale Press.

Wilkins-Laflamme, Sarah. 2017. "The Religious, Spiritual, Secular and Social Landscapes of the Pacific Northwest: Part 1." *UWSpace.* http://hdl.handle.net/10012/12218.

–. 2018. "The Religious, Spiritual, Secular and Social Landscapes of the Pacific Northwest: Part 2." *UWSpace.* http://hdl.handle.net/10012/13406.

Wolf, Edward C., Andrew P. Mitchell, and Peter K. Schoonmaker. 1995. *The Rain Forests of Home: An Atlas of People and Place.* Portland: Ecotrust/Pacific GIS/Conservation International. https://ecotrust.org/wp-content/uploads/Rainforests_of_Home.pdf.

2 On Religion, Irreligion, and Settler Colonialism in the Pacific Northwest: A Snapshot from the Field

CHELSEA HORTON

I usually pick up *Coast Mountain Culture* (*CMC*) when I happen upon it. Advertisements abound, but I like the photography and tidbits, such as a recent report on a short-lived, late-1990s effort to use dachshunds to help curb an invasive deer population on Haida Gwaii. Featured midway through the Winter 2018–19 issue is an image that stopped me in my tracks. Sandwiched between a two-page tourism spread and an article on snowmobile ski touring is a reproduction of Cree artist Kent Monkman's 2018 painting *The Scoop*.[1] In this vivid piece, priests and nuns in robes and habits and Mounties in red serge are ripping young Indigenous children from the arms of devastated women. Other youth lay splayed on the ground, while a trio escapes at a run in the distance. The painting clearly connects the Canadian residential school system, in which Christian missionaries and police enforcement were intimately implicated, and the "Sixties Scoop" of Indigenous children into the child welfare system.

Potent as it is, it is more than Monkman's painting that I find so striking. It is also its placement in the magazine, completely void of contextualization, save a three-word reminder to readers that this is "The Wicked Issue" of *CMC*. The on-the-nose inference here, bolstered by the introduction to the issue, is that *The Scoop* depicts something dreadful (not "wicked" as in cool, as the term is also deployed in the region). The subtext is an apparent assumption on the part of *CMC*'s Vancouver Island–based editorial team that this image and its stripped-down presentation would resonate with its Pacific Northwest audience, or at least readers in Canada. This speaks to growing public awareness of the living history of settler colonialism in Canada, bolstered to a significant degree by the Truth and Reconciliation Commission, which investigated the operation and implications of Indian residential schools in this country.

The qualitative research conducted for this project suggests that Monkman's image as presented in *CMC* would indeed be likely to register with BC readers. In interviews and focus groups in Victoria and Vancouver, project participants spoke directly of the subjects of colonialism, reconciliation, and resurgence.[2] This was partly a product of the design of our project. We posed questions concerning Indigenous-settler relationships, and our research networks led us, via snowball sampling, to some participants who share a particular interest in these issues. Also, we opened each of our focus groups with an acknowledgment of local Indigenous territories. This choice, too, primed participants for discussion. And the discussion that emerged demonstrates that awareness and action concerning the living history of settler colonialism are noticeably more robust among people in British Columbia than in Washington and Oregon today. This difference was also evident in internal research team discussions for this project.

Echoes of the frontier were also audible in focus group discussions and interview responses. This surfaced most prominently in a focus group of adherents in Portland. In reflecting on what makes the Pacific Northwest distinct, and what accounts for religious flexibility in the region, participants in this group – two Jews, a Lutheran, a Catholic, a Buddhist, and a Baha'i – expressly invoked and plugged themselves into a pioneer genealogy of adventure and innovation.[3] "Pioneering spirits," Bruce commented in the course of lively exchange, "It was with us a century or two ago, but it's still here." "That sense of arriving in Portland and being free," Leonard shared of his experience, "I know that's true." As observed by others in this volume, the Pacific Northwest has long been storied as exceptional, freed geographically and psychologically from the fetters of family and staid institutionalism and power, including organized religion. This, the story goes, is the ethereal frontier of freedom, where hardy folk carve their own (spiritual) path, from the nineteenth-century mining claim and saloon, to the 1950s family heading out hiking on Sunday, to the 1970s feminist coastal commune, to today's DIY art collective and slick yoga studio in the heart of the city (Block 2016; Duntley 2017; Killen and Silk 2004; Marks 2017; Todd 2008). The participants in this project who engaged a frontier framework were not blind to past violence and dispossession of Indigenous peoples in the Pacific Northwest. Nevertheless, the residue of the pioneer frontier functions to obscure Indigenous peoples, sovereignty, and living histories of settler colonialism in the region.[4]

In this chapter, I situate the subject of religion and irreligion in the Pacific Northwest in the context of settler colonialism.[5] My approach is at once modest and fundamental. It is modest in the sense that I draw on existing literature to sketch key features of settler-colonial policy and practice as they developed in what became the Canadian and American components of the Pacific Northwest and feature, through this project's qualitative research, a fresh range of settler voices on Indigenous-settler relationships in the region today. It is fundamental, in the sense that settler colonialism is a core context in which all residents and scholars of the Pacific Northwest are implicated and have a responsibility to contemplate. As historians Mary-Ellen Kelm and Keith Smith explain succinctly, "Settler colonialism is a variant of imperialism in which the settlers come to stay, to seek out lives and identities grounded in the colony and for whom Indigenous people, their rights to land and resources, are obstacles that must be eliminated" (Kelm and Smith 2018, 1–2; Veracini 2017). In the Pacific Northwest, where the relationship to place is commonly storied and experienced as a profound and inalienable feature of the region, it is vital to contemplate settler claims to place and narratives of belonging.[6]

Such contemplation includes attention to the category of the Pacific Northwest itself and its current bioregional cognate, Cascadia, both of which can obscure Indigenous peoples and relationships to place.[7] One focus-group participant in Seattle, for example, who works with a local Cascadia-oriented nonprofit, spoke eloquently about the cultivation of Indigenous-settler solidarities in Cascadia via an "antiborder" philosophy and shared affective ties to place, without addressing the overlay of this perspective on Indigenous territories and territoriality. Significantly, one Indigenous person whom we approached about participating in an interview for this project declined in part because of discomfort with the category of "Cascadia." Sylvia, an Indigenous woman whom we interviewed in Victoria, shared that she thinks in terms of territory, not region. To facilitate comparison with existing survey data, the Pacific Northwest Social Survey (PNSS) conducted for this project was framed according to provincial, state, and national borders, a formulation that does not necessarily reflect Indigenous, or regional Cascadian, forms of identification.

This chapter, then, engages with the volume's core question concerning the relevance of the Canada–United States border on several registers. On the one hand, neither the border nor the framework of Cascadia defines or contains Indigenous peoples in the Pacific Northwest. And there are broad settler-colonial strategies that are shared across the border. There are, simultaneously, significant distinctions, both in historical process and contemporary remembrance and narration. In what follows, I accordingly tack back and forth across the border, though I focus most closely on Canada. This focus reflects trends in historiography and our fieldwork alike. In view of a marked unfamiliarity with Canada among American research participants and colleagues, it also signals an effort to share with American readers the Canadian context. Further, this focus on Canada complements the following chapter by Suzanne Crawford O'Brien, which is grounded more in the American context and literature.

For me, this project is not an abstract exercise. I am a spiritual but not religious maritime creature of white settler heritage whose family has lived on the West Coast for four generations, five counting my nieces and nephews. I grew up in the Vancouver area on the territories of the Tsleil-Watuth, Skwxwú7mesh, and xʷməθkʷəy̓əm peoples. I now reside in Snaw-Naw-As Territory on Vancouver Island. My relationship to the ongoing history of settler colonialism in the region is thus profoundly different than that of, say, a Syrian mother recently arrived in the small town of Smithers in northern British Columbia or an African American grandfather in Seattle. Yet all non-Indigenous residents of the Pacific Northwest are, each in their own way, inheritors and beneficiaries of the dispossession of Indigenous lands and waters and the allied logics that undergird this process.[8]

Setting Settler Colonialisms in the Pacific Northwest

As Suzanne Crawford O'Brien elaborates in Chapter 3, the Pacific Northwest was and remains home to diverse Indigenous peoples whose spiritual, economic, and legal orders are tied to particular places. Explorers and traders from Spain, Russia, Britain, and the United States all travelled portions of the Pacific coast in the eighteenth century, setting off processes of place-name reinscription that continue to shape settler-colonial geographies in the region (Murphyao and Black 2015). None of these nations laid exclusive claim to the Pacific Northwest as a whole in this period, however. While Lewis and Clark's storied American sprint across the West culminated on the coast a decade after Alexander Mackenzie's overland arrival farther north in 1793, fur trade economics, not permanent settlement, was the primary vector of exchange with Indigenous peoples, lands, and waters in the early nineteenth century.[9] This exchange was social and political too. Many employees of the Hudson's Bay Company (HBC), the British operation that consolidated control of the Pacific Northwest fur trade in 1821, entered local kinship networks through relationships with Indigenous women. These fur traders included men of Orkney, French Canadian, Hawaiian, and Iroquois heritage, not just English and Scottish.[10] Indigenous communities exercised strong agency in the maritime and terrestrial fur trades alike. At the same time, they experienced dramatic depopulation via epidemic disease that accompanied, and sometimes preceded, non-Indigenous visitors.

Britain and the United States agreed to joint occupation of the Pacific Northwest in 1818. Five years later, the Monroe Doctrine articulated American aspiration and the policy of territorial expansion, tied to a vision of Manifest Destiny that saw American settlement of an empty Western frontier as preordained. Artist John Gast would later capture this civilizing thrust in his 1872 painting, *American Progress,* which depicts an angelic blond-haired woman, clad in a clingy white robe and trailing telegraph wire, bringing light and settlement to the "savage" West.[11] In 1893, historian Frederick Jackson Turner famously declared the frontier constitutive of American pioneers and democracy.

Protestant missionaries, who first arrived in western Oregon in 1834, were key to this pioneer project. Catholic missionaries followed later that decade and had stronger ties to French Canadian ultramontanism (Killen 2000). Strong resentment simmered against the British HBC on the part of American settlers who began to arrive via the Oregon Trail in the same decade. The Oregon Treaty of 1846 situated the mainland boundary separating British and American territories at the forty-ninth parallel.

While porosity persisted across the border, settler-colonial policy and practice also diverged on either side of the forty-ninth after 1846 (Crawford O'Brien, this volume; Marshall 2018). The Oregon Territory was created in 1848, Washington Territory in 1853, and statehood followed in 1859 and 1889, respectively. American settlement north and south of the Columbia River swelled relative to Indigenous and fur trade societies. Settlement was spurred by the 1850 Homestead Act, which offered free land to settlers, and was supported by a formal military presence. Aiming to extinguish Indigenous land title and accelerate assimilation, Governors Palmer (Oregon) and Stevens (Washington) met in council with Indigenous peoples in the 1850s to negotiate a series of treaties that affirmed rights to fishing and hunting and education and health care. The treaties also produced a new reservation geography that assembled Indigenous peoples onto finite parcels, thus restricting access to landscapes of sacred and seasonal harvesting significance (Harmon 2008). In 1869, under President Grant's Peace Policy, administration of reservations was parcelled out to particular Christian denominations, intensifying sectarian conflict between missionaries and their efforts to promote agrarian Christian civilization among "Indians," a malleable category produced in and by the context of colonialism itself (Prucha 1988; Harmon 1998).

In contrast to Washington and Oregon, and much of Canada as well, few treaties were negotiated with Indigenous peoples in the territories that became British Columbia. In 1849, Vancouver Island became a British colony under the administration of the HBC. Between 1850 and 1854, HBC chief factor and the colony's second governor James Douglas entered a series of fourteen treaties with Salish peoples on southern Vancouver Island, in the region surrounding Fort Victoria, and with Salish and Kwakwaka'wakw peoples in coal-rich areas farther north. With the exception of Treaty 8, which includes the northeastern portion of what is now the province, no further historical treaties were negotiated on Vancouver Island or the mainland, which became a British colony in 1858 in the context of the Fraser River gold rush.

Officials set out a number of Indian reserves on Vancouver Island and the mainland in the early colonial period. By the time British Columbia entered Confederation in 1871, many of these had been clawed back. The new province vigorously denied Indigenous land title, leading to sustained disagreements with Indigenous peoples and the federal government alike. By 1876, when the first Indian Reserve Commission was established to allot reserve lands in the new province, settlers had already acquired significant swaths of land through pre-emption and purchase (Harris 2002). As historian Paige Raibmon has demonstrated, the process of "unmaking Native space" proceeded through "microtechniques of dispossession," through mundane settler practices of the everyday, as well as formal policy (Raibmon 2008). Policy was a blunt instrument too, however, witnessed especially in the Indian Act, a sweeping piece of federal legislation first introduced in 1876 that continues to govern relations between the Canadian state and those defined by the Act as "Indians" (Kelm and Smith 2018).

Christianity was also intimately bound up in the project of settler colonialism, permeating what religious studies scholar Pamela Klassen (2016) has called settler cosmologies of land. In a context where "the Bible and the plough" were promoted as the twin pillars of progress, Indigenous practices such as the Potlatch on the Northwest Coast, which include the ritual redistribution of wealth, simultaneously offended Christian and capitalist sympathies (Miller 2000, 254–62). Just how contemporaneous irreligion in the Pacific Northwest informed settler-colonial policy and practice in the region is a question calling for investigation.[12]

In support of their civilizing missions, the Canadian and American states both criminalized Indigenous spiritual practices in the 1880s (Irwin 2000; Miller 2000, 212–15). Christianity was most directly marshalled in service of settler colonialism in the context of education. Catholic and Protestant churches established mission schools in British Columbia, Washington, and Oregon during the second half of the nineteenth century. Some mission schools in the American Pacific Northwest received federal funding until the turn of the twentieth century. In Canada, conversely, churches were paid by the federal government to operate schools well into the second half of the twentieth century. Architects of Canada's residential school system, which coalesced in the 1880s, drew inspiration from the first large-scale American Indian boarding school that opened in Carlisle, Pennsylvania, in 1879 under the direction of former military commander Richard Pratt. The second such institution in the United States, Chemawa Indian School, opened in Oregon in 1880. Pratt's oft-cited aim to "kill the Indian in him and save the man" well captures the goal of cultural genocide that these institutions embodied.[13] Federal law in both Canada and the United States was used to mandate student attendance and impose stiff penalties on resistant families. However, where most off- and on-reservation federal boarding schools in Washington and Oregon were closed by the 1930s, many residential schools in British Columbia remained in operation into the 1970s and some beyond this (Crawford O'Brien 2013, 84–88; Marker 2015; TRC 2015). These schools, which often moved children great distances from their home communities, sought to disrupt and destroy Indigenous kinship systems, languages, and lifeways. The intergenerational impacts of the physical, emotional, spiritual, and sexual abuse and deaths commonly suffered at these institutions are rife (TRC 2015; Crawford O'Brien, this volume; Al Jazeera Staff 2021).

Indigenous children, families, and communities exercised agency and resistance in engaging with residential and boarding schools (Miller 1996, 343–74; TRC 2015; Wellington 2019). By bringing together children from broad backgrounds, these institutions also contributed to the production of new intertribal relationships and political alliances. This process was also propelled by the migration of more Indigenous people into urban centres after the Second World War. In the United States, postwar relocation programs contributed to heightened urban Indigenous migration while termination policies aimed to sever historical treaty relationships and erase tribes altogether. A special issue of the *Oregon Historical Quarterly* dedicated to the Stevens and Palmer Treaties reports that 62 of the 109 tribes and bands subject to the US Termination Act of 1954 were in Oregon. Some of these tribes have since been restored via a federal acknowledgment process.

In Canada, many of the key postwar legal cases that have clarified the contours of Aboriginal rights, especially since these rights were affirmed but not defined in the country's 1982 Constitution Act, have come out of British Columbia. These cases are a product of both a long history of Indigenous rights activism in the province and British Columbia's historical stance on rights and title that rendered this work so pressing. Since the early 1990s, a modern treaty negotiation process has also been underway in the province.

It was likewise in this decade that survivors brought residential schools to growing public awareness by way of lawsuits against the federal government and churches involved in the system. The Truth and Reconciliation Commission was one strand of an out-of-court settlement agreement stemming from these suits. In 2008, the Conservative prime minister, Stephen Harper, issued an apology on behalf of the Canadian government for residential schools even as he elsewhere denied a history of colonialism in Canada (Coulthard 2014, 105–30). Churches and religious orders involved in the system have also offered formal apologies; the Pope has refused to do so on behalf of the Catholic Church at large. Public and political momentum of this order has not been witnessed in the United States. Notably, however, in Seattle in fall 1987, ten prominent Protestant and Catholic leaders extended a formal apology to Indigenous peoples of the Pacific Northwest for the historical involvement of their churches in the destruction of Indigenous spirituality. This public declaration included a call for church communities to "stand in solidarity" with Indigenous peoples protecting their spiritual freedom (Magnuson 1987).[14]

In Canada today, other settler-colonial institutions interconnected with residential schools – including Indian Hospitals, day schools and the experiences of day scholars, and the Sixties Scoop and subsequent child welfare practices – are now the subject of public investigation and litigation. The final report of a controversial National Inquiry into Missing and Murdered Indigenous Women and Girls was released in June 2019. The report characterizes violence against Indigenous women, girls, and 2SLGBTQQIA people in Canada as the product of "a race-based genocide."[15] An announcement by Tk'emlúps te Secwépemc in late May 2021 confirming that the remains of 215 children had been discovered on the site of the former Kamloops Indian residential school (IRS) in British Columbia has prompted ongoing investigations and announcements of unmarked graves uncovered at other former IRS sites in BC and elsewhere in Canada (Al Jezeera 2021; Tk'emlúps te Secwépemc 2021).

A Snapshot from the Field

These living histories surfaced in different ways in the 2018 fieldwork for this project. The subject of Indigenous-settler relations sometimes arose subtly in interviews and focus groups, as in the invocation of the frontier discussed in my opening. We heard explicit critiques of the frontier narrative as well, which came from millennials who organically wove a critical analysis of settler colonialism into their reflections.[16] We also asked settler participants directly about their relationships with Indigenous people. The snapshot that emerged reveals current contemplation and action related to the history of settler colonialism by religious and irreligious participants in British Columbia. The conversation we observed in Washington and especially Oregon, by contrast, was more muted.

This cleavage was noted by some research participants. An Episcopalian leader we met in Portland, for example, contrasted subdued attention to Indigenous-settler relations at his church with the regular practice of territorial acknowledgment among his Anglican colleagues in British Columbia. The protocol of territorial acknowledgment is shared by many Indigenous communities in the Pacific Northwest and is increasingly common among settler people and institutions in British Columbia as well. In British Columbia, such acknowledgments frequently reference the unceded nature of the ancestral territory in question, underlining that these lands have not been surrendered by their Indigenous owners through treaty or other means. Reverend Olsen in Portland observed, "That's kind of pro forma, right? That's one of the major differences." Olsen recalled his reaction when he learned from an Anglican friend in Vancouver that he and his colleagues offer an acknowledgment each time they gather as a community: "And I'm like, 'Oh my gosh, that's really significant,' 'cause that's never even, hasn't really ever been, on my radar screen, really." He noted that there had been some thematic events hosted at his cathedral where he'd been "asked to do an introduction, and to name, 'We recognize that we are on the lands of the,' I forget, 'the Clackamas, the Tualatin, and the Kalapuya.'" Such special events, Olsen explained, have been attended by tribal members and have included recognition of settler occupation, but they are "less a kind of pro forma." That Reverend Olsen did not readily recall the names of the Indigenous peoples on whose Traditional Territory his cathedral is situated underlines his observations. His use of the term "pro forma" is also apt in pointing out both the commonplace nature of this practice in British Columbia today and the real risk of it being a token gesture occurring in the absence of actual relationships with local Indigenous peoples.[17]

An Anglican leader with whom we spoke in Victoria explained that reconciliation work between settler and Indigenous people is part of his diocese's contemporary culture, if not the quotidian consciousness of his specific suburban congregation, which includes a former residential school employee in her nineties. Reverend Wilson shared: "I haven't stood up in the pulpit and described the residential schools as a genocide, which I do in other circumstances, but [what] it really comes down to is, How do nice people like [this woman in my church] get involved in genocide?" Reverend Wilson noted that the bishop of his diocese, Logan McMenamie, prioritized reconciliation while also attracting critique by placing himself at the centre of this effort. Reverend Wilson gave the particular example of a prominent walk for reconciliation that the bishop conducted in 2017, which, he said, some dismissed as "the Logan show." A Victoria focus-group participant, who has professional ties to the Anglican and United Churches in Victoria, also referenced the bishop's walk in the course of a sustained rumination on truth and reconciliation. Benjamin observed, "That was quite a powerful thing and a visible thing. I think we're still, in many ways, listening for truth rather than even being able to talk about reconciliation and deconstructing a lot our own both internal and external colonial symbols."

Catholics whom we spoke with in Victoria likewise reflected on personal and institutional relationships with Indigenous people. However, in our interactions, these research participants did not broach the subject of residential schools. Throughout our interview with Reverend Travis, who had been in relationship with Coast Salish communities for over forty years, he foregrounded the imperative of forging relationships of respect with growing Indigenous communities in the context of reconciliation, rising secularism, and the international composition of today's priesthood. Reverend Travis explained:

> So that's what I'm trying to create opportunities for – for the non-Indigenous
> Catholic population. It's not easy, though, because you've got, in some places,

real long systemic racism. It's really built in. And it's not easy to overcome ... [We] just have to try and get the right fit where they get an openness to this culture, where they're open to learning, where they have a sense of appreciation.

This ethic of appreciation, without sustained attention to historical missionary violence and its living legacies, suffused the reflections of Reverend Travis.[18]

In Vancouver, a Filipino Catholic deacon, Daniel Mendoza, likewise reflected on relationships with Indigenous people, though in a more aspirational manner. The subject arose in Deacon Mendoza's response to a question concerning issues of conflict that he has observed between the church and surrounding society: he flagged residential schools. Mendoza articulated a sense of congruence between Indigenous peoples and Filipinos based on their common histories of colonialism and communalism and their relationship to nature and sense of humour. He explained that he aimed to mobilize this affiliation in the mission field. When asked how the Pope's refusal to issue an apology for the Catholic Church's role in residential schools might bear on such efforts, he did not have a ready response. While Deacon Mendoza observed that the subject of residential schools was not firmly on the radar of the Filipino community, a Filipina Catholic participant in the Vancouver adherent focus group, which included a former residential school student, expressed both familiarity and remorse for this history, as did a Chinese evangelical Christian participant who grew up in Greater Vancouver.

A Chinese evangelical pastor and entrepreneur with whom we also spoke in Vancouver reflected on nascent (sometimes, even necessarily, fumbling) relationship-building efforts underway among a community of pastors to which he belonged. Evan Wong recalled the challenge he faced in trying to identify the local First Nation (what he called "tribe," a term that is more anachronistic in Canada than the United States) on whose territory his suburban church is situated. Google, he explained with an honest chuckle, was not especially helpful. He turned next to his member of Parliament and Elections Canada. Wong explained that he has since been in dialogue with an Elder at the local First Nation, working to cultivate opportunities for connection. He gave the example of a Good Friday community dinner that his church, which is predominantly second- and third-generation Chinese, hosted for the neighbourhood:

But then we made sure to invite them, to invite them because they are part of the community. To instill that into my congregation, that they *are* part of the community. They are, and we need to make sure that we acknowledge that we are blessed by their gracious offer and hospitality of allowing us to use unceded territory for our events.[19]

Notably, the pastor did not specify whether a direct offer of hospitality had been explicitly sought or extended by the local First Nation to his church community. His reference to unceded territory may signal familiarity with the local historical landscape; it is also possible that he has adopted this wording without a deep understanding of its significance. As Rachel Brown outlines in Chapter 10 in this volume, familiarity and aspirations toward developing relationships are being cultivated among racialized adherents of minority religions in British Columbia as well. The fact that the Sunni Muslim leader with whom we spoke in the Vancouver area felt compelled at the end of our interview to circle back to relationships with Indigenous peoples and apologize for not having more to say on the subject is indicative of the live nature of these conversations.

This contrasts with the relative quiet in the United States, highlighted by Reverend Olsen in Portland. The evangelical leaders we interviewed in that city were all the more blunt in reporting that Indigenous-settler relationships are simply not on the radar, publicly or in their church communities, in any substantial way.[20] As one Pentecostal leader, Pastor Novak, put it: "Portland is the whitest city in America. And it wrings my heart. So I can say with great confidence, and this is a sign of great problems, that's not even a conversation Portlanders are having right now." Another nondenominational pastor, Armando, situated this silence in the context of Oregon's acute history of racial exclusion, a connection likewise underlined by participants in our millennial focus group in Portland. Rachel, a Reform Jew who had relocated to Portland the previous year, described her dissatisfaction with the fact "that there's so much history here, and it's either built over, whitewashed, or completely ignored," a sentiment that was echoed by participants with long ties to the area. As also noted by Rachel Brown in this volume, the Reform rabbis with whom we spoke in Portland and Seattle both reported having interacted with Indigenous peoples in interfaith contexts, but infrequently.[21] Rabbi Levi in Portland underlined that even this infrequent interaction, and acknowledgment and political inclusion of Indigenous peoples more generally, is much more robust than he experienced living and working on the East Coast.

A Jewish millennial we met in Seattle, who has Métis heritage and grew up in xʷməθkʷəy̓əm territory in the Greater Vancouver area, intentionally connects his religiosity to the context of settler colonialism. In response to a question concerning whether and how Indigenous peoples' presence in the Pacific Northwest informs how focus-group participants live in and imagine the region, Andrew shared:

> In terms of myself, I find it hard to disconnect Seattle, because I've grown up in this region. I think that it's always encouraged me as a Jew to take a post-colonial understanding of how Judaism has evolved under the influence of

dominant colonizing cultures around it. I think it's also, I've always felt that it seems necessary or obvious that my religiosity and my paradigm has to account for my status as a settler in this area.

He later referred to the territorial acknowledgment with which we opened the focus group: "I think that my religiosity has been always informed by the experience and context of colonialism and acknowledgment (like you began with) ... that I adhere to a tradition that came here by virtue of colonialism and violence, even if it itself, unlike some other religious traditions, did not bring directed violence toward the Indigenous inhabitants of this area."

This perspective contrasts with the experience of another religious millennial in Seattle, Chinese Catholic Fiona, a self-identified transplant from California who explained that before her move five years previous, "I didn't know that when people here said 'Seattle Native,' they meant something different [than someone who grew up in Seattle], right?" Her exposure has since come in the context of her downtown church, which features Indigenous art and outreach service efforts. "So I haven't had a very complex or deep dive into what that means for that area," Fiona added, "but I know at least that 'Seattle Native' means something different than someone from Seattle."

Whereas Andrew and Fiona reflected on Indigenous-settler relations in the context of their own religiosity, millennials with whom we spoke in British Columbia drew a clear correlation between colonialism and irreligion among their peers. This dynamic had been evident to millennial Muslim Kamal since arriving in Vancouver from Toronto (and South Africa before that) in 2016. Building on observations from another participant, Ainsley, who reflected on her sense of exclusion as a white queer feminist from the Christian faith of her ancestors, Kamal observed:

I think, as a result of colonialism, the avenues of spirituality are so narrow, like the church or nothing, and a lot of the guys I went to school with, they didn't agree with the church, so they became atheist, so there's no other room to explore, and this is a question I've been having since I got here. Because the church is responsible for colonialism, residential schools, I wouldn't want to be associated with something like that. The Pope is not apologizing. These are, like, big things, right? So, if you, because I don't have access to any other tradition, then, and the one that I do have doesn't seem right for me, then you switch to "agnostic," "atheist," or I have my own individual spirituality.

In Victoria, Samuel and Kayla both observed millennial disinterest and distress with organized religion, which, Kayla noted, her peers immediately connected to colonial institutions such as residential schools and Indian Hospitals.

Lindsay, who grew up in an irreligious household and converted to evangelical Christianity as a young adult, connected this to her upbringing:

> The story I was told about what Christians are, what religious people are, is "They're bad. They're bad people who do bad things and hurt people." And it was kind of in the story of being educated about what it means to be a white person on colonized lands, et cetera, et cetera. So, like, very much a moralistic, antireligious – but subtle, subtle – teaching. And I think that my impression is that attitude that religiousness is bad because religious people hurt Indigenous people and other oppressed minorities; I suspect that that's a relatively distinct Cascadia thing, that that's here. And I suspect that that's a lot to do with the historical relationship that's unique to this place, with Indigenous people and that, kind of, special case.

When asked to elaborate on this special context, Lindsay pointed to the (lack of) treaties, prominent pipeline debates, and efforts to indigenize public school curriculums in British Columbia.

Notably, it was in Portland that we heard an especially perceptive, and unprompted, reflection on Indigenous-settler relations that also connected history, place, religion, and race. In ruminating on his experience as an African American leader of a liberal religious congregation in Portland, Reverend Richards shared that "part of my discipline here has been to try to figure out how to be a minister of colour ministering to an overwhelmingly white congregation in a vastly white city." Part of this work, he explained, has been to pursue relationships with historically marginalized communities. Significantly, the first example of such relationship building that Richards supplied was a collaboration with the Grand Ronde Council on a land acknowledgment for use at his community's downtown Portland church, an effort that grew out of interaction through an ecological justice initiative. When asked to elaborate on the regional nature of his experience of race and place, Richards spoke of the history of settler colonialism, underlining his church's direct role in missionary civilization efforts in the West. He explained: "And so part of what needs doing for this congregation and this place is a holding up of that history and to say, 'Well, alright, how does that impact who we are today? How does that impact how this church is shown?'" For Richards, this includes paying attention to the specific activist issues that his church has "shown up around," which, he noted, tended to exclude historical issues. Connecting this specifically to the Northwest, Richards reflected, "It's my experience that people who grew up here have a very deep sense of place," "one that does not have much room in it for diversity of people." While such a sense of connection may exist elsewhere, Richards observed: "There is something about the commitment to this place, and Portland particularly. I think it may be true more broadly, the kind of arrogance that comes with the fact that we think we've got it pretty well figured out here. You know, 'Way ahead on environmental, way ahead.' Which is actually not so much true anymore." The Reverend stopped at this point, saying, "I'm rambling." Far from a ramble, his observations offer piercing insight into silences and exclusions produced by the intense commitment to place that is such a prominent feature of Portland and the Pacific Northwest more generally.

As underscored in my opening, settler commitment and claim to place can (re)produce colonial erasure by obscuring Indigenous peoples and territories. However, it can also spark a connection. As other contributors to this volume observe, environmental efforts to protect land and water are strong in the Pacific Northwest, and Indigenous people occupy significant leadership and symbolic roles. Rising expressions of and exposure to Indigenous teachings concerning the interconnection of the human and nonhuman worlds is contributing to a discourse on and practice of what we might call, riffing on Paul Bramadat's chapter in this volume, a relational naturalism in the region. Our fieldwork reveals that such a perspective resonates with settlers of religious and irreligious identification alike, on both sides of the border. In this sense, shared Indigenous teachings such as respect, stewardship, and "all is one" serve to bind Indigenous peoples but also serve as a beacon for settlers seeking to be in right relationship with all living beings in the region.[22] As Suzanne Crawford O'Brien notes in the next chapter, in the wake of the 1974 Boldt Decision that affirmed treaty fishing rights in Washington, momentum and collaboration have emerged among settler and Indigenous communities especially around salmon stewardship in that state, a trend observed by Christian research participants in Seattle.[23]

There is a long and ongoing history of settler projection and appropriation of the imaginary "ecological Indian" in the Pacific Northwest, a trend both critiqued and embodied by various participants in this project, including a dedicated atheist student of a Native American–inspired tracker school.[24] In Victoria, focus-group participant Gloria positioned herself within this history as she shared an anecdote about meeting the late Anishinaabe author Richard Wagamese at a book event in town. Gloria recalled admitting to Wagamese, "I was that white guy in your book *The Quality of Light*. I was the white guy. I wanted to be an Indian because they're so attached [to the land]." Gloria shared with emotion that it is through more recent exposure to the history, ceremony, and community of her Indigenous neighbours, exposure that has come through contributions she has made to community initiatives such as the repatriation of stolen ancestors from museum collections, that she has come to a place where she identifies as pre-Christian and observes a personal spiritual practice that includes a mix of Asian-informed practices and being in nature.

In Vancouver, millennial focus-group participant Nicholas, a British graduate student who has lived in the region for a number of years, invoked the possibility of coming into relationship with Indigenous peoples, lands, and lifeways via solidarity on the environment. Tacking back to Kamal's reflections on colonialism and religion discussed above, Nicholas suggested that a move to atheism is not the only option for those disaffected from Christianity: "I just want to say that the older tradition of nature connecting spirituality, that's been on this land, is available to people who are willing to do the work and if that's what you want. The Watch House, without going into too much detail, is a place of ceremony where you can find community, spirituality, and environmentalism." The Watch House, or Kwekwecnewtxw (a place to watch from), was erected by Coast Salish leaders and community members in Burnaby, a suburb of Vancouver, in opposition to the Trans Mountain pipeline expansion project. Nicholas's comment about the need "to do the work" gestures at processes of relationship building that are underway in the region, in this case in the context of an Indigenous-led movement for environmental justice and Indigenous rights. The virulent racism that erupted in winter 2020 in tandem with solidarity actions across Canada in support of hereditary Wet'suwet'en leaders who were opposing the construction of an LNG pipeline through their territory in northern British Columbia was, simultaneously, a raw reminder of the fraught and fragile nature of Indigenous-settler relations in this region and country (Sterritt 2020).

On Religion, Irreligion, and Settler Colonialism in the Pacific Northwest

There is much to unpack in all of this. In foregrounding settler reflections on Indigenous-settler relations in British Columbia today, and contrasting them with a relative quiet and a more explicit frontier narrative south of the border, it is by no means my intent to reinscribe the benevolent peacemaker myth on which Canada has long nourished itself (Regan 2010, 83–110). Indeed, current momentum concerning reconciliation, resurgence, rights, land, and law in British Columbia has emerged out of the acutely unsettled and fresh nature of settler-colonial history here and the strength and leadership of Indigenous peoples in living and sharing their stories of resilience and sovereignty.

Reconciliation is a contested project, rejected by some outright and critiqued by others as a token state-sponsored effort to seek closure, instead of relationship, and to perpetuate a colonial politics of recognition instead of Indigenous self-determination (see, for example, Coulthard 2014; McCall and L'Hirondelle Hill 2015). The Truth and Reconciliation Commission, specifically, has been criticized for perpetrating violence by placing the retraumatizing burden of public truth telling on the shoulders of survivors. Ethnic, critical race, and Indigenous studies scholars Eve Tuck and K. Wayne Yang (2012) underlined succinctly several years ago that "decolonization is not a metaphor." Territorial acknowledgment alone will not restore Indigenous land, law, and language. Nor will apologies, acts of contrition, and calls for change foster mutually respectful relationships absent sustained action.

The voices of settlers shared here add texture to these complex conversations. They also suggest that BC readers would indeed be likely to situate Monkman's *The Scoop,* decontextualized in the pages of "The Wicked Issue," in a living history of violence against Indigenous families and Indigenous lands. Further, a deep devotion to place woven through the pages of *CMC* and the reflections of participants in this research simultaneously call up the obfuscation of Indigenous peoples' presence and a potential space for collaborative relationship building. As Suzanne Crawford O'Brien takes up further in the next chapter, there is much to contemplate in the specificities of settler colonialism within, and beyond, the border in the Pacific Northwest.

NOTES

1 Monkman is a member of the Fisher River Cree Nation in Manitoba.
2 On reconciliation and resurgence (as complementary, not antagonistic, projects), see Asch, Borrows, and Tully (2018).
3 See also Portland interviews with Father Biali; Pastor Shannon. For archival and interview data see https://www.uvic.ca/research/centres/csrs/.
4 Existing literature on irreligion and place in the Pacific Northwest that engages frontier narratives gestures to the context of settler colonialism without engaging it in depth. See, for example, Block (2016) and Duntley (2017).
5 I use "irreligion" flexibly to include that whole banner of identification and practice ranging from ardent atheism to the more fuzzy "spiritual but not religious."
6 For a study that undertakes this work on Vancouver Island, see Black (2017).
7 On colonial contours of Cascadia, see Decolonizing Cascadia? (2014).
8 On the category of settler, see Battell Lowman and Barker (2015).
9 Mackenzie's arrival is celebrated, with discernable Canadian patriotism, in the opening pages of *CMC*.
10 Historian Jean Barman has been seminal in teasing out these relationships. This section draws on her overview history in Barman (2008). See also Barman (2020).
11 Jack, a Salish artist we interviewed in Seattle, shared with us a painting he was contributing to an Indigenous project in the city that responded to Manifest Destiny; Jack's piece riffed directly on Gast's.
12 Marks (2017, 214–15) and Wickwire (2019, 79, 187) both plant compelling seeds for such investigation in British Columbia.
13 For a recent revisiting of Pratt, see Lomawaima and Ostler (2018). The journal issue in which this article appears is dedicated to boarding schools and, telling of a common trend of limited cross-border historiographical engagement, is largely silent on the Canadian context.
14 On church apologies, see also Seattle interview, Mark.

15 2SLGBTQQIA: two-spirit, lesbian, gay, bisexual, transgender, queer, questioning, intersex, and asexual.

16 See, for example, the comments of Jeremy, Ainsley, and Kamal in the Vancouver millennial focus group and Andrew in the Seattle millennial focus group.

17 On the politics of territorial acknowledgment, see CBC Radio (2019) and Vowel (2016).

18 See also the reflections of Joan, Victoria adherent focus group.

19 There is a long history of Indigenous-Asian interaction in the region. See O'Bonsawin and Price (2020).

20 Another blunt moment arose in an early research team meeting for this project when an American team member expressed shock at the amount of time and energy Canadian team members dedicated to discussions of Indigenous research ethics and Indigenous-settler relations. With a shake of the head, this person exclaimed, in effect, "We just don't give a shit in the US." That is not to say that this individual does not consider these issues worthy of consideration but simply that they are not on the public or most academics' radar in any substantial way.

21 On Indigenous-Jewish interactions, see also Leonard, Portland adherent focus group; George, Vancouver interview.

22 See, for example, Stanley, Portland adherent focus group; Keith and Sunny, oral-history interviews. The potential of alliance-building through connection to place is not restricted to settlers who fit the conventional environmentalist bill. See Grossman (2017).

23 See Seattle adherent focus group, Mark Seattle interview.

24 Patrick, oral-history interview. See also Tamara, Portland adherent focus group; Rose, oral-history interview. For a compelling analysis of this history in Seattle, see Thrush (2007).

References

Al Jazeera Staff. 2021. "Canada Pledges Millions to Search for Residential School Graves." *Al Jazeera*, August 10. https://www.aljazeera.com/news/2021/8/10/canada-pledges -millions-to-search-for-unmarked-indigenous-graves.

Asch, Michael, John Borrows, and James Tully, eds. 2018. *Resurgence and Reconciliation: Indigenous-Settler Relations and Earth Teachings*. Toronto: University of Toronto Press.

Barman, Jean. 2008. "Cascadia once upon a Time." In *Cascadia, the Elusive Utopia: Exploring the Spirit of the Pacific Northwest*, edited by Douglas Todd, 89–104. Vancouver: Ronsdale Press.

–. 2020. *On the Cusp of Contact: Gender, Space, and Race in the Colonization of British Columbia*, edited by Margery Fee. Madeira Park, BC: Harbour.

Battell Lowman, Emma, and Adam J. Barker. 2015. *Settler: Identity and Colonialism in 21st-Century Canada*. Black Point, NS: Fernwood.

Black, Kelly. 2017. "An Archive of Settler Belonging: Local Feeling, Land, and the Forest Resource on Vancouver Island." PhD diss., Carleton University.

Block, Tina. 2016. *The Secular Northwest: Religion and Irreligion in Everyday Life*. Vancouver: UBC Press.

CBC Radio. 2019. "'I Regret It': Hayden King on Writing Ryerson University's Territorial Acknowledgement." *Unreserved*, January 18. https://www.cbc.ca/radio/unreserved/ redrawing-the-lines-1.4973363/i-regret-it-hayden-king-on-writing-ryerson-university -s-territorial-acknowledgement-1.4973371.

Coast Mountain Culture. 2018–19. "The Wicked Issue." Special issue, *Coast Mountain Culture* (Winter).

Coulthard, Glen. 2014. *Red Skin, White Masks: Rejecting the Colonial Politics of Recognition*. Minneapolis: University of Minnesota Press.

Crawford O'Brien, Suzanne. 2013. *Coming Full Circle: Spirituality and Wellness among Native Communities in the Pacific Northwest.* Lincoln: University of Nebraska Press.

Decolonizing Cascadia? Rethinking Critical Geographies' Conference Organizing Committee. 2014. "Decolonizing Cascadia?" *ACME* 13 (3): 595–604.

Duntley, Madeline. 2017. "Place and Spirituality in the Pacific Northwest." *Oxford Research Encyclopedia, Religion.* https://doi.org/10.1093/acrefore/9780199340378.013.564.

Grossman, Zoltán. 2017. *Unlikely Alliances: Native and White Communities Join to Defend Rural Lands.* Seattle: University of Washington Press.

Harmon, Alexandra. 1998. *Indians in the Making: Ethnic Relations and Indian Identities around Puget Sound.* Berkeley: University of California Press.

—, ed. 2008. *The Power of Promises: Rethinking Indian Treaties in the Pacific Northwest.* Seattle: University of Washington Press.

Harris, Cole. 2002. *Making Native Space: Colonialism, Resistance, and Reserves in British Columbia.* Vancouver: UBC Press.

Irwin, Lee. 2000. "Freedom, Law, and Prophecy: A Brief History of Native American Religious Resistance." In *Native American Spirituality: A Critical Reader,* edited by Lee Irwin, 295–316. Lincoln: University of Nebraska Press.

Kelm, Mary-Ellen, and Keith Smith, eds. 2018. *Talking Back to the Indian Act: Readings in Settler Colonial Histories.* Toronto: University of Toronto Press.

Killen, Patricia O'Connell. 2000. "Writing the Pacific Northwest into Canadian and U.S. Catholic History: Geography, Demographics, and Regional Religion." *Historical Studies* 66: 74–91.

Killen, Patricia O'Connell, and Mark Silk, eds. 2004. *Religion and Public Life in the Pacific Northwest: The None Zone.* Walnut Creek, CA: AltaMira Press.

Klassen, Pamela. 2016. "God Keep Our Land: The Legal Ritual of the McKenna-McBride Commission, 1913–16." In *Religion and the Exercise of Public Authority,* edited by Benjamin Berger and Richard Moon, 79–94. Oxford: Hart.

Lomawaima, K. Tsianina, and Jeffery Ostler. 2018. "Reconsidering Richard Henry Pratt: Cultural Genocide and Native Liberation in an Era of Racial Oppression." *Journal of American Indian Education* 57 (1): 79–100.

Magnuson, Jon. 1987. "Affirming Native Spirituality: A Call to Justice." *Christian Century* 104 (37): 1114–17.

Marker, Michael. 2015. "Borders and the Borderless Coast Salish: Decolonising Historiographies of Indigenous Schooling." *History of Education* 44 (4): 480–502.

Marks, Lynne. 2017. *Infidels and the Damn Churches: Irreligion and Religion in Settler British Columbia.* Vancouver: UBC Press.

Marshall, Daniel. 2018. *Claiming the Land: British Columbia and the Making of a New El Dorado.* Vancouver: Ronsdale Press.

McCall, Sophie, and Gabrielle L'Hirondelle Hill. 2015. *The Land We Are: Artists and Writers Unsettle the Politics of Reconciliation.* Winnipeg: ARP Books.

Miller, J.R. 1996. *Shingwauk's Vision: A History of Native Residential Schools.* Toronto: University of Toronto Press.

—. 2000. *Skyscrapers Hide the Heavens: A History of Indian-White Relations in Canada.* 3rd ed. Toronto: University of Toronto Press.

Murphyao, Amanda, and Kelly Black. 2015. "Unsettling Settler Belonging: (Re)naming and Territory Making in the Pacific Northwest." *American Review of Canadian Studies* 45 (3): 315–31.

National Inquiry into Missing and Murdered Indigenous Women and Girls. 2019. *Reclaiming Power and Place: Executive Summary of the Final Report.* https://www.mmiwg-ffada.ca/final-report/.

O'Bonsawin, Christine, and John Price, eds. 2020. "(Un)settling the Islands: Race, Indigeneity and the Transpacific." Special issue, *BC Studies* 204 (Winter 2019–20).

Oregon Historical Quarterly. 2005. "The Isaac I. Stevens and Joel Palmer Treaties, 1855–2005." Special issue, *Oregon Historical Quarterly* 106 (3).

Prucha, Francis Paul. 1988. "Two Roads to Conversion: Protestant and Catholic Missionaries in the Pacific Northwest." *Pacific Northwest Quarterly* 79 (4): 130–37.

Raibmon, Paige. 2008. "Unmaking Native Space: A Genealogy of Indian Policy, Settler Practice, and the Microtechniques of Dispossession." In *The Power of Promises*, edited by Alexandra Harmon, 56–85. Seattle: University of Washington Press.

Regan, Paulette. 2010. *Unsettling the Settler Within: Indian Residential Schools, Truth Telling, and Reconciliation in Canada.* Vancouver: UBC Press.

Sterritt, Angela. 2020. "Rise in Anti-Indigenous Racism and Violence Seen in Wake of Wet'suwet'en Protests." *CBC News*, February 27. https://www.cbc.ca/news/canada/british-columbia/rise-in-anti-indigenous-racism-violence-requires-allyship-accountability-say-victims-advocates-1.5477383.

Thrush, Coll. 2007. *Native Seattle: Histories from the Crossing-Over Place.* Seattle: University of Washington Press.

Tk'emlúps te Secwépemc. 2021. "Remains of Children of Kamloops Residential School Discovered." *Tk'emlúps te Secwépemc*, May 27. https://tkemlups.ca/remains-of-children-of-kamloops-residential-school-discovered/.

Todd, Douglas, ed. 2008. *Cascadia, the Elusive Utopia: Exploring the Spirit of the Pacific Northwest.* Vancouver: Ronsdale Press.

TRC (Truth and Reconciliation Commission of Canada). 2015. *Honouring the Truth, Reconciling for the Future: Summary of the Final Report of the Truth and Reconciliation Commission of Canada.* Ottawa: Truth and Reconciliation Commission of Canada.

Tuck, Eve, and K. Wayne Yang. 2012. "Decolonization Is Not a Metaphor." *Decolonization: Indigeneity, Education & Society* 1 (1): 1–40.

Veracini, Lorenzo. 2017. "Decolonizing Settler Colonialism: Kill the Settler in Him and Save the Man." *American Indian Culture and Research Journal* 41 (1): 1–18.

Vowel, Chelsea. 2016. "Beyond Territorial Acknowledgements." *âpihtawikosisân*, September 23. https://apihtawikosisan.com/2016/09/beyond-territorial-acknowledgments/.

Wellington, Rebecca. 2019. "Girls Breaking Boundaries: Acculturation and Self-Advocacy at Chemawa Indian School, 1900–1930s." *American Indian Quarterly* 43 (1): 101–32.

Wickwire, Wendy. 2019. *At the Bridge: James Teit and an Anthropology of Belonging.* Vancouver: UBC Press.

3

Border Crossings: Indigenous Spirituality and Culture in Cascadia

Suzanne Crawford O'Brien

On August 30, 2010, a Seattle police officer shot and killed John T. Williams, a Ditidaht First Nation carver from Vancouver Island, British Columbia. The officer was fired but faced no other penalty. Enraged and in grief, Seattle's intertribal, international Indigenous community responded with ceremony: they carved a memorial pole on Pier 57, where visitors could learn about Williams's life and death. On February 26, 2012, they carried the pole to its final destination near the base of the iconic Space Needle. The accompanying public ceremony testified to a history of police and state violence against Indigenous peoples, but in doing so, it transformed the narrative. Williams's brother explained his motivation in carving the pole: "They took something beautiful. Let's give Seattle something beautiful back." This work of art, he hoped, would become a "symbol of peace for many generations" (Kershner 2013). It was a public reclaiming of place, and justice, positioning Indigenous peoples as the voices of moral authority within an immoral state.

Like the previous chapter in this volume shows, Indigenous communities in Cascadia experienced colonialism in various and brutal ways. Their cultures were appropriated by or simply overlooked in settler colonial societies inspired by idealized notions of the frontier and informed by narratives that non-Indigenous settlers were the rightful inheritors of the land. As Chelsea Horton makes clear, this colonial history took different legal and political forms in Canada and the United States. Despite these divergent histories, Indigenous communities throughout Cascadia continue to share much in common. Bound by kinship and cultural ties that predate colonialism, Indigenous communities regularly cross the border for economic, social, and spiritual reasons, taking part in cultural movements, fighting to protect waterways and endangered species, and supporting one another in the face of two settler-colonial regimes. In this essay, I argue that Indigenous spiritual and cultural traditions in this region –

with their emphasis on individual journeys, family connections, and intimate relationships with water and land – have supported survival, resistance to settler colonialism, and revitalization of Indigenous communities north and south of the border. For millennia, Cascadia has been predominantly Coast Salish territory. In the twentieth century, the Coast Salish were joined by other Indigenous peoples from throughout North America, creating vibrant and diverse Indigenous communities, particularly in urban centres such as Vancouver and Victoria in Canada and Seattle, Tacoma, and Portland in the United States (Harmon 1998). As regional hosts, the Coast Salish share their culture, arts, and spirituality to anchor and animate Indigenous moral and political activity and activism, both within their own tribal groups and in the wider public sphere.

Indigenous communities thus stand in some degree of contrast to those predominantly Euro-American groups discussed in other chapters of this volume. While Indigenous communities do share with their fellow Cascadians a growing discomfort with religion as a category and an institution, this does not necessarily mean they are also participating in the region's growing movement toward secularism (Wilkins-Laflamme 2018). By contrast, Indigenous communities are, in growing numbers, engaged in a spiritual and cultural revitalization that is inspiring stronger ties to the religio-spiritual traditions of their ancestors, even as participation in Christian institutions associated with settler colonialism may be on the wane.

Multicultural, International

Indigenous religious and cultural life in Cascadia is diverse and complex. While much of the region is Coast Salish territory, the Coast Salish comprise dozens of tribal nations and communities. Moreover, these communities are linguistically diverse: Coast Salish is a language family that includes thirteen different dialects. But these communities are also connected through a network of relationships that are complicated, but not halted, by an international border. As Sylvia, a Coast Salish woman from Victoria explained,

> [We're] from [the Gulf Islands] all the way down to Portland ... We have lots and lots of relations ... In Tribal Journeys, we paddle as a community ... from Kulleet Bay ... down to Puyallup. And we'll paddle all the way down there ... [For my family, home] wasn't one spot, it was these places ... Yeah, we just, would just, drive across, all the time ... and up until recently, they'd tell you if you're going across the border, if you have your status card, they'll let you cross without a passport, but my niece said the other day that she barely made it across with her status card.[1]

As Sylvia explained, local tribal affiliations exist alongside a broader regional identity:

> So, definitely, there's this place – my grandmother always, always, always [talked] about the fact that we're Coast Salish. So, there's also that bigger connection to being Coast Salish and talk about the fact that we have similar cultures and traditions and languages ... Coast Salish people all have Big Houses. And we have particular ceremonies and celebrations that go on in the Big House, and those are very similar in all of those communities.

The United States–Canada border complicates these relationships. As Ainsley, a Vancouver millennial participant explained: "Well, for Indigenous people ... it split families historically, and [presents] legal differences that creates problems around mobility, immigration, and things like that." But Indigenous interviewees noted the border could be used strategically: at different times, families fled north or south to evade various government officials and protect children from residential schools. Others travelled for seasonal work. Some families maximized social benefits by moving back and forth across the border. Sylvia noted:

> We used to just go back and forth all the time. And there were all kinds of funny incentives, like food stamps ... Some of our families were pretty darn poor. You could get food stamps in the States ... You could say, "Oh, I've got ten nieces and nephews with me." But my aunt would get food stamps, and we would all be picking berries, and it was almost like quite a communal thing that our family did.

Movements of Indigenous peoples across borders brought diverse populations to Vancouver, Victoria, Seattle, and Portland (the four urban centres of Cascadia, where over four-fifths of the population resides). In the United States, federal relocation policies brought Indigenous peoples to cities. First Nations people from British Columbia, drawn by family ties, economic opportunity, and cultural affiliation, joined them. In the United States, 78 percent of Indigenous people live off-reservation, and 72 percent live in cities (many maintaining second homes on reservations).[2] Portland's Indigenous community is affiliated with over three hundred different tribes, and the Seattle Indian Health Board regularly serves patients from over two hundred different tribes. A 2011 combined survey of Seattle, Tacoma, and Olympia found that of those who self-identified as "Native American" or "Alaska Native," 29.5 percent were Coast Salish, 8.7 percent were Cherokee, 5.6 percent were Yakama, and 56.2 percent were categorized as "Other" (National Urban Indian Family Coalition 2011).

These urban communities needed spaces where people could come together. In 1958, Seattle women formed the American Indian Women's Service League. Led by Pearl Warren (Makah) and Ella Aquino (Lummi/Yakama), the league published a newsletter, and in 1960 they opened the city's first Indian Center, offering social services and gathering places. In 1968, the league organized an international urban Indian conference, hosting participants from the United States and Canada. And in 1970, league members supported members of the activist organization Indians of All Tribes during their occupation of Fort Lawton, when they climbed a security fence "armed with sandwiches and coffee" (Thrush 2007). That occupation proved to be successful, resulting in what would become the Daybreak Star Cultural Center.

Daybreak Star and its parent organization, United Indians of All Tribes Foundation, provide preschool, family services, outpatient treatment programs, an Elder nutrition program, a youth home, homelessness services, and a workforce development program. It hosts an intertribal powwow, exhibits the work of Indigenous artists, and provides space for ceremonies and sweat lodges. As Harold, a Yakama tribal member who serves as executive director of the centre explained, it was intentionally intertribal from its inception:

> [All the local tribal communities] just pitched in and said, "We want to help" ... There's so much sweat equity that went into this by the local Natives. They just put their heart and soul into it. And it's been a stronghold ... I would say there's no one central tribe that seems to be dominant over the others. I think we have counted seventy different representations we serve a year ... There's twenty different coastal tribes, Canadian people, people who come down from Alaska, people from Oregon, east of the mountains, they all collect here. In fact, if you could, if you really want to see sheer, a real diverse collection of Native people, come here July 20, 21, 22, [when] we have our annual powwow. [On] any one given day, six thousand people here ... You'll see a lot of coastal people, a lot of Plains people, Plateau people, Southwest people, people [from] as far east as Wisconsin. They just all come here to have a great time and practise their culture.

Thirty miles down the Interstate 5 corridor in Tacoma, the Puyallup Tribe provides another example of urban Indigenous cultural diversity. In 1976, Puyallup tribal members occupied the former site of Cushman Hospital, in the end securing land on which to build their health and wellness centre. Supported by the 1976 American Indian Self-Determination and Education Assistance Act, the tribes reclaimed control of health, education, and social services. Today, the Puyallup Tribal Health Authority cares for thousands of people, representing dozens of different tribal communities, and is a leader in culturally appropriate care, with a successful medical residency program and an integrative cancer treatment centre. The Puyallup tribal school is the largest BIA-constructed school in the country, serving students from over sixty different nations.

George, an Indigenous man whose ancestors hail from Alberta and who now lives in Vancouver, British Columbia, explained that foundational values within Coast Salish culture helped make this openness to other Indigenous cultures possible:

> They always raise their arms and thank you and acknowledge you, acknowledge your time, your presence ... Just going and just kind of saying, "You know what? I think you're great. And hopefully we can work together. It's up to you whether we do or not, but you guys are fantastic" ... And that's a very Salish attitude ... So you have this whole, sort of, urban tradition without, kind of, you're not on your Traditional Territory; you're on someone else's Traditional Territory. But that's allowed, because the Salish just want acknowledgment of their Traditional Territory, and that acknowledgment is super powerful.

Within this context, people's experiences of religion are complex and multi-faceted, combining dozens of distinct Indigenous traditions and settler-colonial religious traditions.

Religion, Spirituality, and Traditional Ways of Life

Go looking for "religion" in Indigenous communities and you may run into trouble. Survey data and interviews show that Indigenous respondents frequently distinguished between religion and traditional culture, or spirituality. Among First Nations respondents in British Columbia, Washington, and Oregon, the term "spirituality" was often used to refer to personal, private spiritual relationships with the natural world and the traditional ways of one's ancestors. "Religion," by contrast, was more often used to refer to forms of settler-colonial Christianity. Harold, director of a large intertribal organization in Seattle explained: "We don't use the word 'religions'; we just say 'sacred beliefs.' Our beliefs are nothing near of what European Christian society views of what's considered religion. Ours is more or less centred on certain trees or certain rocks, certain river bends, landmarks that are significant." Traditional forms of prayer and spirituality take place while gathering materials for basketry, carving, preparing traditional foods, fishing, hunting, sharing a song, or making offerings for the dead. However, rarely do Indigenous peoples describe these activities as "religion." For Jack, a Coast Salish traditional storyteller living in Seattle, spirituality can be found in storytelling:

But I do feel my spirit is connecting with the spirit of the story because I was taught that a story is a living thing. To speak the story, you bring it in front of people, and it stays alive by the moisture of your breath; it lives and breathes by the moisture of your breath. So, at one level, I don't consider myself a spiritual person, but at another level, if I'm helping the spirit of a story come before us and do its work, then that's a good thing.

Marie, a Coast Salish woman who lives on a reserve in the Fraser Valley near Vancouver, British Columbia, articulates this further, explaining that she is not religious but does follow her peoples' traditional ways. Asked to clarify, she explained:

The traditional and the cultural is just the surrounding of where we lived. How we lived is how we survived. So how we lived was just being together. We'd sing together, just, funerals and weddings and births, baptisms of any sort, just the gatherings still kept us alive. Oral history, also, helped us survive ... They would talk about the higher spirit, which was Xa:ls. And learning who Xa:ls was, was like God.

The private and personal nature of Coast Salish spiritual life is another reason project participants may feel it diverges from their understanding of what is meant by the term "religion." At the heart of this tradition are intimate relationships with spirit powers that include plants, animals, and ancestors. Communities have learned that protecting these deeply personal spiritual experiences requires keeping them away from the public eye: negative experiences with insensitive visitors have meant that many ceremonies are now closed to outsiders. George also observed this regard for personal privacy:

And [this Nation] does not open their spiritual tradition to anyone who's not [from the Nation] ... If you're a Kwakwaka'wakw student, and you're down here hanging out with the Salish students, the Kwakwaka'wakw are *extremely* open about their spiritual traditions ... Cormorant Island is pretty remote, and Vancouver is not. [Chuckles.] You preserve your traditions by making it private, right?

Winter Spirit dancing, also called Seowyn, Big House, or Smokehouse, is one of the most spiritually significant activities of Coast Salish spiritual life, and it is guarded from intrusion (Amoss 1970; McCormick Collins 1974; Bierwert 1999; Crawford-O'Brien 2014a). Jack explained that this sacred tradition is not categorized as "religion" by its participants:

We don't even call it religion. It's called the Smokehouse. It's called Seowyn. The Seowyn is the belief, the smokehouse, the place where they practise it. And the belief that you have the spirit of your ancestors inside you. And that through ceremony, that spirit ancestor will come out and teach you a song and dance, which you share with the community during the wintertime, in these smoke-houses. I don't think most white people, religion, they can't understand that. In fact, the early ones said: "This is obviously demonic possession, so we have to forbid the Native people from [it]." And so there were laws in Canada. Down here, there were policies set aside to punish Native people for practising that religion, that belief, the Smokehouse.

For Harold, it was the individualized nature of these traditions that set them apart from settler-colonial Christianity:

Smokehouse is more of a people have visions regularly, and they communicate their visions to the people. If it's something that seems to really take hold on the people, then they hang on to that spiritual guidance, that vision. A lot of times, it's usually in the form of animal. It could be like a wolverine, a wolf, a killer whale. Something guides their everyday decisions, so when they go to smokehouses, everyone has their own guidance mechanism that helps them through their lives. So, they don't necessarily have a preacher that tells them you should do this, or in the Bible it says this.

Many respondents emphasized that Indigenous spiritual traditions were ways of life rather than sets of particular rituals that have to be followed, doctrinal beliefs that must be adhered to, or a clerical hierarchy to which one must submit. Rather, for Indigenous peoples in Cascadia, spirituality often entails healing from trauma, restoring healthy, balanced relationships between oneself, one's human community, and the spiritual world. Sylvia, a Coast Salish woman from Vancouver Island presently living in Victoria, made this point regarding a spiritual mentor and friend:

He said: "For me, healing is about every day striving to be a better person today than I was yesterday and praying to be a better person tomorrow than I was today" ... And he said that what he knew is that there was a power that was greater than him, and the power that he believed in was the Creator, or what some people will call Chichelh Siya:m ... Chichelh Siya:m is like the highest respected person there can be ... It's about sacred bathing holes; it's about our traditional medicines; it's about our singing, drumming, dancing, language; it's about our teachings. And that's called our *snuw'uyulh,* and you know so people say, "You need to take care of your snuw'uyulh so you'll walk in a good way."

We [also] talk about the responsibility of having a name ... So, because I have my grandmother's name, I'm taught that I carry my grandmother's spirit and her ways of knowing and being ... Whether I'm behaving well or not, reflects my grandmother ... The other teaching that was really significant in the work that I have is [Hul'q'umi'num' phrase]: "Please bring in your good feelings." And my old auntie, when we were talking about "please bring in your good feelings," she said, "[Sylvia], I challenge you for one day to try, live your life with a good mind and a good heart ... " *Uy'skwuluwun* is "to be of a good mind and a good heart.

Sylvia emphasized that there is no one "right" way to learn to live with right mind and heart. For many, these lessons are found in intimate engagement with the natural world. For her, these spiritual lessons are found in water:

[For] Coast Salish, [it] is our connection to the land and the water. Like, there's a real special bond with ... the water, with the land ... Auntie told me that, before you ever got on the water, that you would go, and you would thank the water for everything they provide us ... Before you stepped foot into the canoe, you would bless the water, and you would ask the water to help guide you and direct you to where you are going ... I have this real connection. I have this real need to be on the water.

Jack also reflected on his Coast Salish tradition:

[Cedar and salmon are] two [of the] most powerful elements of this world that we live in. The Native people say: "It's the salmon's world" ... We should just be grateful that we live in the world of the salmon because they provide every-thing ... and they ask for nothing in return. The cedar tree, which are all around us, gives you everything you need to live in the world, you know, clothing, your houses, your canoes, your boxes, your ropes, your nets, your baskets, and it's a gift-giver ... So, the tribes of this area, I really believe, looked at this and said: "So, we have to be like that. We must give and expect nothing in return." This is a culture of gratitude. They give thanks constantly. They are always thanking each other, thanking the plants, the animals. They're thanking everything.

This distinction between spiritual traditions that emphasize personal healing and gratitude and settler-colonial religion can also be seen in this study's survey data. The Pacific Northwest Social Survey (PNSS) defined "religion" as "affilia-tion with a specific religious organization, belief in God, other religious beliefs, going to church or other religious education, prayer, reading scripture." For many of our survey respondents and interviewees, this definition likely seemed to exclude much of Indigenous spirituality. A commonly heard refrain was, "we do not have a religion. We have a way of life." This way of life has little to do with adhering to a formalized set of beliefs, attending church services, or reading scripture and more to do with fishing, hunting, making nettle tea, or pounding cedar bark. While scholars of religion would still find much that is "religious" in Indigenous spiritual traditions (ethical values, sacred places, rituals and ceremonies, oral traditions, and sacred symbols), within Indigenous communities, the term "religion" is more likely to be employed to distinguish between Indigenous ways of life and settler-colonial institutions.

Throughout North America, the great majority of Indigenous people also identify as Christians. While Indigenous Christianity stems from a complex legacy of colonialism, missionization, and boarding schools, it has nonetheless become a central feature of much of Indigenous North American life (see Archambault, Thiel, and Vecsey 2003; Bradford and Horton 2016; Kidwell, Noley, and Tinker 2001; McNally 2000; Treat 1996). In some regions of North America, Indigenous affiliation with Christianity (often maintained alongside some form of Indigenous beliefs) may be as high as 82 percent (Garroutte et al. 2008). But these numbers appear to be the lowest in the Pacific Northwest. In a 2011 survey of First Nations people in British Columbia, only 43 percent identified as Christian (nearly half of these were Catholic), while 53 percent claimed "no religion." At the same time, 53 percent said that religious beliefs were very or somewhat important. In our Pacific Northwest Social Survey, Indigenous people were less likely to believe in God according to the dictates of a particular religion (19 percent of Indigenous people agreed with this notion, while 22 percent of British Columbia's general population agreed, and 35 percent of Oregon's and Washington's general population agreed) and were far more likely to think about God as a higher power (17 percent of Indigenous people agreed to this claim, compared to 9 percent of British Columbia's general population and 5 percent of Oregon's and Washington's general population). While Indigenous respondents were much less likely to self-identify as religious, they were much more likely to self-identify as spiritual. Ninety-four percent of Indigenous survey respondents identified as spiritual in contrast to 74 percent of the general population of British Columbia and 77 percent of the general population of Oregon and Washington. Indigenous survey respondents were four times more likely to say that they engaged in a solitary spiritual activity each week than the general population. And 64 percent of Indigenous respondents indicated that they found spirituality within outdoor activities, compared to 51 percent of the general population in British Columbia and 48 percent of the general population in Oregon and Washington. These statistics suggest Indigenous survey respondents were less likely to identify with organized religion and more likely to see themselves as participating in individual cultural or spiritual practices, particularly those that include engagement with the natural world.

Although Indigenous people in Cascadia are less likely to identify as Christian than elsewhere in Indigenous North America, the church remains a vibrant part of life, even if it is a legacy of settler colonialism. Harold explained:

> You'll see churches on every single reservation in the Lower 48. Some small villages of less than a thousand people will have as many as seven or eight different Christian denominations there ... They actually used to gain federal funding to say, "Hey, we're going to give you money, so you go right on those reservations and you quell those Natives, you pacify them, you get them to buy into your religion, and then we're going to turn them into white people. We don't want them to be Red savages, we want them to be like white people." It never really took off, a lot of Natives will still practise their Christianity, but in large part they are hanging on to their Native sect of beliefs.

For previous generations, conversion was a way to survive. Sylvia described how this worked in her family, where her older relatives,

> identify as being Christian as well ... And sometimes she would even say things like, "Oh, that Indian stuff. That Indian stuff." And yet when ... [my son] got his name, she was like: "Are you going to have *sxwayxway* dancers? Did you make sure you talked to so-and-so about that name?" And so, all of these real, traditional protocols, right? ... Becoming a Christian often came out of a shame-based place ... If she could just be a Christian like all of the other settler people in the community, then she could be just like them. And there was lots of shame in the day of what it meant to be Indigenous ... And you see a lot of that ... around residential school is that shame-based identity. So that, because of shame, they just walked away from things, and language, culture, tradition.

The Indian Shaker Church is one way many Indigenous people found to be "Christian as well." A movement that spread across borders, the Shaker Church began in 1883, when John Squisachtun-Slocum (Squaxin) became ill and died. Three days later, during his funeral, Slocum returned to life, informing a shocked group that he had travelled to heaven, consulted with the Creator, and returned to build a new church for Indigenous people. They were to abandon settler vices: drinking, smoking, gambling, and fighting, and return to traditional ways. If they did this, Creator would send them a new medicine. A year later, John Slocum was again near death. His wife, Mary, prayed for him and began to shake, receiving a spiritual song. Slocum was miraculously healed. Known by manifestations of spiritually given song and supernatural healing, the Shaker

Church soon spread throughout Washington, Oregon, northern California, Idaho, and British Columbia.

Despite opposition from Euro-American missionaries and government agents, the movement survived and continues as one of the most important manifestations of Indigenous religious life throughout the Pacific Northwest. In the late nineteenth and early twentieth centuries, many traditional spiritual leaders joined the church, finding a way to care for their communities that reflected traditional worldviews, strengthened relationships, and evaded the worst of settler-colonial suppression. The church united the region in a new way, as Elders, ministers, and church members visited one another and attended regional gatherings. As Harold noted, the Shaker Church integrates Indigenous ways with Christian practice:

> They have their own take on religion which kind of moulds Native American beliefs, spiritual beliefs, into Christianity, if you can believe that. A lot of it is Catholicism, along with the bells, the crosses, and the emblems that you see in these churches, but yet they are moulded into how our Native people believe their connection to God ... the Shaker. They don't believe in the writings of the Bible. They just kind of constantly discuss things as a people, as a religious sect, and they make their own decisions based on that.

For Sylvia, a First Nations Coast Salish woman interviewed in Victoria, the Shaker church provided an access to spirituality for those drawn to Christianity but who still identify as Indigenous:

> We have a church, and you've probably heard of it in the Coast Salish community, called the Shaker Church. Now that is very, very Christian. You know, they've got their little altar and their crosses. And [a W̱SÁNEĆ Elder], who I just love and adore, and respect so much, is part of the Shaker faith. And you can tell by the way she does opening prayers. And from my teachings, I don't judge those people at all for needing that Christianity ... because I think that, you know, there's something about spirituality. I think that can bring us such inner peace, however that comes to us.

The Indian Shaker Church provides a stirring example of creative resistance that had the effect of strengthening Indigenous connections across the region, in the face of colonialism's disruptive influences. Particularly important during the years when it was illegal for Indigenous communities to conduct ceremonies such as Potlatches or healing rites such as soul retrieval ceremonies (from 1883 to 1978 in the United States, and from 1884 to 1951 in Canada), the Indian Shaker Church provided a way for Indigenous healing and spiritual traditions to survive in the guise of Christianity. As Indigenous peoples emphasized the veneration of Jesus, the Creator, the Holy Spirit, and the symbol of the cross, they simultaneously preserved Indigenous songs, worldviews, ethics, forms of social organization, and modes of economic exchange. With the overturning of these punitive laws in the latter half of the twentieth century, many members of Indigenous communities turned instead to reclaiming precolonial traditions and practices. In the contemporary context, as Nate observed, the Shaker Church has come to embody a very Christian practice, albeit in a distinctly Indigenous form (Amoss 1982; Barnett 1957).

Tactics of Settler Colonialism

First Nations people throughout Cascadia also share a history of settler colonialism. This larger project worked effectively to separate people from their land, fracture cultures, eradicate languages, and restrict access to traditional resources and territories. Perhaps the most destructive tactic was the removal of children from their families and communities. Indigenous children in the United States and Canada alike suffered under coercive policies that forcibly removed them from homes and placed them in religiously affiliated boarding schools. Indigenous children suffered horrific rates of sexual, physical, and mental abuse in these institutions, the legacy of which has carried on for generations. As a result, (institutionalized, settler-colonial) religion is indelibly associated with the violence and sexual abuse perpetrated on Indigenous children. When Sylvia asked her father-in-law about his experiences with the Canadian residential school system,

> he just absolutely snapped and said, "I'm *not* talking about it. Never ask me again. Don't ever bring up the subject again. I do not want to talk about it." So we don't know what happened to Dad. We know he was really angry. We know that when Dad died, he said: "Do *not* have a church service. Do *not* bury me in a church graveyard. You do not have *anything* to do with religion at my funeral." Nothing. So, all I knew growing up was from these snippets of stories that religion was a bad thing. Yeah. So that's kind of me and religion. Yeah.

Exact statistics were not kept, but at least 100,000 Indigenous children in the United States and 150,000 Indigenous children in Canada were taken from their families, and thereafter allowed only limited contact with them. As Sylvia recalled:

> I remember him saying he was hungry all the time; I remember him saying his mother passed away, and she was buried in Alert Bay. And he was in Alert Bay, and they wouldn't let him go to the funeral, and he said he could literally see

the funeral procession from the top floor of the school at St. Mike's, and they wouldn't let him leave to go to it. And then that summer, because his mother had died, him and his brothers and sisters were classified as orphans, and he said he stood on the top floor of the St. Mike's looking at all the fishing boats bringing all the children home in different directions, and him and his brothers and sisters would not leave the school that summer.

These policies impacted future generations. Nate noted, "I didn't grow up speaking [our Coast Salish language], and my mom and uncles don't. My grandma's from Squamish, but she doesn't speak anymore. I suppose from residential schools ... Her fingers [were] pinched with pliers for speaking her language and stuff like that, so she doesn't speak any more." The trauma of residential schools became part of everyday life in First Nations communities: if a person struggled with mental illness, the community understood the source. Reflecting on her upbringing among Coast Salish communities in British Columbia, Sylvia recalled, "And so I would hear things like: 'Oh, don't worry about Auntie so-and-so. She went to residential school.' So, we just learned. It just became so commonplace to hear this excuse of 'they went to residential school.' And it could be about anger; it could have been about addiction; it could have been about food."

Policies to remove children were not limited to residential schools. For decades, the United States promoted the out adoption and fostering of Indigenous children to Euro-American homes. Before the 1978 Indian Child Welfare Act, up to 35 percent of Indigenous children in the US were removed from their homes, with 85 percent of them relocated into non-Indigenous American families. In Canada, the 1960s policy known as the Sixties Scoop promoted the removal of First Nations children from their homes and adoption out to white families. Perhaps twenty thousand First Nations children were taken from their families as result of this policy (Crey and Fournier 1998).

While Indigenous peoples in both countries suffered from similar policies, they differ as to how these stories have become part of national conversations. Beginning in the 1990s, the wider Canadian public began acknowledging this staggering history of abuse, recognizing the link between trauma and struggles with suicide, addiction, mental illness, incarceration, and poverty. A Truth and Reconciliation Commission was established in 2008, as part of the Indian Residential Schools Settlement Agreement, to document the history and lasting impacts of the residential school system. Funding was established to provide cash payments for pain and suffering, and mental health care and trauma counselling for survivors and their descendants. In 2008, the Conservative prime minister, Stephen Harper, issued a formal apology for the policies that supported residential schools and the devastation they caused. By contrast, while similar abuse occurred in the United States, government officials have not offered apologies or formally acknowledged the effects of such policies, and remarkably few non-Indigenous people are even aware of this history (Lomawaima and Child 2000).

In a similar fashion, the United States and Canada both experience disproportionate rates of violence toward Indigenous people, while they differ in the degree to which the issue is acknowledged or addressed. Indigenous communities have pointed out that Indigenous women are far more likely to experience violence than non-Indigenous women and are far more likely to be attacked by non-Indigenous men. The highest number of cases is in British Columbia. In 2016, the Canadian federal government declared a national crisis, establishing the National Inquiry into Missing and Murdered Indigenous Women and Girls. While the inquiry has received criticism, it is nonetheless illustrative of a level of public awareness and political will. News coverage ensured Canadians were aware of the crisis, as it received attention at the provincial and federal level. This attention was due, in part, to the activism of First Nations women. The February 14th Women's Memorial March began in Vancouver, British Columbia, in 1991, honouring Indigenous women who have been victims of violence, and the march has spread to more than twenty communities across Canada.

While similar rates of violence against Indigenous women exist in the United States, non-Indigenous American citizens are much less likely to be aware of the crisis, and lawmakers are less likely to prioritize the issue. This may be changing. The US Senate declared May 5, 2018, a National Day of Awareness for Murdered and Missing Native American Women. Washington State House Bill 2951, calling for an investigation into violence against Indigenous women in Washington, passed unanimously through both the House and Senate and was signed into law on June 7, 2018.

Revitalization and Renewal

If Indigenous communities throughout Cascadia share an experience of settler colonialism, they also share an active engagement in the revitalization of Indigenous spirituality and culture. As communities revive traditions, Knowledge Keepers travel widely, crossing borders to assist others in reclaiming and sometimes reimagining songs, dances, ritual practices, and skills. Members of smokehouses visit one another, leading events such as naming ceremonies, giveaways, healing ceremonies, and all-night winter spirit dancing. As Marie, a First Nations woman from the Fraser Valley outside of Vancouver, British Columbia, explained, this exchange of ideas across borders is vital to cultural renewal: "I think the strength is sometimes when, we do have a Big House or a Longhouse, where a lot of the teachings come from those main speakers that travel all over, from Lummi or Saanich or Port Hardy, coming all to the smokehouse and spend some time in there."

Intrinsic to this process is language revitalization, as more and more tribal programs, colleges, and universities offer Indigenous language courses (Hermes, Bang, and Marin 2012; Shreve and Littlebear 2019; Meek 2012). Such programs employ new technologies, digitizing information and providing new ways to learn. During his interview in Victoria, Nate reflected on the connection between Indigenous cultural and linguistic revitalization:

> More and more people [are] doing the [language] immersion program, for instance. You can't really learn the language without learning about the cultural and spiritual things with it, too, because lots of words, they tie to specific stories or places, and then there's [a] creation story with that place. They kind of get linked together ... If you have more people speaking [our language], then you probably have more people thinking about what's the worldview that informs it or comes with it, that animates it ... The more you bring these sorts of teachings, laws, and language forward more, then Indigenous spirituality comes along with it.

As Indigenous communities negotiate the path toward cultural and spiritual revitalization, they draw on deep wells of spiritual resources. As Sylvia said:

> I think that we will see a resurgence of Indigenous spirituality, I truly do, in the future. I think we have young people that are sick and tired of the impact of colonization. And the things that we can do to say, "I'm tired of being a victim. I'm tired of being defined by colonization. I'm tired of all of this." And the way that we can claim back what we need to is through what it means to be home and what it means to be an Indigenous person. And so I truly believe, I think that we are quite a bit more spiritual in discussing spirituality and in discussing Indigenous ways of knowing and being in my little family now than we were twenty years ago.

As an Indigenous person relocated to Vancouver, British Columbia, George argued that Indigenous oratory was an important part of this revitalization movement:

> [There's this] whole thing around these great orators, you know. Like the speech and the ability to move people with words is really highly regarded here ... In the Salish world, this happens all the time ... And I would say, in comparison to Toronto and other big cities, that just the awareness of Indigenous issues is light years ahead of other cities. It's very interesting. And I think that's largely through the work of people like Chief Dan George ... And I think there's always

that tradition here of people, like Ian Campbell [from the Squamish Nation], now running for mayor. I think the whole Longhouse tradition and all that kind of stuff really produces these amazing speakers.

For Jack, sharing traditional Coast Salish stories – both within and without Indigenous communities around Seattle and Portland – was another way that oratory was being employed to speak to contemporary concerns:

> Nothing makes me happier than to have a little kid come up and tell me, "You know that story you told about the beaver in the field, I can tell that story now" ... Because within those stories, they learn philosophy, they learn wisdom, they learn values, they learn morals. All the things that we would need to teach our children are in those stories. So I just look at a little kid in a preschool telling an old Indian story that they heard from me or another storyteller, that's the most – that's resistance. That is, just, this little kid's going to grow up remembering one story, and hopefully more.
>
> So, I use storytelling as a springboard to philosophy, essentially, and change. If you're an addict, addicted to alcohol, and I tell you a monster story, in that monster story, is there anything that you might find? 'Cause I'm not gonna find it for you. You've got to find it yourself, about how you can transform your life and overcome the monster.

Tribal Journeys (Canoe Journey) is a particularly powerful way cultural revitalization crosses international borders, building connections throughout the region. Begun in 1989, hundreds of canoes and thousands of people participate in various ways. Canoe families, as participants call them, travel from as far away as Alaska, British Columbia, and California, joining pullers from Oregon and Washington (Johansen 2012). Each year, a different Washington State or BC tribal community hosts the final landing. Throughout this week-long gathering, families, Elders, and community leaders present at protocol, sharing songs, dances, and oratory.

This revival of canoe culture has had far-reaching consequences for cultural renewal. As Jack explained:

> Canoe Journey [is] where a lot of the local tribes and families create canoes, and they go on a journey together, and they go to different destinations every year, and they share their songs and dances and ceremonies ... To do that, you have to remember, How did my ancestors carve a canoe? And how did they paint it? Where's the artwork? What songs did they sing? And when they got to a village, what protocol things did they have to do? So, in itself, it helped get so many things back in front of us that were kept from us.

Revitalizing canoe culture means reclaiming their identity as people of the water and demanding their space alongside the ferries and barges that ply these waterways. It has instilled pride in young people, inspiring them to learn about their traditional ways of life. Many pullers describe spiritual experiences on the water, visions they have had of old ones, songs they have heard, and encounters with eagles, whales, or salmon. Even the act of coming to shore can be transformative, as pullers learn the proper protocols, modes of speech, songs, dances, and oratory required of them. Participating in Journey requires working throughout the year, making cedar regalia, carving a paddle, or weaving a basket hat to give away, not to mention the commitment to physical training and sobriety. Throughout Cascadia, Tribal Journeys has inspired a renewal in cultural and spiritual traditions, embodying in a remarkable way the people's relationship with their natal waters.

Political Activism

A commitment to political activism likewise unites First Nations throughout Cascadia, even as they face different legal and political challenges. The battle for fishing rights is one such shared experience. Throughout the twentieth century, tribal people in western Washington continued to exercise their treaty rights to fish, even in the face of police brutality and arrest. During the 1960s and '70s, these acts of political resistance were increasingly publicized, becoming known as "fish-ins" and garnering broad support. They culminated in the 1974 Boldt Decision, which determined that treaties guaranteed Washington tribes the right to half the harvest, the right to fish in "usual and accustomed" places, and the right and responsibility to comanage the fisheries (Wilkinson 2000; Reid 2015). Soon after, the Northwest Indian Fisheries Commission was formed to monitor, regulate, and restore fisheries. In the decades since, tribes have come to hold considerable legal, political, and symbolic power over state and federal policies related to water, fish, and game. As Roger, a non-Indigenous American man from Seattle, noted:

> We partner with them a lot on habitat projects. They're comanagers of fish in the State of Washington, so tribes are a very big deal ... But I mean the Boldt Decision was like *Brown v Board of Education* in terms of the impact it's had on how we manage all kinds of resources. And it's ongoing, you know ... Yeah, tribes are like, they're not gone. They're, like, major, major, major players.

Tribal rights to fish have repeatedly been upheld in the courts. But more than this, courts have upheld tribes' rights for fish to *exist*, ruling that because tribal people have a right to fish, the state and federal governments have an obligation to protect fish habitat, ensure fish passage, and maintain clean, cool, navigable waterways. The legal consequence is that tribal treaty rights ensure that fish and marine life also have rights.

Following the Boldt Decision, some Coast Salish communities in Washington opened their first salmon ceremonies to the public, hoping to communicate who they are, what they value, and how non-Indigenous American allies can join in their work. Built on stories tracing tribal lineage back to the mythic past, first salmon ceremonies uphold a worldview in which salmon are relatives. In one story, a young woman is transformed into a salmon, marries a salmon, and has salmon children, who are returned to their human form by Grandmother Cedar. In another, a young man is nearly drowned and goes under the sea to visit the salmon, where he learns they live in villages much like his own (Crawford O'Brien 2014b).

While stories and particulars of practice differ, the heart of the ceremony remains the same: once the salmon runs begin, a certain number of days must pass before fishing can commence. The first salmon is caught and brought to shore, sung in, and welcomed like an honoured guest. It is carefully cooked, filleted, and distributed to those present – everyone should have a bite. Finally, all of its bones are gathered carefully, placed on a bed of cedar branches, and returned to the water. The rite ensures the renewal of salmon people and their annual return: should they be mistreated, the salmon will stop coming back. When open to the public, these ceremonies provide a valuable teaching moment, an opportunity to explain why salmon matter, and how they ought to be treated. It is a dramatically different way of thinking about fish: not as resource, but as relatives, not as things to be caught, but as beings that offer themselves up to sustain the life of others.

These ceremonies are part of a broader commitment to restoring salmon habitat and watersheds found in this region. Jack reflected on his western Washington Coast Salish community's work:

> There were two dams built along [a river in our territory]. You probably heard about the dams coming down. And the Indigenous people didn't do it for political reasons, they didn't do it for economic reasons, they only did it because that river is life, and the salmon that come up them are the centre of the universe, the world. And anything that destroys them has to be challenged and fought. So, for one hundred years, over one hundred years, they fought to have those dams come down. And they were told at every turn, "You can't do it. It's impossible. You can't take down dams this big – no one in the world has intentionally done this. You can't do it!" But they came down a few years ago, and the river is free again. And the salmon are coming back up the river again.

> And so what was wrong can be set right ... But it means they passed that commitment on to their children, their grandchildren, who carried it as strongly as they did, and they made sure it happened.

In British Columbia, this fight to protect tribal sovereignty, subsistence rights, and resources has taken a different track. First Nations legal and political concerns in British Columbia also centre on land claims, resource rights, and the legal status of Indigenous peoples. Washington tribes, however, have their subsistence rights written into 1855 treaties that have been repeatedly upheld in federal courts. In British Columbia, most First Nations did not sign treaties and do not have protected treaty rights. The Calder Decision (1973) and the Canadian Supreme Court case *Delgamuukw v Britsh Columbia* (1997) prompted the modern negotiation of treaties. The *Sparrow* case (1990) determined that First Nations people had the right to fish for food and ceremonial purposes ("food fish"), but – in contrast to Washington tribes – not the right to sell such fish commercially. The *Sparrow* victory was further insufficient because it failed to offer legal protections to those resources themselves. As Sylvia explained, her Coast Salish communities on Vancouver Island

> lived on those seafoods ... For me right now, my desire to look at water and our concern about water is the fact that ... for the last two years, because there hasn't been enough sockeye, for there to be a food fish ... I have a licence to get X amount of sockeye, for our own, for food and ceremony ... And we haven't even been able to get that ... We need to be really concerned about how we're treating the water.

Indigenous tribes in Oregon and Washington have access to a set of legal tools to protect fish and habitat, while also ensuring them powerful roles in resource management. By contrast, in Canada, a different historical experience has inspired a commitment to revitalizing Indigenous legal traditions (Miller 2008). Nate explained his work recovering Indigenous law among First Nations communities in Victoria: "I tend to emphasize a way that really focuses on all of those underlining beliefs and worldviews and so forth, because," when it comes to beliefs and laws, "you can't really know one without the other."

Neither salmon nor oil spills respect national borders. And so Indigenous communities throughout Cascadia must also collaborate in their battles to protect water and sea life and to combat climate change. In ceremonies of protest, sacred symbols, regalia, oratory, and carefully crafted ritual spaces convey messages of Indigenous sovereignty, the personhood of the natural world, and a transformed relationship with the earth and its waters. Ritual studies scholar Elizabeth Currans argues that in such ceremonies of protest, public spaces are reclaimed, held, and transformed (Currans 2015). And as religious studies scholar Dennis Kelley (Chumash) argues, as ceremonies become means of protest, they provide transformative spaces for experiencing what communities understand to be the sacred (Kelley 2014). This bringing of the sacred into secular space manifests a new way of being in the world. When Idle No More activists occupy a shopping mall with a deafening drum circle, they do more than shock or inconvenience shoppers: they demand a transformed way of seeing the world. When a totem pole is carried through the streets of Seattle, or a protest is held to halt a coal-export terminal or pipeline, Indigenous activists cross boundaries and borders to support and fight for one another. For Indigenous communities throughout Cascadia, the work of protest and activism is a sacred and vital part of spiritual life, what scholars of religion would call public religion.

***

This snapshot of Indigenous religious life in Cascadia illuminates the complex interplay of the regional and international, the spiritual and the political. Our interviews challenge notions of a monolithic Indigenous culture, instead reminding us of the incredible diversity of Indigenous communities in Cascadia. Our data likewise challenge our very understanding of what constitutes religion and the role it plays in people's lives. The emphasis on individual spirituality, family connections, and intimate engagement with Cascadia's lands and waters undergirds Indigenous resistance to colonialism, anchoring and animating political activism and cultural renewal (Hilbert 1986). In contrast to the secularizing movement away from religious institutions among the general population in Cascadia, Indigenous communities appear to be trending toward a renewal of commitment to the spiritual traditions of their ancestors. The values of hospitality and generosity and events such as first salmon ceremonies, Tribal Journeys, and environmental activism provide Indigenous communities opportunities to reclaim their heritage, share their sacred teachings, and invite newcomers to learn how to live in better relationship to this sacred place.

NOTES

1 For archival and interview data, see https://www.uvic.ca/research/centres/csrs/.
2 In the United States, the term "reservation" is used, while in Canada the term is "reserve."

REFERENCES

Amoss, Pamela. 1970. *Coast Salish Spirit Dancing: The Survival of an Ancestral Religion.* Seattle: University of Washington Press.
—. 1982. "Resurrection, Healing and the Shake: The Story of John and Mary Slocum." In *Charisma and Sacred Biography,* edited by Michael A. Williams, 87–109. Oxford: American Academy of Religious Studies.

Archambault, Marie Therese, Mark G. Thiel, and Christopher Vecsey, eds. 2003. *The Crossing of Two Roads: Being Catholic and Native in the United States*. Maryknoll, NY: Orbis.

Barnett, Homer G. 1957. *Indian Shakers: A Messianic Cult of the Pacific Northwest*. Carbondale: Southern Illinois University Press.

Bierwert, Crisca. 1999. *Brushed by Cedar, Living by the River: Coast Salish Figures of Power*. Tucson: University of Arizona Press.

Bradford, Tolly, and Chelsea Horton. 2016. *Mixed Blessings: Indigenous Encounters with Christianity in Canada*. Vancouver: UBC Press.

Crawford O'Brien, Suzanne. 2014a. *Coming Full Circle: Spirituality and Wellness among Native Communities in the Pacific Northwest*. Lincoln: University of Nebraska Press.

—. 2014b. "Salmon as Sacrament: First Salmon Ceremonies in the Pacific Northwest." In *Religion, Food and Eating in North America*, edited by Benjamin Zeller, Marie Dallam, and Reid Neilson, 114–32. New York: Columbia University Press.

Crey, Ernie, and Suzanne Fournier. 1998. *Stolen from Our Embrace: The Abduction of First Nations Children and the Restoration of Aboriginal Communities*. Vancouver: Douglas and McIntyre.

Currans, Beth. 2015. *Marching Dykes, Liberated Sluts and Concerned Mothers: Women Transforming Public Space*. Urbana: Illinois University Press.

Garroutte, Eva, Heather Anderson, Patricia Nez-Henderson, Calvin Croy, Janette Beals, Jeffrey Henderson, Jacob Thomas, and Spero Manson. 2009. "Religiosity and Spiritual Engagement in Two American Indian Populations." *Journal for the Scientific Study of Religion* 48 (3): 480–500.

Harmon, Alexandra. 1998. *Indians in the Making: Ethnic Relations among Indian Identities around Puget Sound*. Berkeley: University of California Press.

Hermes, Mary, Megan Bang, and Ananda Marin. 2012. "Designing Indigenous Language Revitalization." *Harvard Educational Review* 82 (3): 381–402.

Hilbert, Vi. 1980. *Ways of the Lushootseed People: Ceremonies and Traditions of Northern Puget Sound Indians*. Seattle: United Indians of All Tribes Foundation.

Johansen, Bruce. 2012. "Canoe Journey and Cultural Revival." *American Indian Culture and Research Journal* 36 (2): 131–41.

Kelley, Dennis. 2014. *Tradition, Performance and Religion in Native America*. New York: Routledge.

Kershner, Jim. 2013. "The John T. Williams Memorial Totem Pole." *History Link*. https://www.historylink.org/File/10299.

Kidwell, Clara, Homer Noley, and George Tinker. *American Indian Theology*. Maryknoll, NY: Orbis.

Lomawaima, K. Tsianina, and Brenda Child. 2000. *Away from Home: American Indian Boarding School Experiences, 1879–2000*. Phoenix, AZ: Heard Museum.

McCormick Collins, June. 1974. *Valley of the Spirits: The Upper Skagit Indians of Western Washington*. Seattle: University of Washington Press.

McNally, Michael. 2000. "The Practice of Native American Christianity." *Church History* 69 (4): 834–59.

Meek, Barbara. 2012. *We Are Our Language: An Ethnography of Language Revitalization in a Northern Athabaskan Community*. Tucson: University of Arizona Press.

Miller, Bruce Granville. 2008. *Be of Good Mind: Essays on the Coast Salish*. Vancouver: UBC Press.

National Urban Indian Family Coalition. 2011. "Seattle [statistical profile]." Accessed November 27, 2013. http://nuifc.org/?p=510.

Reid, Joshua. 2015. *The Sea Is My Country: The Maritime World of the Makahs*. New Haven, CT: Yale University Press.

Shreve, Bradley, and Richard Littlebear. 2019. *Language Revitalization at Tribal Colleges and Universities: Overviews, Perspectives, Profiles, 1993–2018*. Mancos, CO: Tribal College Press.

Thrush, Coll. 2007. *Native Seattle: Histories from the Crossing-Over Place*. Seattle: University of Washington Press.

Treat, James. *Native and Christian: Indigenous Voices on Religious Identity in the United States and Canada*. Abingdon, UK: Routledge.

Wilkins-Laflamme, Sarah. 2018. "The Religious, Spiritual, Secular and Social Landscapes of the Pacific Northwest: Part 2." *UWSpace*. http://hdl.handle.net/10012/13406.

Wilkinson, Charles. 2000. *Messages from Frank's Landing: A Story of Salmon, Treaties, and the Indian Way*. Seattle: University of Washington Press.

4 But People Tend to Go the Way Their Families Go: Irreligion across the Generations in the Pacific Northwest

TINA BLOCK AND LYNNE MARKS

In a recent interview for the Cascadia research project, Reverend Wilson, a member of the Anglican clergy in Victoria, British Columbia, pondered the reasons behind the comparatively large population of religious Nones in the Pacific Northwest.[1] He observed: "There's a whole lot more people in BC who have come from somewhere else or moved around in BC, whereas when I was ministering in St. Catharine's, Ontario, it was not at all unusual to find people who would be fourth, fifth generation." He went on to speculate:

> I think as you go across Canada, with Quebec being the major exception, you
> get consistently more religious as you go [east]. That's changing, but it's as a
> general rule, I think it still holds more or less true, and I think that has a lot to
> do with the rootedness of people in a place. Whereas, interestingly enough, I
> don't think people are rooted as strongly in community around here, and so they
> perhaps are looking toward other things to give meaning in their life. Because
> their parents are in the States, or they're back in Ontario, or whatever.

Reverend Wilson is not alone in attributing the unique irreligion of the Pacific Northwest to the "rootlessness" of its inhabitants. Scholars, as well as religious and cultural observers, have long pointed to the transience of the region's population to explain its secularity (Stewart 1983, 32; Burkinshaw 1995, 4; Block 2016, 155–56). British Columbia, Washington, and Oregon have, by statistical measures, constituted a distinctly irreligious region since the early days of European settlement (Marks 2017; Killen and Silk 2004; Pasquale 2007; Block 2016); the region has also been characterized by high levels of mobility and in-migration (Barman 1996, 343; Stark and Bainbridge 1995, 94; Burkinshaw 1995, 4). While we acknowledge the importance of high mobility and fewer family ties to the distinctively irreligious nature of the region, our focus here is on the passing down of irreligion through the generations in a number of settler families who have resided in the Pacific Northwest since the 1920s or earlier. Northwest ir-religion was reproduced and sustained not only by those who moved to the region and left families behind but also by and within settler families that were "rooted" in the region for much of the twentieth century.

In 1912, the Reverend J.H. White, Methodist superintendent of missions in British Columbia, remarked on the growing entrenchment of religious disdain and indifference in the province:

> The most alarming feature of the situation is the growing indifference and often hostility toward the churches and even towards the Bible and religion generally. A few years ago though men might be very rough and even dissipated they had a background of Christian training and tradition to which appeal could be made. A new generation is grown up who have been trained in a different school. There is little use appealing to a man to remember his mother's prayers and his father's God if his mother never prayed and his father scouted [dismissed] religion.[2]

In White's view, the most "alarming" aspect of British Columbia's irreligion was that it was being reproduced across generations. This essay demonstrates that the Pacific Northwest is indeed home to many families that have trans-mitted various forms of religious disinterest and disbelief across the generations. We show that the original motivations for irreligion within these families varied and included religious indifference, a general hostility to religion and the churches, a belief that science and rationality precluded religious belief, an association between irreligion and socialist/progressive politics and, in a few cases, personal trauma leading to a loss of faith. The transmission of irreligion in these families could come from an irreligious mother or father, or both parents, and ranged from explicit passing on of unbelief to more implicit model-ling of irreligion. How irreligion was understood, experienced, and transmitted varied within and between these families according to class, education, and gender. Long-standing secular families of the Pacific Northwest did not cause the region's distinct irreligion, but like the many "rootless" individual migrants to the region who abandoned religion along with their eastern family connec-tions, these largely secular families helped to normalize irreligion in the Pacific Northwest. Such families also reproduced irreligion over time. They were thus one of the secularizing forces that reduced the relevance of religion in many areas of public and private life in the Pacific Northwest; they help to explain why the region has been at the forefront of North American secularization over the twentieth and into the twenty-first century.

This research contributes to the rich scholarship on religious disaffiliation, irreligious socialization, and secularization in North America and Europe (see

Brown 2001, 2017; Clarke and Macdonald 2017; Baker and Smith 2009; Thiessen and Wilkins-Laflamme 2017). While our work is informed by burgeoning scholarship on the rise of religious Nones, it departs from that scholarship in foregrounding the experiences of those who were influenced by a secular up-bringing rather than those who rejected a religious one (Clarke and Macdonald 2017; Brinkheroff and Mackie 1993). We offer historical perspectives on the ex-isting literature by considering the intergenerational transmission of irreligion within a comparatively unchurched regional context and over a substantial frame of time. Although families with one or more irreligious member are far more common today than they were in the early part of the twentieth century, such families have always been more preponderant in the comparatively secular Pacific Northwest than in other regions. Our work builds on the work of other scholars who have shown that the irreligion of those raised in irreligious house-holds can be reinforced by an increasingly secular culture around them (Thiessen and Wilkins-Laflamme 2017). In addition to considering a longer time frame than previous scholars, we base our analysis on in-depth oral interviews and look closely at experiences both within and between families. We also argue here that place mattered – that the transmission of irreligion across the gen-erations was enabled by, and experienced differently within, the Pacific North-west, a region where dismissing the churches or being a religious None was normalized (or at least tacitly accepted) much earlier than elsewhere in North America. We also suggest that the process was mutually reinforcing, with the presence of these long-standing secular families further normalizing irreligion in the region.

This chapter is based primarily on twenty-four semistructured oral interviews conducted by the Cascadia research team.[3] In a number of cases, the project team had the opportunity to interview more than one member of the same family. Seventeen of the interviewees were male, and seven were female; all were white, and a majority were middle-class and of British or Scandinavian and Christian background.[4] Although just over half of the interviewees were baby boomers, other generations were also represented.[5] In addition to sharing long histories in the region, the interviewees were all, to varying degrees, nonreligious and came from families that had at least one irreligious member reaching back a minimum of three generations. We use "irreligion" interchangeably with terms such as "nonreligion" and "secularity" and define it broadly to include everything from affirmed atheism to religious indifference. As scholars have shown, and as the interviews in this study made clear, how irreligion is lived is complicated, rarely conforms to any singular pattern, and often shifts, even over the course of an individual's lifetime (see Brown 2017). To capture the threads of irreligion in Pacific Northwest families, then, it is important to conceptualize the term broadly.

Irreligion as Family Tradition

The majority of our interviewees were very clear that irreligion was a part of their family tradition for a very long time. As Sunny from Vancouver noted, irreligion was "just the way we've been for a long time." Charles's family had been actively irreligious since the early twentieth century in Oregon, a pattern that existed on both sides of the family. Charles's father publicly rebuked the minister at his mother's funeral for mentioning an afterlife, as he knew she would not have approved. Charles's father also interrupted the minister at his own wedding in the 1960s for daring to mention God, after having been instructed not to make any religious references. As Charles said: "He was standing at the altar, and he cut off the preacher because just out of habit he said 'brought together by God.' And my dad went, 'Stop. Backup,' and then made him redo it. That earned him a lot of brownie points with my mom's family [who were also irreligious]." Patrick saw the irreligion over several generations of his family, since at least the early twentieth century, as being an active and positive phenomenon, in that, in his words, it meant that "he was not indoctrinated" in religion. In Phoebe Murphy's family, neither parent, both of whom were born in the 1920s, was religious, and her father was actively against religion, having come from an irreligious working-class English family and having seen much suffering in his Second World War service. He told her that religion was a waste of time and questioned how there could be a God with so much suffering in the world. In this context, there seemed to be no space for Phoebe to be religious. When she told her father that she had to say the Lord's Prayer in school, he "hit the roof" and told her, "You don't have to do that if you don't want to." She said that she gradually came to see things her father's way: "I eventually didn't believe in it either." It was clear in several other families that parents influenced their children to be irreligious, both by example and by teaching. Steve was proud of his "iconoclastic" and irreligious grandmother who lived an intellectually alternative lifestyle in 1920s Vancouver. His father was also irreligious and certainly encouraged those values in his children. Steve noted that his father encouraged him to read Bertrand Russell to help him understand a rational, atheist worldview.

In a number of families, the intergenerational transmission of irreligion was more complex. For some parents, their hostility to religion, and particularly their disdain for the religious indoctrination of children, made them careful not to indoctrinate their children with irreligion (see also Thiessen and Wilkins-Laflamme 2017). This was true even in families that were dismissive of religion. David Martin was born in 1948 in Oregon. His grandmother and parents made fun of religious people, and his grandmother, who was born in the late nineteenth century in Portland, would enjoy being particularly bawdy and irreverent when religious people came to proselytize. Nonetheless, his parents told the children when they were about seven that they had to go to church to be "exposed" to "some form of religion," so that they could then decide for themselves whether they wanted to be religious. After a year of going to church, they were given the choice of whether to continue attending, and they both decided that they would "rather sleep in" and that religion more generally was not for them. In Rose's family, which had lived in both Oregon and Washington from early in the century, both her parents and grandparents thought all aspects of religious practice and theology were "hilarious." Nonetheless, once every two or three years, the grandparents took the children to church because their father thought "they should be exposed to it," but in Rose's words, it was like "going to the circus."

In some families, such decisions were more fraught. Charles's paternal grandparents had had no patience for religion when his father was growing up in Oregon in the 1940s, and his great-grandparents were "both antitheist ... antireligious," so there was no sense that being religious was an option. At first, his father struggled against his parents' and grandparents' nonbelief but then came to identify as irreligious. However, Charles's father was concerned that Charles should work out his religious-irreligious beliefs for himself. Charles was certainly raised in a nonreligious household. As he said, "It honestly didn't even occur to me that anyone believed in God until my early teens." However, Charles noted, his father "was worried that I was an atheist only because that's what my parents told me to believe. And it was like, it was really important to him that I actually came up with my own beliefs, and I believed things because I thought them through on my own." So Charles's father wanted his son to go to church to decide for himself. But his irreligious mother opposed this, because she was worried that he would end up being converted to evangelicalism. As Charles recalled, his father "felt that by not having me go to church, that I had been sort of deprived of that opportunity and that I could never really be sure if I was just sort of following in my parents' footsteps."

Charles's father was somewhat unusual in that, among our interviewees, it was more common for irreligious mothers to be concerned about exposing children to some religious teaching. For example, Helen (born in 1928 in a small BC town, with an atheist father and a religious mother) was an unbeliever, but with regard to her children, she said that "the kids had to go to Sunday school. I wanted them to know what it was all about and maybe in later life they can do whatever they like. And as it is, none of them have had anything to do with it." She had always been open about her unbelief with her children and acknowledged that "it maybe rubbed off." Joyce, born in Abbotsford, British Columbia, in 1952, said that her irreligion "was probably because my mom and dad didn't go to church" and because her mother was particularly irreligious. Nonetheless, she made her kids go to a church group, at least a few times when they were growing up, "only because I thought. Well, I don't want to be the one saying ... you know. I never pushed 'don't believe in God' with the kids. That wasn't my intent, and I wanted them to ... make some choices themselves."[6]

Gender and Class

Some women may have been more concerned about not indoctrinating their children in irreligion because of the long-standing gender ideology that defined women as naturally more religious than men. From the nineteenth century on, women in Anglo-American culture were expected to train their children in religion and morality (see Brown 2001). The limited historical literature on unbelief suggests that, at least until the 1960s, men were much more likely than women to be irreligious, to define themselves as atheists or unbelievers, and to stay away from church. Even in the 1960s and later, as more women left the churches, men were still overrepresented among unbelievers (Brown 2012; McLeod 2007). In her chapter in this volume, Sarah Wilkins-Laflamme draws on recent data to show that men constituted a majority (53 percent), albeit slight, of the religious None population in both British Columbia and Washington-Oregon.

Our interviews to some extent reflected this pattern, especially in families from more working-class backgrounds and often from Finnish and Swedish communities, which were particularly common ethnic origins in the Pacific Northwest. In families such as Keith's and Simon's, men were irreligious for several generations, while the women were Christian and regular church attenders.[7] Keith's grandfather on his mother's side came from Finland to Oregon in the early twentieth century and ultimately settled in Washington State. He was a commercial fisherman and was always irreligious, while his wife was a regular churchgoer. Keith recalled his grandfather making fun of Christianity, saying such things as "so a man knocks up a virgin and he makes a big deal religion out of it," comments that his grandmother responded to by going "ballistic, just ballistic." Keith lived with his grandparents for a while as a young boy, and his grandmother tried to get him to go to church. He went a few times, but then, when he was eight, he quit and refused to go any longer. He said that he would stay home with his grandfather instead and "play canasta and snap." His grandfather clearly encouraged Keith's irreligion. Keith's father, a commercial diver, was also irreligious, and also came from a long line of irreligious men and churchgoing women, this time from Sweden. As Keith's son Simon noted, the men in his family were "kind of famously hilariously irreligious, just antichurch, offensively antichurch. Often ... my father, his father, my grandfather on the other side, none of them ever expressed any kind of religious conviction of any kind. I don't remember any of them going to church."

Women, on the other hand, did attend church and tried to get their children and grandchildren to do so as well. Other studies suggest that the pattern of female piety and male irreligion was common among resource-based, working-class communities in late nineteenth- and early twentieth-century British Columbia. For working-class men in those communities, irreligion was part of a broader antipathy toward middle-class culture and convention (Marks 2017).[8] The interviews in this project suggest that this pattern was not limited to the turn of the century but persisted throughout the twentieth century and was evident in both British Columbia and Washington-Oregon.

While it was particularly common in working-class families, this gendered pattern was also evident in the families of other interviewees. For instance, Patrick, who was born in 1945 into a middle-class irreligious family, and whose family had been in the American Pacific Northwest since before 1900, noted that in his family "the men didn't go to church. The men went fishing, and the men made up excuses not to go to church. Then, in my household, it wasn't even discussed. My dad just never went." Scott, who was born in 1948 into an irreligious, non-churchgoing rural family in Washington State, noted that in families in his rural area where one partner went to church, it was typically the wife: "The men in the farming community did not, were the ones that didn't really have any type of church. If there were families that did go to church, it was primarily the females that got them involved, the mothers." In several families, then, there was a long-standing pattern of churchgoing women and of non-churchgoing, often profoundly irreligious, men. Although women sometimes became annoyed with male irreverence toward religion, the pattern of female piety and male irreligion caused relatively little tension and seemed to be at least tacitly accepted within these families.

Although the families interviewed for this project generally reflected the more common pattern of female religion and male irreligion, a few of the interviewees came from families where mothers were irreligious and fathers were very Christian. In these cases, the women came from multigenerational irreligious families and brought their irreligion with them into their marriages. When these women married religious men, it could create real tensions in the family and the marriage. For example, Raymond was born in 1942 in British Columbia, and his mother was irreligious because she was raised by totally nonreligious parents. As Raymond said, his mother's parents, who came to British Columbia in the early twentieth century, would enter churches for weddings and funerals, but "they never went to church. They didn't participate in any kind of religious identities." He noted that his grandfather's brothers and sisters and his mother's siblings were also irreligious. Raymond's mother was raised in Victoria in the 1920s and '30s and remained irreligious her entire life, stating that religion was "gullible nonsense." She married a Protestant evangelical man, and religious differences led to a lot of arguments between them. They divorced after Raymond left home. Raymond's father forced the children to go to church with him, although Raymond stopped going "at an early age"; his siblings, however, continued to attend and ended up becoming evangelical Christians. Marsha reported on a similar but even more tense environment in her birth family. Again, her mother was irreligious while her father was an evangelical Christian. Marsha's maternal grandparents were Finnish communists who came to Alberta in the early twentieth century. As communists, they were antireligious and passed that on to Marsha's mother. Marsha noted that the relationship between her parents was quite tense. Her father forced the children to go to church; he beat up her older siblings for refusing to go, so Marsha recognized that she had no choice but to attend. This left her with a lifelong hatred for religion. Her mother did not argue against the children going to church but refused to go herself.

Those families characterized by male religiosity and female irreligiosity experienced the most conflict and tension, which may reflect that this pattern contradicted dominant gender norms. While men were expected to be less religious, women continued to be viewed as the keepers of the faith, especially within families. But a number of interviewees challenged these gender expectations, including Steve Rogers' grandmother, whose irreligion seemed to be part of a more broadly anti-establishment worldview and lifestyle. Steve's great-grandmother arrived in British Columbia from Scotland in the very early twentieth century with five daughters but without her husband. Steve thought that his great-grandmother, his grandmother, and all of his aunts were irreligious, but only his grandmother combined irreligion with involvement in various iconoclastic discussion groups in Vancouver, whom, he believed, discussed a range of heterodox spiritual and political issues. She and her children were abandoned by her husband, and although she worked to support them, she lived separately from her children, who were raised by one of her sisters. Gendered patterns of irreligion could thus follow somewhat conventional patterns, with religious wives and antireligious husbands, but long-standing secular traditions in certain Pacific Northwest families could also result in families with irreligious mothers and evangelical fathers, while for some women, like Steve Rogers' grandmother, abandoning religion could be linked to a broader rejection of traditional gender norms.

As we have seen, irreligion, particularly among men, was clearly part of white, working-class tradition and culture in some Pacific Northwest families extending back to the late nineteenth or early twentieth centuries.[9] Irreligion was also associated in certain cases with the more educated middle classes. Sarah, a millennial who took part in a Portland focus group, noted that some of her family had been in the Pacific Northwest since the 1890s and that, in her family, there was "a lot of class issues tied in with religion ... There's a lot of going back and forth between atheism and really fundamental[ist] Christians ... And even forty years ago, if you were educated you were atheist in my family." Henry, whose family was religious, noted a similar pattern among his father's mountain-climbing friends, who were more educated than his father. He said that most of them were engineers and that they did not attend church. This was in the 1930s, and he noted that "it really was social class, social educational level. So those people ... did not attend church." This pattern was also common in other interviewees' families, particularly among those whose parents or grandparents were academics. For example, Charles's family had roots in the Pacific Northwest back to the nineteenth century, and his family had been irreligious for at least four generations. His grandfather, who would have been born in the 1930s or earlier, was a math professor. He apparently told Charles that, for him, like for other scientists, "religion got in the way of their research." Rose's grandfather was a music professor, born in the early part of the century, and both her grandparents and parents were irreligious and made fun of religion, something Rose attributed to the fact that her family was composed of "educated liberals."[10]

The border made a difference to the association between education and irreligion. The link between higher education and secularity was clearly and frequently made in the American oral-history interviews but was absent from the Canadian ones. In Chapter 5 of this volume, Sarah Wilkins-Laflamme shows that while there was a significant education gap between religious Nones and the religiously affiliated in Washington and Oregon, with the more highly educated being more likely to be Nones, no such gap existed in British Columbia.[11] Wilkins-Laflamme suggests that religious Nones have been fairly evenly distributed among all levels of education in the province.[12]

The Roots of Irreligion

While irreligion was handed down from generation to generation in many Pacific Northwest families, the motivations for becoming irreligious differed. One recurrent theme is that of religious indifference – religion, or at least church-going, was seen as unimportant, and other things, such as spending time outdoors, more worth doing. As Paul Bramadat shows in Chapter 1 in this volume, revering and connecting to nature are central to how the Pacific Northwest is both imagined and experienced. One of our interviewees, Scott, described how three to four generations of his family farmed near Spokane. According to Scott, no one in his family went to church, or seemed to care about religion, until his mother converted to Christianity. He recalled that before her conversion they preferred to go fishing or boating or spending time outdoors on Sundays. Most of his relatives did not go to church, and that was common among the families in that part of his farming community. When asked if spending time outdoors was in any way a spiritual experience for his family (as it is for some in the Pacific Northwest today), he said no: "It was pretty straight-forward – just immersing yourself in the outdoors on the weekends." For Sunny's family, which came to British Columbia in the early twentieth century, church-going was just "not part of their life at all." She also noted that although she had some religious friends growing up, for those friends whose families had been in British Columbia for a few generations, churchgoing was not part of their traditions. Nature and the outdoors were important to Sunny's family, and swimming, hiking, and other outdoor sports were things that they very much enjoyed doing. At least for more recent generations, this involvement with nature seemed to have more of a spiritual dimension than it did in Scott's family. When Sunny spoke of her parents and herself, she made explicit connec-tions between their sense of spirituality and their relationship with the Pacific Northwest's natural world. After pointing out that her father fit into the "spirit-ual but not religious kind of framework," she remarked: "The role of the natural world in that is one that does resonate really strongly for him." Sunny also de-scribed herself as "spiritual but not religious": "I, yeah, derive a great sense of connection from the natural world and from this place specifically. I feel very connected to this region in particular."

While some families had long traditions of indifference to religion and the churches, others included threads of anticlericalism and more active forms of irreverence toward religion. This was certainly true of many of the interviewees from working-class backgrounds. For most, however, anticlericalism does not seem to have been central. Rather, most of the interviewees were part of families that were either dismissive of religion or actively hostile toward it. For a number of irreligious families, this hostility toward religion focused on the irrationality of religion and on the need to understand the world in rational, scientific ways.

Callum Brown argues that this approach was much more common among men who came to atheism as teens or adults than among women (Brown 2017, 115–21). We found this to be true to some extent, but when patterns of unbelief are passed down from generation to generation, this more rational, irreligious approach was shared by both men and women. In some cases, this pattern reached back several generations. For instance, Raymond Murphy's grandparents dis-missed religion as "superstition" in the early twentieth century, as did he and his mother. A number of other interviewees also spoke of their parents' and grandparents' dismissal of religion as superstition. In a few cases, such as that of Steve Rogers' father, who encouraged him to read Bertrand Russell, the focus on the rational reasons for being an atheist were particularly explicit, as was the case for Charles's grandfather, who saw religion as being contrary to his aca-demic, scientific worldview. Others saw religion as a crutch. For example,

Marsha observed that her mother "said religion is for people who aren't strong enough to handle it on their own, to handle life on their own." Patrick shared a similar view, although he was the only one to talk about this in an explicitly gendered way, referring to irreligious male role models. Perhaps because his father never went to church, Patrick stated that, "in terms of deep-seated prejudice, I still regard a religious man as weak."

While Callum Brown has shown that personal trauma could lead people, particularly women, to atheism, this did not emerge as a predominant theme in our interviews (Brown 2017, 91–96). Marsha stated that she rejected religion largely because of the violent, controlling way in which religion was imposed on her and her siblings by their father, although she was likely also influenced by her mother's irreligion. Robin and his daughter Ainsley noted that Robin's father appeared to be totally uninterested in religion, largely because of all of the deaths (of his parents and siblings) that he had experienced at a fairly young age. Phoebe Murphy's father's irreligion was further fuelled by his service in the Second World War, during which, as Phoebe reported, he saw "terrible things." The fact that trauma was not central to most of our interviews may be explained by the long-standing culture of irreligion within these families, making religion less something that one suddenly rejected, as a result of trauma, than something that was just not part of the world in which one had been raised.

In a number of families, irreligion evolved out of, and was associated with, a progressive focus. As Sarah Wilkins-Laflamme shows in this volume, religious Nones in the Pacific Northwest and elsewhere are more likely to hold left-wing attitudes. The association between leftist political views and irreligion has deep roots in the region. Marxist ideology has long held particular appeal not only in British Columbia but in the broader Pacific Northwest (see Schwantes 1979, 220–23; Taft 1983). In early twentieth-century British Columbia, working-class Marxists generally rejected religion as "the opium of the masses" (Marks 2017). In some families, a left-leaning focus was passed down through the generations with irreligion. Sometimes it was linked to ethnic political traditions. For example, Marsha's grandparents were communists who had emigrated from Finland. Their daughter, Marsha's mother, retained both their politics and the atheism linked to it. As Marsha said, in explaining her mother's and grandparents' irreligion, they were "Red Finns." Craig's family was irreligious for at least a few generations, and during the 1930s, his grandfather was the assistant editor of a socialist newspaper in Vancouver. Craig noted that his parents and grandparents were "freethinkers" along a number of political and cultural dimensions, not just in relation to religion. Among the irreligious American interviewees, no one identified family members as having been explicitly socialist, but a number talked about irreligious parents and grandparents as having been "New Deal Democrats," or radical liberals.[13]

Dealing with Stigma

During the twentieth century, it was more acceptable to be irreligious in the Pacific Northwest than it was in the rest of North America. However, people of "no religion," and especially unbelievers and atheists, continued to find themselves in a minority situation in certain parts of the region into the 1980s and beyond, particularly in the United States. Even in the increasingly secular Pacific Northwest, irreligious families could encounter problems with social acceptance and a lingering stigma, although that stigma seemed to decline over the course of the century. The existence and force of this stigma varied by locale as well as by the type of irreligion – with affirmed atheists eliciting the most disapproval.

Some interviewees who simply did not go to church, but did not claim a particular "unbeliever status," noted that their irreligion and that of their families did not create any issues or stigma for them. For instance, Scott, who grew up in what he defined as a primarily irreligious farming region near Spokane in the 1950s, noted that since no one in his region went to church, being irreligious did not create any difficulties for him or for anyone else in his family. Robin, who grew up in Vancouver and then Victoria in the 1950s and early 1960s, noted that some of his neighbours attended church, but others did not, and the fact that his family generally did not go to church did not cause them any difficulties.

However, in many cases, interviewees talked about the stigma that they, their parents and grandparents faced for being part of an irreligious family, particularly in smaller communities, and especially if they identified explicitly as unbelievers. This was certainly true of the Murphys, who grew up in a small town in British Columbia in the 1950s. Phoebe Murphy had antireligious parents, while her husband, Raymond, had a mother and grandparents who explicitly rejected religion. The Murphys noted that most people in the community went to church regularly and that their irreligious parents were clear that they needed to be cautious about not alienating their more religious neighbours. As Phoebe told us, her parents went to weddings and funerals in church to "not make waves," although they did not attend church beyond that. Although Phoebe's father told her she did not have to, she mouthed the Lord's Prayer in school so she would fit in. Phoebe also noted that it was ironic that her irreligious parents pushed her to get married in a church, although neither she nor her fiancé were religious in any way. Her parents insisted on this to please her mother's mother, who was a churchgoer, and more generally to appear "respectable" within the larger community. Raymond Murphy said that when he joined the military reserves in British Columbia in the 1960s, "I'd run into problems because, you know, you had to put down a category and, you know, being agnostic or atheist was not considered part of the categories that you could. You had to be, you had to be something, you know." He noted that even in the 1990s, when he had a job with a Christian employer in Vancouver, he had to be careful not to talk about his atheist views.

Other interviewees noted that their irreligious parents were aware of the risks of being open nonbelievers in their communities. Craig, who was from an irreligious BC family, was advised when he went to school in the late 1940s "to put down 'Anglican' because of the stigma attached to anything else." Charles, who grew up in Idaho in the 1980s, noted that he was kicked out of Scouts because his parents were atheists. Charles mentioned that his irreligious father was rather proud of this. Keith talked about living in a community in the Puget Sound area in the 1980s where most people were Christians: "[My wife] and I were not included in or invited to some of [our son's] friends' events because, I think because we were not religious." The fact that he acknowledged challenging religion when he was invited to people's homes suggests that this lack of inclusion was not just about his irreligion but his vocal hostility to religion.

On the broad spectrum of irreligion, it was nonbelievers, and particularly atheists, who reported that they experienced the most social exclusion and stigma. "Atheist" clearly remained a contentious word well into the late twentieth century, and irreligious people in both Canada and the United States were aware of the dangers of calling themselves atheists (Block 2014; Edgell, Gerteis, and Hartmann 2006). Certainly, in the United States from the 1940s to the 1970s, atheism was explicitly linked to communism and all that was un-American (Brown 2012, 253). Patrick, whose parents and grandparents were irreligious, noted that, growing up in Oregon in the 1940s and '50s, his parents "just didn't talk about it, because in my lifetime, you didn't label yourself anything, because atheists were something bad." Roy, who also grew up in Oregon in the 1950s, noted that his father was always an atheist "but would never say that out in the community." In the 1970s in Salem, Oregon, Rose, who was irreligious from an irreligious family, shocked another young girl in her class by telling her that she did not believe in God. When she went home and told her mother, her mother said, "Well, honey, you probably shouldn't talk about the fact that you don't believe in God to other children."

Other irreligious interviewees had clearly internalized the negative connotations of the word. Helen, who was born in 1928 in British Columbia, had never been a believer, but she said that "I never did like that name 'atheist.' It just, I think, 'a nonbeliever' just seems to make me feel more comfortable. As though you had some disease or something, you're an atheist ... No, I just don't believe. There was a time when I didn't like to tell people that I was this. But now it doesn't bother me."[14] Other interviewees observed that it has become easier in recent years to call yourself an atheist in the Pacific Northwest. David Martin noted that although there was some lingering social concern about being an atheist in the region, the situation in the Pacific Northwest "ain't like Indiana. Or Oklahoma." Craig recalled that Vancouver, where he grew up and went to university, was more open to irreligion, even in the 1960s and 1970s, than the Canadian prairie academic institution where he worked until the late twentieth century. The American interviewees suggested that not all areas of the Pacific Northwest were open to irreligion, pointing out that in eastern Oregon and eastern Washington there continues to be a stigma attached to being irreligious, let alone being an atheist. We did not hear such comments explicitly about any specific subregions of British Columbia. Nonetheless, there have typically been more religious Nones in urban than in rural areas. Not surprisingly, most interviewees suggested that in Portland, Seattle, Victoria, and Vancouver there is no stigma attached to defining oneself as an atheist.

The existence of this stigma, at least in past decades, explains some of the complexities of what we might call "lived irreligion." The more common term, "lived religion," reflects the way people actually live religion in their own ways, with their own rituals and practices that might have some connection to official religious doctrines and rituals but could also diverge from them significantly. The practices of lived religion, as Robert Orsi (1997) and others have noted, hold meaning and significance for the individuals involved and can sometimes serve as creative and subversive strategies to help them survive oppressive religious and social structures. Similarly, we argue that lived irreligion can involve practices and strategies that are understood to be "religious" and thus might appear inconsistent or contradictory but are used by irreligious people in contexts where they knew that their lack of belief was not accepted within the larger community. For example, we found that irreligious people who were quite hostile to the churches and religion in general might, nonetheless, send their children to Sunday school, or attend local weddings and funerals in church, or even let their children go to church camps or youth groups because, despite their personal beliefs, they or their children wanted to feel part of local communities.

As we noted earlier, when irreligious parents sent their children to Sunday school, this was sometimes to "expose them to both sides" so that they could make their own choices about religion. However, it was often also (or instead) done to "not make waves" in local communities. Steve Rogers noted that although his father was an atheist and would not go to church, his mother made them go to church in the 1950s:

> I think part of the reason we went to church was Nanaimo was a small town at that time, and ... my mom had a network of friends, and it was kind of what you did ... She thought there might be some stigma associated with us not going. It was for the show, you know, to sort of be accepted ... Keep the waters calm and everything.

Robin also noted that in the 1950s his mother, who was hostile to religion and the churches, may have "wanted to fit in" in the Vancouver neighbourhood where they lived, which explains why she made her sons go to Sunday school, at least briefly.[15]

The complexities of lived irreligion extended beyond just avoiding stigma in local communities to include more positive efforts to incorporate religious traditions within families. Sometimes people maintained what might look like religious practices in their lives even if they did not believe in God, because of the importance of family or ethnic traditions. Arthur, who was born in Seattle in the 1930s and raised Anglican, lost any belief in religion quite early in his life, but he still says grace at major family dinners, a practice he describes as a long-standing family "tradition" that is important to him for "historical" rather than religious reasons.

In other irreligious families, particularly in those communities where they were in the minority, children would sometimes attend church youth groups or camps because that was a way to spend time with their friends. For example, Sunny's parents met at an evangelical youth event in Vancouver in the 1960s, though both were irreligious and from largely irreligious families. Nonetheless, they went with their more Christian friends, as a social outing. In the late 1980s, Simon attended an evangelical Christian youth group in the Puget Sound area, again because that was where his friends were, although his father (and Simon himself) drew the line at continued involvement when the youth group leader tried to pressure him to become religious. Craig noted that in the 1950s his irreligious parents sent him "to Anglican church camps several times out in the Okanagan in summertime, because it was a camp. And I reacted [negatively] to the teachings of the people in charge but got along very well otherwise with the situation and people there ... I didn't find the counsellors particularly religious ... But the swimming was good." These patterns suggest that Pacific Northwest irreligious families who saw themselves as a minority in their communities allowed their children to get involved in church youth activities for social reasons. While they may have attended some of these groups, or gone to Sunday school, our interviewees told us that it never "stuck." Their lived irreligion was flexible, allowing for sporadic engagements with religion and inclusion in social communities that happened to be religious. However, the irreligion that they had learned from their parents, and often their grandparents, remained central to their worldviews.

***

Families who have deep irreligious roots reaching back to the early twentieth century and who maintained and passed on that irreligion into the late twentieth and early twenty-first centuries remain a minority in the Pacific Northwest.

Among the growing group of Nones in the region, they have been outnumbered by those who abandoned the religion in which they were raised, either as teens or adults, while residing in the Pacific Northwest or after moving here. However, the presence in the Pacific Northwest of families who for several generations were completely indifferent to religion, or actively hostile to it, may have created cultural space for the normalization and expansion of irreligion that happened earlier and more quickly in the Pacific Northwest than in the rest of North America. As sociologists of irreligious socialization have noted, learning to be irreligious in one's family of origin is an increasingly important mechanism for becoming irreligious, and such irreligion is then further reinforced by the increasingly secular society in which those "raised irreligious" find themselves (see Thiessen and Wilkins-Laflamme 2017). Although more research needs to be done on the prevalence and impact of long-standing irreligious settler families in the region, their existence adds another dimension to our understanding of how the Pacific Northwest has been and remains at the forefront of secularization in North America.

NOTES

Acknowledgments: We would like to thank the anonymous reviewers for their insightful feedback and the entire Cascadia research team for their helpful comments on earlier drafts of this chapter. We are especially grateful to Chelsea Horton for her extensive work on the oral histories for this project. Finally, we would like to acknowledge and give special thanks to the interviewees for so generously sharing their memories.

1 For archival and interview data, see https://www.uvic.ca/research/centres/csrs/.
2 Reverend J.H. White to Reverend Allen, April 22, 1912, United Church of Canada Archives, Toronto, Methodist Church Missionary Society Fonds, Fonds 14, Series 4: Home Mission.
3 We also draw evidence from focus groups conducted by the Cascadia research team, as well as on two oral-history interviews that were conducted for Tina Block's "Oral Histories of Unbelief in British Columbia and Ontario" project, the transcripts of which will soon be made available in Thompson Rivers University's digital repository, TRUSpace. One of those interviewees (Helen) was born in Chase, British Columbia, in 1928, and fits the criterion of intergenerational secularity reaching back to the early years of the twentieth century. The other (Joyce) was born in Abbotsford, British Columbia, in 1952; it is not certain how long her family resided in the Pacific Northwest. Pseudonyms are used to protect the anonymity of participants.
4 While most interviewees were raised within broadly Christian cultures (even if they or their parents rejected most or all of such culture), one interviewee was raised in a secular Jewish household (Eugene). Because all of the interviewees were white, our analysis focuses on the intergenerational transmission of irreligion among white settler families; the question of how or whether irreligion was reproduced among racialized communities of the Pacific Northwest demands further research. The greater preponderance of male interviewees may partly reflect the fact that some participants were located through secular humanist organizations. Seven of the twenty-four interviewees were recruited through these organizations (with two of the seven from one family), and men typically outnumber women on their membership lists. We used secular humanist/atheist groups as one source of interviewees, as it was difficult

to locate those who had been irreligious in the Pacific Northwest for three generations solely through newspaper ads and word of mouth – although the majority of our interviewees were ultimately located in this way. The fact that almost a third of the interviewees were located through secular humanist groups could have created some bias in the narratives they produced, as these groups sometimes reproduce certain narratives about secularism and the process of rejecting religion. However, since the interviewees talked not only about their own move to irreligion but also the experiences within their families over at least three generations, we did find considerable variation in how they discussed the nature and development of irreligion in their families.

5   One respondent was born in the 1920s, one in the 1930s, eight in the 1940s, five in the 1950s, four in the 1960s, three in the 1970s, and two in the 1980s or later.

6   *Oral Histories of Unbelief* project interviews: Helen, personal interview by Tina Block, March 10, 2017, Kamloops, British Columbia; Joyce, personal interview by Kelsey Hine, July 4, 2016, Kamloops, British Columbia.

7   For the men in such families, irreligion ranged from staying away from religious institutions and being generally indifferent to religion, to more actively rejecting religious belief and expressing hostility toward religious institutions, particularly the churches.

8   There were additional interviewees who pointed to a thread of working-class male irreligion, including Helen, personal interview by Tina Block, March 10, 2017, Kamloops, British Columbia.

9   While irreligion was especially common among men in families with working-class roots, in a few cases, it was the norm for both husband and wife; see Cascadia oral-history interview with Sunny. On working-class irreligion in early twentieth-century British Columbia, see Marks (2017).

10 Also see Cascadia oral-history interview with Christopher (in Portland). Christopher's grandfather was a history professor, and both his grandparents and parents were irreligious.

11 The pattern that Wilkins-Laflamme identified for the American Pacific Northwest also seems to hold true for the rest of the United States. See Pew Research Center (2017).

12 Interestingly, census evidence from almost fifty years ago suggests that this phenomenon has a long history in British Columbia. While income is not an exact proxy for education level, the two measures are closely related. The 1971 census indicates that people of "no religion" in British Columbia were more evenly dispersed across income groups and less concentrated in upper-income brackets than their counterparts in other provinces. See Block (2016).

13 See Cascadia Oral History interviews with Keith, Charles, Simon, Rose, and David Martin.

14 "Oral Histories of Unbelief" project interview, Helen.

15 It seems that Robin may have only attended for a few months.

REFERENCES

Baker, Joseph, and Buster Smith. 2009. "The Nones: Social Characteristics of the Religiously Unaffiliated." *Social Forces* 87 (3): 1251–63.

Barman, Jean. 1996. *The West beyond the West: A History of British Columbia.* Rev. ed. Toronto: University of Toronto Press.

Block, Tina. 2014. "Ungodly Grandmother: Marian Sherman and the Social Dimensions of Atheism in Postwar Canada." *Journal of Women's History* 26 (4): 132–54.

–. 2016. *The Secular Northwest: Religion and Irreligion in Everyday Postwar Life.* Vancouver: UBC Press.

Brinkerhoff, Merlin, and Marlene Mackie. 1993. "Nonbelief in Canada: Characteristics and Origins of Religious Nones." In *The Sociology of Religion: A Canadian Focus,* edited by W.E. Hewitt, 109–32. Toronto: Butterworths.

Brown, Callum. 2001. *The Death of Christian Britain: Understanding Secularisation, 1800–2000.* London: Routledge.

–. 2012. *Religion and the Demographic Revolution: Women and Secularisation in Canada, Ireland, UK and USA since the 1960s.* Woodbridge, UK: Boydell Press.

–. 2017. *Becoming Atheist: Humanism and the Secular West.* London: Bloomsbury Academic.

Burkinshaw, Robert. 1995. *Pilgrims in Lotus Land: Conservative Protestantism in British Columbia, 1917–1981.* Montreal/Kingston: McGill-Queen's University Press.

Clarke, Brian, and Stuart Macdonald. 2017. *Leaving Christianity: Changing Allegiances in Canada since 1945.* Montreal/Kingston: McGill-Queen's University Press.

Edgell, Penny, Joseph Gerteis, and Douglas Hartmann. 2006. "Atheists as 'Other': Moral Boundaries and Cultural Membership in American Society." *American Sociological Review* 71 (2): 211–34.

Killen, Patricia O'Connell, and Mark Silk, eds. 2004. *Religion and Public Life in the Pacific Northwest: The None Zone.* Walnut Creek, CA: AltaMira Press.

Marks, Lynne. 2017. *Infidels and the Damn Churches: Irreligion and Religion in Settler British Columbia.* Vancouver: UBC Press.

McLeod, Hugh. 2007. *The Religious Crisis of the 1960s.* Oxford: Oxford University Press.

Orsi, Robert. 1997. "Everyday Miracles: The Study of Lived Religion." In *Lived Religion in America: Toward a History of Practice,* edited by David Hall, 3–21. Princeton, NJ: Princeton University Press.

Pasquale, Frank. 2007. "The 'Nonreligious' in the American Northwest." In *Secularism and Secularity: Contemporary International Perspectives,* edited by Barry Kosmin and Ariela Keysar, 41–58. Hartford, CT: Institute for the Study of Secularism and Society.

Pew Research Center. 2017. "In America, Does More Education Equal Less Religion?" Pew Research Center, Polling and Analysis, April 25. https://www.pewforum.org/2017/04/26/in-america-does-more-education-equal-less-religion/.

Schwantes, Carlos. 1979. *Radical Heritage: Labor, Socialism, and Reform in Washington and British Columbia, 1885–1917.* Seattle: University of Washington Press.

Stark, Rodney, and William Bainbridge. 1985. *The Future of Religion: Secularization, Revival, and Cult Formation.* Berkeley: University of California Press.

Stewart, Bob. 1983. "That's the BC Spirit! Religion and Secularity in Lotus Land." *Canadian Society of Church History Papers:* 22–35.

Taft, George. 1983. "Socialism in North America: The Case of BC and Washington State, 1900–1960," PhD diss., Simon Fraser University.

Thiessen, Joel, and Sarah Wilkins-Laflamme. 2017. "Becoming a Religious None: Irreligious Socialization and Disaffiliation." *Journal for the Scientific Study of Religion* 56 (1): 64–82.

Second to None: Religious Nonaffiliation in the Pacific Northwest

SARAH WILKINS-LAFLAMME

"I'm Jeremy. I'm thirty. I have a little business here. I do, like, web development and stuff, and lots of different work. And I'd also be under the kind of irreligious banner." Jeremy, one of the millennials who took part in the Vancouver focus group conducted in 2018 by the Cascadia research team, would probably not typically mention his irreligious identity when introducing himself.[1] Nevertheless, he does so when prompted or when it comes up in conversation, as it did in the focus group. Although for the most part an unseen phenomenon in day-to-day life, irreligion in the Pacific Northwest does come up when researchers start asking about it.

In response to the question "What, if any, is your religion (even if you are not practising)?," the most common answer given in the Canadian and American Pacific Northwest is not a specific religious tradition or denomination as such. Instead, according to data from the 2017 Pacific Northwest Social Survey, an estimated 49 percent of British Columbians and 44 percent of residents in the states of Washington and Oregon say they have no religion. Commonly referred to as "religious Nones" by researchers, this group is the largest (non)religious tradition in British Columbia and the second largest in Washington and Oregon (just below the 46 percent of residents affiliated with Christian traditions). This high rate of individuals with no religious affiliation explains why the Pacific Northwest has been called the "None Zone" (Killen and Silk 2004) since it has proportionately more religious Nones than anywhere else in North America.[2]

The None phenomenon in the Cascadia region is not the product of a recent spontaneous shift in people's identities and affiliations. Nonreligion has a long history in the region, as Tina Block (2016) and Lynne Marks (2017) explore in their work and their jointly authored chapter in this volume. Even though most European settlers in the nineteenth and early twentieth centuries identified as Christians, Christianity never became as integral to the societies of British Columbia, Washington, and Oregon as it did elsewhere on the continent. For example, rates of regular church attendance in the region have always been lower than national averages. With no one religious group having established strong ties with overall regional culture, and with individual and family ties to faith groups often being more precarious in the region, religious affiliation was not as resistant to decline in British Columbia, Washington, and Oregon compared with elsewhere on the continent as forces of moral liberalism, individualism, and pluralism became prevalent in Canadian and American societies from the 1960s onwards (Clarke and Macdonald 2017; Putnam and Campbell 2010). Nowhere did the normative expectations of belonging to a religion erode among such a large segment of the population as in Cascadia.

Using a variety of high-quality survey statistics along with interview and focus-group data gathered in 2017–18 by the Cascadia research team,[3] I explore some of the key contemporary realities and dynamics of the religious None phenomenon in British Columbia, Washington, and Oregon as they stand in the second decade of the twenty-first century. What do religious Nones look like, and what experiences do they have in a region where they are so predominant? The focus here is on the substantive secularity of many of the region's residents: exploring less what this None population is not (religious) and more who they are demographically and politically; their diversity of worldviews, identities, beliefs, and practices; along with how these religious Nones perceive, and interact with, more religious populations in a society now notably defined by the coexistence of secular and religious groups. The goal is to better understand this key Cascadian population, which may be a harbinger of things to come for the rest of North America.

Sociodemographics

Religious Nones, or those who say they have no religion when asked, come in all shapes and sizes: they are of all genders, of all ages, of all races and ethnic backgrounds, of all education levels, of all income strata, and of all political affiliations. My colleague Joel Thiessen and I (Thiessen and Wilkins-Laflamme 2020), along with other researchers (see, for example, Baker and Smith 2015; Beaman and Tomlins 2015), have found this to be the case for Nones in Canada and the United States. Others have explored this reality across Europe (see, for example, Bullivant and Lee 2012; Zuckerman, Galen, and Pasquale 2016). This demographic and political diversity of Nones is also present in Cascadia: we find religious nonaffiliation among all sociodemographic groups in British Columbia, Washington, and Oregon.

That said, several clear sociodemographic patterns do exist when it comes to religious Nones in Cascadia, matching many trends found elsewhere in North America and Europe. This is an indication that, although there are religious Nones of all stripes, the processes leading to their growth are more prevalent among certain subpopulations in the region. The proportions in Table 5.1 from Statistics Canada's 2011 National Household Survey and Pew's 2014 Religious Landscape Study illustrate some of these trends. Although the results in Table 5.1 also indicate some smaller gender and income differences, the focus here is on three of the most pronounced sociodemographic distinctions between religiously affiliated and unaffiliated populations in the region: religious Nones are younger on average; more likely to be white, Indigenous, East Asian, or born in the country; and more likely to have a university education in Washington and Oregon.

Age

First, religious Nones are disproportionately younger than those who affiliate with a religion: 48 percent of Nones in British Columbia and 36 percent in Washington and Oregon are under the age of thirty-five, compared with 36 percent and 26 percent among the religiously affiliated of all traditions in Cascadia North and South.

How might we explain this prominent nonreligion trend among youth in the region? Following the secular transition framework (Voas 2008; Thiessen and Wilkins-Laflamme 2020), the None phenomenon is understood here as a consequence of long-standing, progressive, and generational religious decline over time, driven by changing socialization patterns and social environments among an important segment of the Cascadian population.

Tina Block and Lynne Marks's chapter in this volume shows that family histories of irreligion in the region go back further in time and are more common than elsewhere on the continent. This, in turn, has helped shape a social environment more accepting of nonreligion even before the 1960s, especially among certain ethnic, class, and gender subpopulations in the area. Nevertheless, there are also many families in the region whose older members were more religious, and the acceptability of nonreligion still had its limits throughout much of the nineteenth and twentieth centuries. Then, especially during the 1960s, many adults began to decrease religious group activities that had once been prevalent during their childhood. Religious identification and occasional involvement with a religious group (e.g., for religious holidays or rites of passage) persisted for many of these individuals, though, as they maintained social and cultural ties to their faith tradition and experienced remaining normative expectations and pressures surrounding religion (Day 2011; Meunier and Wilkins-Laflamme 2011; Thiessen 2015; Voas 2009).

When these pre-Boomers and Boomers went on to have children of their own, more of these children did not attend religious services regularly with their parents or receive regular religious education at school or home compared with those among prior generations. Younger birth cohorts grew up in much

TABLE 5.1 Sociodemographic characteristics among religious Nones and the religiously affiliated, British Columbia, 2011, and Washington and Oregon, 2014 (%)

		Under 35	Male	University-educated	Household income below $50,000	Foreign-born	Black	Hispanic	Indigenous	East Asian	Other non-White racial identity	White
British Columbia	No religious affiliation	48	53	22	32	22	<1	<1	6	16	4	72
	Rest of BC population	36	45	22	31	34	1	1	4	8	22	64
Washington and Oregon	No religious affiliation	36	53	36	54	7	1	5	n/a	n/a	14	80
	Rest of Washington and Oregon population	26	47	26	58	14	3	11	n/a	n/a	10	76

NOTES: *N* (BC) = 117,592; *N* (Washington and Oregon) = 1,133. Percentages weighted to be representative of the general population.
SOURCES: Statistics Canada (2015); Pew Research Center (2014).

more secular social environments than in the past. This, in turn, has driven larger numbers of members of younger generations to not see the need to have any ties, including identity ties, with religion (Crockett and Voas 2006; Manning 2015; Thiessen and Wilkins-Laflamme 2017).

Race and Ethnic Background

Second, in comparison with those affiliated with a religion, religious Nones are less likely to be foreign-born: only 22 percent of BC Nones were born outside of Canada, compared with 34 percent of religiously affiliated individuals in the province; only 7 percent of Washington and Oregon Nones were born outside the United States, compared with 14 percent among the religiously affiliated populations of the two states.

This trend is not unique to Cascadia but is seen across most of North America and Europe. Although nonreligion is a phenomenon present in many non-Western societies (see Zuckerman, Galen, and Pasquale [2016] for world region rates of nonreligion), it is not as commonly found outside of traditionally Christian North American and European nations. Consequently, most non-Western immigrants recently settled in Cascadia and elsewhere in Canada and the United States arrived with strong existing ties to a faith group or tradition; or, in other words, with lower rates of religious nonaffiliation. An exception to this trend is those migrants from East Asia, numerous in Cascadia, who have high rates of religious nonaffiliation, at least in part because Western religion labels do not apply well to their family's spiritual practices and beliefs (Bramadat and Seljak 2005; Skirbekk et al. 2012).

Nevertheless, many Cascadian religious Nones come from white Caucasian families of European descent who were once linked to liberal Protestant denominations and, to a lesser extent, to Roman Catholicism, and who have since left these Christian identities behind (Bibby 2011; Clarke and Macdonald 2017; Sherkat 2014). In addition, a large portion of the Indigenous population in the region does not identify with a religion (53 percent of Indigenous populations in British Columbia, according to Statistics Canada's 2011 National Household Survey); they understand religious labels as a further dimension of settler colonialism removed from their own spiritual and community traditions.[4] And once individuals from different backgrounds have lived in the area for a generation or two, the more secular social environment of Cascadia influences many of them to spend their energy on other activities, beliefs, and identities than those considered religious.

Education

Third, there is an educational divide between Nones and the religiously affiliated in Washington and Oregon: 36 percent of Nones have a university degree, compared with only 26 percent of the religiously affiliated. This education gap is also present when only looking at younger adults (to control for the Nones' overall younger composition): 29 percent of Nones between the ages of eighteen and thirty-five in Washington and Oregon have a university degree, compared with only a 20 percent rate of university education among young religiously affiliated adults. These educational differences are likely also impacting (the more minor) household income differences seen in Table 5.1 for Cascadia South between religious Nones and the religiously affiliated.

Why is this educational divide present? For many, the years spent at university, especially nondenominational (non-Christian) universities, are a time in a young adult's life when religious ties may weaken (Glanzer, Hill, and Ream 2014; Hill 2011; Mayrl and Oeur 2009). Many university students are no longer living with their parents near their original religious group or congregation; they have other social and educational demands on their time; and they are regularly exposed to new, notably critical and scientific, worldviews in classes and among their peers. Additionally, a social reproduction effect may be at play: those who are born to and raised by parents with university degrees are more likely to go on to university themselves and also to adopt many of their parents' (non)religious attitudes and behaviours.

However, this educational divide is not present in British Columbia, where both None and religiously affiliated populations have the same rate of university education (22 percent). British Columbia is distinct in this sense from many other North American and European regions where we find an education gap between Nones and those affiliated with a religion (Lewis 2015; Schwadel 2015). The None phenomenon seems to have permeated all levels of education equally in the Canadian province. Kelley Strawn (2019) finds that educational differences between religious and nonreligious populations have weakened over time in the United States as the rate of Nones has grown there since the 1990s and nonreligion has become normalized to a greater degree. The lack of an educational divide in British Columbia may be another case of this greater normalization of nonreligion in the province, compared with the American Pacific Northwest.

Sociopolitical Attitudes among Cascadia's Nones

"You know that out West is different. It's a Left Coast," said Catherine, a thirty-nine-year-old religious None living in Victoria, British Columbia. This is even more the case among religious Nones in the Cascadian region: they have, on average, more left-leaning attitudes on a number of sociopolitical issues than religiously affiliated residents, making West Coast Nones one of the most left-oriented subpopulations in North America. The statistics in Figure 5.1, from the 2011 and 2015 Canadian Election Studies as well as Pew's 2014 Religious Landscape Study, indicate that a higher proportion of religious Nones considers

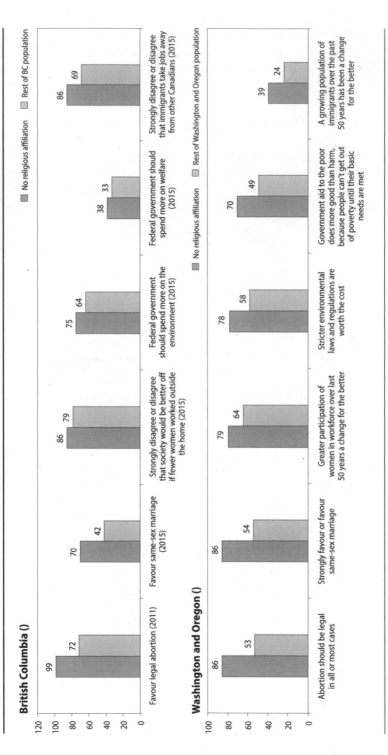

FIGURE 5.1   Left-leaning sociopolitical attitudes, British Columbia (2011 and 2015) and Washington and Oregon (2014)

NOTES: *N* (BC) abortion = 404; same-sex marriage = 777; women in the workforce = 777; women in the workforce = 773; environment = 1,055; welfare = 1,018; immigration = 767. *N* (Washington and Oregon) abortion = 1,078; same-sex marriage = 1,055; women in the workforce, welfare and immigration = 1,125; environment = 1,093. Percentages weighted to be representative of the general population.
SOURCES: Fournier et al. 2017; Pew Research Center 2014.

immigration good for society overall and supports access to legal abortion, same-sex marriage,[5] women's participation in the workforce, and the government's role in protecting the environment, as well as the government's role in addressing poverty.

In fact, in the month leading up to the 2015 Canadian federal election, only 15 percent of Nones in British Columbia identified the more right-leaning Conservative Party as their party of preference, compared with a Conservative preference rate of 30 percent among the religiously affiliated in the province (Fournier et al. 2017). In Washington and Oregon in 2014, only an estimated 20 percent of religious Nones leaned toward the Republican Party, compared with 39 percent of those who were religiously affiliated (Pew Research Center 2014).

The greater prevalence of left-wing attitudes among religious Nones persists even once we control for these Nones being on average younger and university-educated. For example, 96 percent of Nones in Washington and Oregon aged 25–44 years with a university degree favour or strongly favour same-sex marriage, compared with only 58 percent of 25–44-year-old university-educated religious affiliates in Cascadia South.

This gap between less and more religious populations is something we see not only in Cascadia, but also across the rest of Canada and the United States as well as in Europe (Ang and Petrocik 2012; Putnam and Campbell 2010; Wilkins-Laflamme 2016b). Why are so many religious Nones more left on the political spectrum? In my work with Joel Thiessen, we argue that socialization processes and social environments are key to understanding this trend (Thiessen and Wilkins-Laflamme 2020; Wilkins-Laflamme 2016a). During both their childhood and adult years, religious Nones are much more likely to find themselves surrounded by people and living in areas characterized by more left-leaning values. Many Nones in Cascadia come from liberal Protestant family backgrounds (Bibby 2011; Clarke and Macdonald 2017; Sherkat 2014), religious traditions that have also been characterized by more liberal positions on family values, reproductive rights, gender roles, and social justice. Consequently, Nones are more likely to be socialized with these values growing up. This does not necessarily determine that they will share these same values as adults, but it does usually have an important influence on them.

During their young-adult years, many Nones also find themselves attending secular colleges or universities where such liberal views are often prevalent and discussed in classes and clubs and among friends on campus. Such views may also have an impact on those who are more involved with religion who attend such colleges and universities. However, the impact on Nones may be even greater since they are more likely to be primed for these views by their earlier more left-leaning socialization at home.

Individuals also often choose friends and partners with similar values to themselves from the available pool of people around them, and friends and partners then tend to become more like one another as they spend time together. This often reinforces a person's sociopolitical attitudes and values, since most in their circles echo them. These are phenomena that sociologists Paul Lazarsfeld and Robert Merton (1954) classically group under the concept of homophily (Cheadle and Schwadel 2012; Olson and Perl 2011).

By contrast, those more actively involved with a religious group as children and in their adult years are more likely to be regularly exposed to right-leaning values within their families, congregations and faith groups, and their network of friends and acquaintances who often share their own religious identities and beliefs. More religious individuals are also more likely to be exposed to right-leaning values at faith-based schools as well as colleges and universities they are more likely to attend (Nicolet and Tresch 2009; Putnam and Campbell 2010; Raymond 2011; Reimer 2003; Smidt et al. 2010). To be clear, however, not all organized religious groups have right-leaning teachings on sexuality, reproductive rights, family values, gender roles, and the roles and responsibilities of government in society. But, on average, more do than what can be found in general Cascadian popular culture and society.

For some religious Nones, these more right-leaning religious teachings helped them cement their decision to leave their previous religious group or tradition. Many religious Nones, whether having disaffiliated at some point in their lives or having grown up with no religion, also used their more left-leaning issue positions as important boundary markers in constructing and maintaining their own nonreligious identities, or, in other words, to better flesh out and justify who they are and who they are not. The following comment from Jasmine, a religious None from Seattle in her forties, illustrates this boundary-marking process at play between the nonreligious "us" and the religious (especially Christian) "them" or "other":

> I'm really disgusted by what I see the [type of Christian Church] doing ... As a whole, it's just is coming off so incredibly ugly that it makes it hard to even to want to associate myself in any way with that ... definitely how they're talking about women, definitely how they're talking about gay people, definitely – I think the [type of Christian Church] at this point has pretty much aligned itself with racism.

Religious None Identities and Worldviews

Jasmine self-identified as an agnostic in her interview. Her disdain for the church of her youth is evident. Some religious Nones shared Jasmine's nonreligious identity and dislike of church and religion. Yet other Nones indicated an indif-

FIGURE 5.2   Religious nonaffiliation in the Pacific Northwest Social Survey sample, 2017

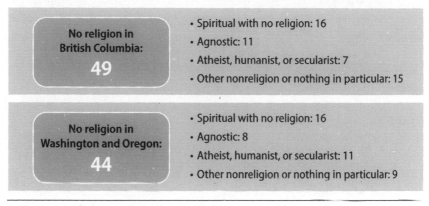

NOTES: *N* (BC) = 359; *N* (Washington and Oregon) = 316. Percentages weighted to be representative of the general adult population.

ference toward all such religious and irreligious labels. Others still showed interest in some spiritual beliefs and practices. Although religious Nones share in common their nonbelonging when it comes to religious groups and traditions and are often removed from most forms of organized religion in their adult years, there is, nevertheless, diversity among religious Nones when it comes to their identities and worldviews and spiritual and secular practices.

When asking "What, if any, is your religion?" the 2017 Pacific Northwest Social Survey gave respondents four "no religion" options to choose from. Figure 5.2 contains the proportional distribution of unaffiliated respondents' selections in both British Columbia and the states of Washington and Oregon. "Spiritual with no religion" is the most popular of these four options in both Cascadia North and South, with an estimated 16 percent of respondents in both subregions selecting this option (representing 33 percent and 36 percent of Nones in British Columbia and Washington and Oregon, respectively).[6] Beatrice, a religious None in her twenties residing in the state of Washington, provided us with an example of this spiritual mindset:

> I'm very, like, connected, I call it. I'm connected to my higher self. And, like, the inner voice, and that's kind of what guides me. And I'm very much, I'm an artist, so I connect to my intuition and kind of the quiet stillness that is within. So, I definitely have a lot, and I draw every day as a part of, kind of, meditation. And to, like, focus on the values that I find important, that I've learned from spirituality. And, like, I try and cultivate that and take that out into my

job and my school. And when I'm, like, you know, if I'm not feeling well, I definitely use spiritual, like, connection and recognition of the divine and my, like, place in the bigger picture.

Jeremy, whom we met at the beginning of this chapter, is another example of someone with a more spiritual identity:

And, yeah, so I mean I'd say I'm also the spiritual thing ... I like finding meaning in things. I like discussing topics about what life is, purpose and what is this all about. It doesn't matter if the person is religious or not. I'm really interested in that stuff. So, it matters a lot to me anyway.

In the 2017 Pacific Northwest Social Survey, an important proportion of Cascadian religious Nones indicated having spiritual experiences outdoors in the natural world: 37 percent and 31 percent for Canadian and US Nones, respectively.[7] Samuel, a millennial religious None from the Victoria focus group, described his spiritual experiences in the outdoors:

I've had spiritual feelings while out surfing, or just being on beaches ... I feel like being kind of immersed in nature in that way, physically being in the ocean, being present there, like, witnessing all of these natural powers, whether or not it's animals or waves coming at you, or whatever. And just, like, seeing the landscape from out there has a very kind of awe-inspiring effect on you. To me, when I think about describing it, it feels profound, it feels spiritual, it feels significant.

Some Cascadia interviewees identified other activities as potentially spiritual, a finding also present in many other qualitative US studies on the topic (e.g., Ammerman 2014; Drescher 2016). Mike, an atheist in his fifties from Seattle, said, for example:

The manifestation of my spirituality probably is in, you know, my love of listening to music and working in my garden. I have a large organic garden, and so I can go out there and work for hours, and I think that that's spiritual. But do I consider it, like, spiritual, like church spiritual? No. It's a different kind. I guess there's all different types of that. I don't really spend much time thinking about that aspect of stuff.

Jack, an artist, storyteller, and educator from a Salish Nation in northwestern Washington, described his storytelling:

So, anyway, that's, as a storyteller, that's how I try to use storytelling. And I'm not quite sure it's a spiritual practice, but I do feel my spirit is connecting with the spirit of the story because I was taught that a story is a living thing. To speak the story, you bring it in front of people, and it stays alive by the moisture of your breath; it lives and breathes by the moisture of your breath. So, at one level, I don't consider myself a spiritual person, but at another level, if I'm helping the spirit of a story come before us and do its work, then that's a good thing.

A number of religious None interviewees, some members of First Nations, some not, also pointed to Indigenous spiritualties playing a crucial role in their understanding of the world. For example, Sunny, a religious None resident of Vancouver Island in her early forties from a British family background, said: "I think teachings around the interconnected nature of everything as one, which are really core teachings in a lot of Indigenous contexts, is one that really just makes a whole lot of sense to me. It really does."

As Figure 5.2 indicates, in British Columbia, the agnostics and "other/nothing in particular" groups come next in size after "spiritual with no religion," representing, respectively, 11 percent and 15 percent of all BC respondents (22 percent and 31 percent of Nones, specifically). In Washington and Oregon, these two groups represented only 8 percent and 9 percent of respondents, respectively (or 18 percent and 20 percent of Nones). Jasmine, introduced earlier, talked about her agnosticism:

Definitely agnostic. I don't go to church anymore. I haven't for many years. I mean, I go on Easter with my mom because it makes her happy, but I don't even do Christmas anymore, so I'm not even a C and E. I'm just an E, but agnostic. I don't – it's hard for me to embrace the label of "Christian." That's not really where I'm at, so ... I think, it's sort of, I mean, I think I am sort of vaguely spiritual in that I feel like there's more, that there's not just what we can see. I think that there's a lot of – you know, there's possibility of all sorts of things, and I'm not discounting the concept of God. I don't know. And I don't know – if there is a God, like, how personal the relationship is. And I, you know, I have a fascination with things like tarot cards and, you know, the general New Age stuff. Whether or not any of that is true either, I have that sort of that same, "Eh, it could be?" It would be kind of nice if it wasn't just we die and then we're dust, you know? I'd like there to be more. But I have a hard time. I'm very skeptical about it all, so. And I love watching ghost shows and things, and it's like, "Oh, yeah, there could be something?" But then the other part of me is like, "Oh, they're just moving that chair with fishing wire," you know? So it's always, it's a back and forth. So I can't claim any one specific thought process.

In Washington and Oregon, it was atheists, humanists, and secularists who took second place among the Nones, with 11 percent of all respondents from Cascadia South choosing this category (representing 25 percent of Nones). Harry, a Portland resident in his seventies, talked about his atheism and more scientific worldview:

> And I'm getting more atheist as time goes on ... Well, my belief is ... the more we're learning over time about the universe and about, and physics, and chemistry, and the more we learn about what's going on, what we think is going on, the more, in my opinion, it becomes more difficult to believe in some of the things that the church preaches.

The start of Harry's quote also reminds us that the Pacific Northwest Social Survey only provides a snapshot in time of the "no religion" categories that respondents chose. These survey data do not capture any potential changes over time or between social contexts for the respondent. The interview data, on the other hand, contain examples of how agnostic and atheist identities may be somewhat interlinked and fluid throughout an individual's lifetime. Simon, a Victoria, BC, resident in his early forties, talked about the evolution of his nonreligious identity:

> I'd say for most of my life I tried to approach this with a degree of humility in the sense of, you know, thinking about myself mostly as an agnostic, you know, sort of rigidly saying, you know, "I don't know, and neither do you." I'd say I've become more of an atheist as I've grown. And I'd say that, you know ... I have just as much certitude in faith that there's nothing up there as the people that have faith, you know. So I guess I'm a ... rationalist atheist.

Washington and Oregon respondents were also characterized by slightly higher rates of frequent participation in organized atheist, humanist, or secularist activities (with groups such as the American Humanist Association, Humanists of Greater Portland, and the Sunday Assembly), although taking part regularly in these kinds of activities remained relatively uncommon overall in both Cascadian subregions: 8 percent of respondents in Washington and Oregon participated at least once a month in atheist, humanist, or secularist organized activities according to the 2017 Pacific Northwest Social Survey, compared with 5 percent in British Columbia. Steve, an atheist in his seventies from Victoria, British Columbia, explained why he was involved with a secular humanist organization in the region:

I'm feeling more disturbed and annoyed almost by the, by religion insinuating itself into people's lives. The abortion debate, I don't like calling it that, it's the antichoice–prochoice debate. It really bugs me when I read "the antiabortion." It suggests, like, somebody is proabortion. I don't think anybody is really for it, but it's things like that, when I think the undercurrent there is religion to a large degree. And that troubles me. And, you know, schools. I didn't realize until I joined the humanist association that they got Bibles out in the schools in Abbotsford, and when I read that, I was just blown away. I was just, like, "What? In this day and age?" So, I'm learning quite a bit ... But I am feeling more troubled by religion and, and more, it's more pronounced I think in the States too ... It's like, you know what, you believe what you want to believe, and I couldn't care less. But when it's influencing political and societal decisions, it's, we need to push back.

At the same time, a quote from Charles, an atheist in his early forties from Portland and involved with a nonreligious organization, hints at the reasons these organizations may not be that popular among their target demographic:

Portland was one of the test cities in the United States to set up [specific non-religious organization]. And they actually came here, and they did a couple, and then they trained some people to keep it going. And it's still kind of going, but for the most part, it was just a miserable failure ... And part of the reason was because, basically, because I was on the phone calls and stuff with sort of helping this happen, and, basically, we couldn't, we couldn't get this little middle sliver between one group of people who said, "The whole reason I'm atheist is that there's no sort of compulsory ... you know, group thing." And then the other side that was saying, "Why even bother to get together if you don't stand for anything?" And between those, that covered 90 percent of the nonreligious groups ... Either one side was, like, "Never organize a regular event." And the other said, you know, that you have to stand for something. You can't just not stand for something.

Christopher, an atheist in his fifties from Portland, gave another reason for not being involved with such organizations: "All my friends are pretty much all atheist, so I don't really have to seek people out to feel at home as far as religion goes."

Why do atheism, humanism, and secularism – identities and positions usually more explicitly against religion – and active participation in related organizations appear to be somewhat more popular in Washington and Oregon than in British Columbia? Richard Cimino and Christopher Smith (2007) argue that some religious Nones become actively involved in nonreligious associations notably in reaction to their real or perceived minority status in society. Similar to Steve's story, Cimino and Smith share interview data from religious Nones in the United States whose interactions with evangelicals contributed to a growing fear of the role that evangelicals play in American society, so much so that some religious Nones became more involved in nonreligious associations to strengthen the secular voice and its impact in society. Stephen LeDrew (2015) adds that nonreligious organizations can be helpful spaces for atheists to "come out" and gather with other like-minded individuals, particularly if they were raised in a religious tradition and find themselves in contexts where religion is more normative.

This may be an indication that levels of participation in atheist, humanist, and secularist organizations are at their lowest in the Pacific Northwest, where nonreligion is so common and accepted among such a large segment of the population. That said, it may also be the reason the US context as a whole, even in the None Zone, seems to have some influence on religious Nones in Washington and Oregon (even on a few Nones in British Columbia, as we saw with Steve). Slightly more Nones in Cascadia South seem to be driven to adopt explicitly antireligious stances and to mobilize to share their views in the face of a nationally and politically dominant conservative American evangelicalism.

Group Closure and Bridging among Nones

Marsha, an atheist in her seventies from Victoria, British Columbia, shared the following about one of her close friends and her own family:

> And she's antireligious now. Totally antireligious. She hates the [specific Christian denomination]. She doesn't like religion of any kind. And so, you know, like I see the negative effects that it's [religion's] had on people, you know ... My older sister never believed either. But we [immediate family] never discussed it. None of us ever, ever discussed religion, we just all knew that we hated it.

Marsha's experience hints at larger phenomena at play among many religious Nones: a certain amount of homophily and group closure that exists among these individuals, as discussed earlier regarding sociopolitical attitudes. How do religious Nones coexist with more religious persons in Cascadia? In fact, most do not come into much daily contact with religious people. As alluded to earlier in this essay, Nones tend to be surrounded by other Nones more often than not, just like those who are actively involved with a faith group tend to have relationships with others who are similarly involved.

How extensive is this phenomenon of homophily among different types of religious Nones? The 2017 Pacific Northwest Social Survey asked respondents

FIGURE 5.3   (Non)religious friend distribution among five close friends, British Columbia, Washington, and Oregon, 2017

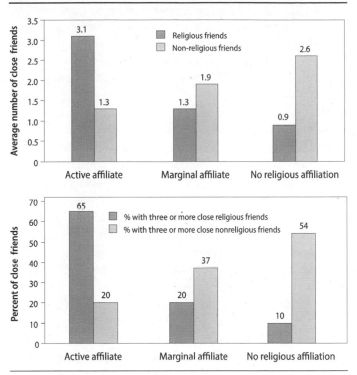

NOTES: *N* active affiliates = 373; marginal affiliates = 449; no religious affiliation = 672.

about their five closest friends and how many they would consider religious or not religious at all. Figure 5.3 illustrates the mean number and some percentages of both types of friends for religious Nones, and how they compare with marginal (attend religious services less than once a month) and active (attend religious services at least once a month) religious affiliates in this regard. It is important to keep in mind here that these data are from the point of view of the respondent, not their friends. These data are based on the respondent's definition of religious–not religious. Additionally, if rarely or never discussed among close friends, the respondents may be making an assumption about their close friends on this trait. Regardless, these data are telling when it comes to how respondents perceive their close friends on the matter of (ir)religiosity.

According to the results in Figure 5.3, active religious affiliates are, by far, the most likely to have religious close friends: an average of 3.1 out of 5 close friends are involved with a faith group among these respondents, compared with fewer than 0.9 out of 5 close friends being religious among religious None respondents. Sixty-five percent of active affiliates have 3 or more (out of 5) close friends who are involved with a faith group, compared with only 10 percent among religious Nones. By contrast, religious Nones have an average of 2.6 close friends who are not religious at all, compared with an average of 1.3 nonreligious close friends among the actively religious. Fifty-four percent of religious Nones have 3 or more close nonreligious friends (out of 5), compared with only 20 percent of active affiliates.

Why do we find these homophily trends among religious Nones and their close friends in the Cascadian region? First, Nones are more likely to be surrounded by other religious Nones in their social environments: at home, in their neighbourhood, at school while growing up, at college or university, and so forth. People make friends from the pool of available individuals around them. That said, the interview data explored earlier also hint at a certain amount of group closure among Nones: some Nones are actively turned off by religion and may consequently avoid people associated with it. When talking of their dislike or discomfort toward religion, many of the Nones interviewed usually spoke at a more general level without necessarily targeting the people who belonged to and practised particular faiths. Robin, an atheist in his seventies from Vancouver, British Columbia, said, for example, "Without being melodramatic, I've always found it [religion] manipulative, destructive, and pretty elitist, to tell you the truth." These attitudes are still likely, however, to colour Nones' views of more religious persons and may affect friendship and relationship decisions. We can see this link in part of the interview with Connor, a Vancouver religious None in his fifties:

> From what I've seen, religion has been the major cause of the vast majority of societal conflicts over the centuries, and that, to me, is a fairly negative thing ... just the behaviour that I have seen among religious people toward each other, and the kind of discrimination and hierarchical pecking order that seem to come into play when people are religious.

Additionally, since religious Nones' social ties are more likely to be with people like themselves in their irreligiosity, this, in turn, can reinforce these Nones' negative views of religion.

In fact, if we look at different Nones' average levels of comfort with different types of individuals hypothetically becoming their in-law by marriage (see Figure 5.4), we can see that some groups with specific (non)religious and (non)-spiritual backgrounds are clearly favoured over others. Atheists and spiritual persons receive the highest comfort scores, on average, from None respondents in British Columbia, Washington, and Oregon. By contrast, evangelical

FIGURE 5.4 Average level of comfort with certain types of persons becoming a relative by marriage, British Columbia, Washington, and Oregon, 2017

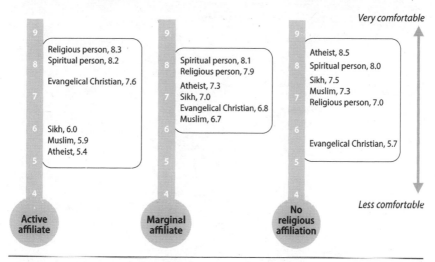

NOTE: 10 = "Very comfortable," and 0 = "Very uncomfortable."

Christians and religious persons are the groups that receive the lowest comfort scores, on average, among Nones.

Consequently, the phenomena of homophily and group closure are not isolated to only the actively and marginally religious, many of whom socialize and prefer members of their own religious and spiritual groups. These phenomena also characterize many religious Nones in Cascadia in that the nonreligious tend to interact more with one another and prefer their own company to interacting with the religious.

That said, many Nones do express some level of comfort and openness toward more religious persons. Only 17 percent of religious Nones gave a score of 4 or lower (indicating discomfort) to a religious person becoming their in-law; 37 percent of religious Nones instead gave the highest scores of 9 or 10 (indicating high levels of comfort) to this group.

Micro-interaction Strategies with Religious Individuals

So what strategies are used by religious Nones when they come into contact and interact with more religious persons, either family, friends, in the workplace, or in any other social setting? How do Nones in Cascadia bridge the religious–irreligious divide when needed in social spaces where religious and secular groups coexist? Four strategies for interaction seemed to come up again and again in the qualitative data, illustrated in Figure 5.5. These four strategies are

FIGURE 5.5   Strategies among religious Nones when interacting with more religious persons

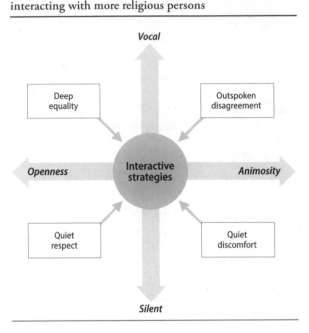

designated here as outspoken disagreement, quiet discomfort, quiet respect, and deep equality. These four distinct approaches fall along two spectrums: whether or not Nones choose to say anything about (ir)religion to the other individual, and how open or closed they are toward the other's religiosity. Some Nones may be prone to using one type of strategy during most interactions with religious individuals, and others may employ different strategies in different contexts as needed.

Mike, an atheist in his fifties from Seattle whom we met earlier, provided an example of the open-disagreement strategy when discussing one of his more religious friends:

> [Catholic friend who volunteers] and I will talk about it [religion] because I'm always giving him gas about his, the grief that he gets from these Catholic people. And I said, "You know, how can you like volunteering and getting shit from people?" I said, "It's because they can't help themselves. They've been processed by this Church. All these years later, they're in their fifties, sixties, even seventies, and they're still in that whole absolutist mindset. And you're outside of the box. They just can't handle that. So you need to find something different to do as far as putting yourself into some community or something like that."

Robin, an atheist in his seventies from Vancouver whom we met earlier, instead talked about his strategy of quiet discomfort:

> If I run into someone who's religious, and they're telling me a religious story, like my sister-in-law or something, I just kind of shrug it off, right. Like, I don't go out afterwards, after she'd gone, and, like, you know, put needles in a little doll or something. I just let it go. But ... and because she does, she believes very seriously as does her husband, in religion. And I just, I just don't get it ... and when we're at a family thing, and he starts trying to tell me about some great thing he's heard or learned, I try to change the subject as quickly as possible.

Kelly, a religious None in her twenties from Seattle, spoke instead about an experience that more closely resembles quiet respect:

> I can really only think of one friend who identifies as religious, and she doesn't, I wouldn't even consider it being a huge identifier for her. I think she goes to church very rarely. I think she went for Easter this year. So no, not, it's never something we've really talked about. I think it's something that's been approached but nothing that we've ever, like, dug deep into and had full conversation about.

With quiet respect, religion is not discussed between individuals, less because of a fear of discord if it were discussed and more because the religious None in question does not see it as all that important to the mutual relationship.

Jayden, a religious None in her twenties from Seattle, adopted a deep-equality strategy with one of her closest friends:

> I have another pretty close [friend], I don't think she even realizes how much I love her, but she's also in the church. And she's a super free spirit. She's like my daily motivation on how I want to be as a person, because she's just very loving, very caring, just, like, wants to participate in the community in any way she can, and she just motivates me so much ... She respects that I don't [go to church] ... We can sit down and talk about how it [religion] informs the way that she's working as a person, I guess. You know. And that's just unique to my relationships and friendships with people. Specifically [with] her and, like, anyone I know that actively believes, I only want to be the most respectful of religion as I can be.

"Deep-equality strategy" refers to when Nones openly discuss in an accepting manner someone else's religion. The term "deep equality" is borrowed here from scholar Lori Beaman's (2014, 96) broader concept of the same name, which she defines as

> a vision of equality that transcends law, politics, and social policy, and that relocates equality as a process rather than a definition, and as lived rather than prescribed. It recognizes equality as an achievement of day-to-day interaction, and is traceable through agonistic respect, recognition of similarity and a simultaneous acceptance of difference, creation of community, and neighbour-liness. It circulates through micro-processes of individual action and inaction and through group demonstrations of caring.

These four interaction strategies could also be used by more religious individuals when interacting with the nonreligious, but the focus here remains on how Nones employ them. With our qualitative data, it is not possible to tell which of the four interaction strategies is most prevalent among religious Nones overall. The quiet strategies came up most often in the interviews, but future research will have to determine whether this is representative of the larger nonreligious population. Our data also cannot identify if certain strategies are especially distinct or more prominent in the Cascadian context, compared with elsewhere in North America. In a region where nonreligion is for the most part socially accepted, does this normalization of nonreligion allow less antagonistic strategies such as quiet respect and deep equality to flourish? Or, on the contrary, does it embolden the nonreligious to be more vocal in their disapproval of religion? Or does it create, first and foremost, a context of indifference among many of the nonreligious who come more rarely into contact with religious persons? Again, future researchers will need to engage in comparative research to answer these questions.

***

So what does a religious None look like in Cascadia? There are so many different ways of being a religious None – from holding beliefs in the supernatural and some connections to the spiritual but away from church doors; to holding a more scientific worldview and disdain for most things religious; to being completely indifferent and oblivious to any of it; to a whole variety of experiences in between. Although there are Nones of all sorts in the region, Jeremy, whom we met at the start of this essay, exemplifies the typical demographic and sociopolitical profile in this subpopulation: young, male, born in North America, coming from a once Christian family, left-value oriented, and university-educated.

Many of the findings here are not necessarily unique to Cascadia; they also characterize religious Nones in other parts of North America. More comparative research is needed to tease out the elements distinct to the Pacific Northwest in this regard. Still, nowhere else on the continent does the phenomenon of nonreligion touch such a large segment of the population as in British Columbia, Washington, and Oregon.

That said, as others in this volume suggest, religion will not be disappearing from Cascadia for the foreseeable future; so coexistence among the diversity of secular and religious groups that we see in the region appears to be the name of the game at present and moving forward. The intent here is not to make a case for which coexistence strategy is better and preferable for shared living and the public good but rather to document and explore all of these realities as they are experienced on the ground by everyday Cascadia residents.

Notes

Acknowledgments: I would first like to acknowledge and thank my colleague Joel Thiessen from Ambrose University: writing our book together on religious Nones in the United States and Canada (Thiessen and Wilkins-Laflamme 2020) has helped develop a great deal of my thinking and arguments in this chapter. I would also like to thank the entire Cascadia research team, especially Tina Block, Paul Bramadat, Chelsea Horton, Patricia Killen, and Lynne Marks for their data collection efforts and constructive feedback.

1 For archival and interview data, see https://www.uvic.ca/research/centres/csrs/.
2 In comparison, only an estimated 20 percent of Canadians living outside of British Columbia and 23 percent of Americans living outside of Washington and Oregon say they have no religion. See Pew Research Center (2014) and Statistics Canada (2017).
3 See the Introduction of this volume for general data-collection details. See also Tina Block and Lynne Marks' chapter in this volume for more details about how and with whom the oral-history interviews were conducted.
4 See, notably, Suzanne Crawford-O'Brien's and Chelsea Horton's chapters in this volume for more on this subject.
5 The seemingly lower levels of support for same-sex marriage in British Columbia than in Washington and Oregon in Figure 5.1 may be an artifact of how the survey question was asked in the 2015 Canadian Election Study (CES). This survey provided respondents with only three answer options (favour, oppose, or don't know/no opinion), rather than a more detailed Likert scale, as in the 2014 Pew Religious Landscape Study. Consequently, BC respondents who did not have as strong opinions on this issue may have selected the third category in larger numbers in the CES (31 percent of all BC respondents in the 2015 CES did so) compared with US respondents who were given more answer options in the Pew survey.
6 This phrase has a similar meaning to the more common "spiritual but not religious" label (SBNR). However, since the survey question is about belonging (to religion) not (religious) behaviour, this answer option was worded as "no religion – spiritual with no religion."
7 For more on this kind of engagement with nature, see Paul Bramadat's and Susanna Morrill's chapters in this volume.

References

Ammerman, Nancy. 2014. *Sacred Stories, Spiritual Tribes: Finding Religion in Everyday Life.* New York: Oxford University Press.

Ang, Adrian, and John R. Petrocik. 2012. "Religion, Religiosity, and the Moral Divide in Canadian Politics." *Politics and Religion* 5 (1): 103–32.

Baker, Joseph O'Brian, and Buster G. Smith. 2015. *American Secularism: Cultural Contours of Nonreligious Belief Systems.* New York: New York University Press.

Beaman, Lori. 2014. "Deep Equality as an Alternative to Accommodation and Tolerance." *Nordic Journal of Religion and Society* 27 (2): 89–111.

Beaman, Lori, and Steven Tomlins, eds. 2015. *Atheist Identities: Spaces and Social Contexts.* New York: Springer.

Bibby, Reginald. 2011. *Beyond the Gods and Back: Religion's Demise and Rise and Why It Matters.* Lethbridge, AB: Project Canada Books.

Block, Tina. 2016. *The Secular Northwest: Religion and Irreligion in Everyday Postwar Life.* Vancouver: UBC Press.

Bramadat, Paul, and David Seljak, eds. 2005. *Religion and Ethnicity in Canada.* Toronto: Pearson.

Bullivant, Stephen, and Lois Lee. 2012. "Interdisciplinary Studies of Non-religion and Secularity: The State of the Union." *Journal of Contemporary Religion* 27 (1): 19–27.

Cheadle, Jacob E., and Philip Schwadel. 2012. "The 'Friendship Dynamics of Religion,' or the 'Religious Dynamics of Friendship?' A Social Network Analysis of Adolescents Who Attend Small Schools." *Social Science Research* 41 (5): 1198–212.

Cimino, Richard, and Christopher Smith. 2007. "Secular Humanism and Atheism beyond Progressive Secularism." *Sociology of Religion* 68 (4): 407–24.

Clarke, Brian, and Stuart Macdonald. 2017. *Leaving Christianity: Changing Allegiances in Canada since 1945.* Montreal/Kingston: McGill-Queen's University Press.

Crockett, Alasdair, and David Voas. 2006. "Generations of Decline: Religious Change in 20th-Century Britain." *Journal for the Scientific Study of Religion* 45 (4): 567–84.

Day, Abby. 2011. *Believing in Belonging: Belief and Social Identity in the Modern World.* Toronto: Oxford University Press.

Drescher, Elizabeth. 2016. *Choosing Our Religion: The Spiritual Lives of America's Nones.* New York: Oxford University Press.

Fournier, Patrick, Fred Cutler, Stuart Soroka, and Dietlind Stolle, principal investigators. 2017. *2011–2015 Canadian Election Study (Dataset).* Accessed March 12, 2017. http://ces-eec.arts.ubc.ca/english-section/surveys/.

Glanzer, Perry L., Jonathan Hill, and Todd C. Ream. 2014. "Changing Souls: Higher Education's Influence upon the Religious Lives of Emerging Adults." In *Emerging Adults' Religiousness and Spirituality: Meaning-Making in an Age of Transition,* edited by Carolyn McNamara Barry and Mona M. Abo-Zena, 152–69. New York: Oxford University Press.

Hill, Jonathan P. 2011. "Faith and Understanding: Specifying the Impact of Higher Education on Religious Belief." *Journal for the Scientific Study of Religion* 50 (3): 533–51.

Killen, Patricia O'Connell, and Mark Silk, eds. 2004. *Religion and Public Life in the Pacific Northwest: The None Zone.* Walnut Creek, CA: AltaMira Press.

Lazarsfeld, Paul F., and Robert K. Merton. 1954. "Friendship as a Social Process: A Substantive and Methodological Analysis." In *Freedom and Control in Modern Society,* edited by Morroe Berger, Theodore Abel, and Charles H. Page, 18–66. New York: Octagon Books.

LeDrew, Stephen. 2015. *The Evolution of Atheism: The Politics of a Modern Movement.* New York: Oxford University Press.

Lewis, James R. 2015. "Education, Irreligion, and Non-religion: Evidence from Select Anglophone Census Data." *Journal of Contemporary Religion* 30 (2): 265–72.

Manning, Christel. 2015. *Losing Our Religion: How Unaffiliated Parents Are Raising Their Children.* New York: New York University Press.

Marks, Lynne. 2017. *Infidels and the Damn Churches: Irreligion and Religion in Settler British Columbia*. Vancouver: UBC Press.

Mayrl, Damon, and Freeden Oeur. 2009. "Religion and Higher Education: Current Knowledge and Directions for Future Research." *Journal for the Scientific Study of Religion* 48 (2): 260–75.

Meunier, É.-Martin, and Sarah Wilkins-Laflamme. 2011. "Sécularisation, catholicisme et transformation du régime de religiosité au Québec: Étude comparative avec le catholicisme au Canada (1968–2007)." *Recherches Sociographiques* 52 (3): 683–729.

Nicolet, Sarah, and Anke Tresch. 2009. "Changing Religiosity, Changing Politics? The Influence of 'Belonging' and 'Believing' on Political Attitudes in Switzerland." *Politics and Religion* 2 (1): 76–99.

Olson, Daniel V.A., and Paul Perl. 2011. "A Friend in Creed: Does the Religious Composition of Geographic Areas Affect the Religious Composition of a Person's Close Friends?" *Journal for the Scientific Study of Religion* 50 (3): 483–502.

Pew Research Center. 2014. *Religious Landscape Study (Dataset)*. Accessed July 2, 2017. http://www.pewforum.org/religious-landscape-study/.

Putnam, Robert, and David Campbell. 2010. *American Grace: How Religion Divides and Unites Us*. New York: Simon and Schuster.

Raymond, Christopher. 2011. "The Continued Salience of Religious Voting in the United States, Germany, and Great Britain." *Electoral Studies* 30 (1): 125–35.

Reimer, Sam. 2003. *Evangelicals and the Continental Divide: The Evangelical Subculture in Canada and the United States*. Montreal/Kingston: McGill-Queen's University Press.

Schwadel, Philip. 2015. "Explaining Cross-National Variation in the Effect of Higher Education on Religiosity." *Journal for the Scientific Study of Religion* 54 (2): 402–18.

Sherkat, Darren E. 2014. *Changing Faith: The Dynamics and Consequences of Americans' Shifting Identities*. New York: New York University Press.

Skirbekk, Vegard, Éric Caron Malenfant, Stuart Basten, and Marcin Stonawski. 2012. "The Religious Composition of the Chinese Diaspora, Focusing on Canada." *Journal for the Scientific Study of Religion* 5 (1): 173–83.

Smidt, Corwin E., Kevin den Dulk, Bryan Froehle, James Penning, Stephen Monsma, and Douglas Koopman. 2010. *The Disappearing God Gap? Religion in the 2008 Presidential Election*. New York: Oxford University Press.

Statistics Canada. 2015. *2011 National Household Survey [Canada] Public Use Microdata File (PUMF): Individual File*. Dataset. Accessed October 2, 2018.

–. 2017. *Cycle 30 (2016), General Social Survey [Canada] Public Use Microdata Files (PUMF): Individual Files*. Dataset. Accessed October 2, 2018.

Strawn, Kelley D. 2019. "What's behind the 'Nones-sense'? Change over Time in Factors Predicting Likelihood of Religious Nonaffiliation in the United States." *Journal for the Scientific Study of Religion* 58 (3): 707–24.

Thiessen, Joel. 2015. *The Meaning of Sunday: The Practice of Belief in a Secular Age*. Montreal/Kingston: McGill-Queen's University Press.

Thiessen, Joel, and Sarah Wilkins-Laflamme. 2017. "Becoming a Religious None: Irreligious Socialization and Disaffiliation." *Journal for the Scientific Study of Religion* 56 (1): 64–82.

–. 2020. *None of the Above: Nonreligious Identity in the US and Canada*. New York: New York University Press.

Voas, David. 2008. "The Continuing Secular Transition." In *The Role of Religion in Modern Societies*, edited by Detlef Pollack and Daniel V.A. Olson, 25–48. New York: Routledge.

–. 2009. "The Rise and Fall of Fuzzy Fidelity in Europe." *European Sociological Review* 25 (2): 155–68.

Wilkins-Laflamme, Sarah. 2016a. "The Changing Religious Cleavage in Canadians' Voting Behaviour." *Canadian Journal of Political Science* 49 (3): 499–518.

–. 2016b. "Secularization and the Wider Gap in Values and Personal Religiosity between the Religious and Non-religious." *Journal for the Scientific Study of Religion* 55 (4): 717–36.

Zuckerman, Phil, Luke W. Galen, and Frank L. Pasquale. 2016. *The Nonreligious: Understanding Secular People and Societies.* New York: Oxford University Press.

6 From Outlier to Advance Guard: Cascadia in Its North American Context

Mark Silk

The purpose of this essay is to place religion in Cascadia in its larger national, indeed transnational, context. That means examining the relationship between British Columbia and the rest of Canada, on the one hand, and between Washington and Oregon and the rest of the United States, on the other, against the background of changes in religious identification and practice in both countries. Of central significance is the striking increase in the proportion of adults in both countries who identify with no religion – what has come to be called the rise of the Nones – over the past several decades. What I want to argue is that where, at the turn of the century, Cascadia stood apart from the rest of Canada and the United States as a place of notably low religious identification, it now appears to be leading the way toward disengagement from institutional religious connections.

In the interest of providing some background for this volume's exploration of religion in Cascadia, let me begin by immodestly taking some credit for opening the discussion of the key issues facing my colleagues. Two decades ago, the Leonard E. Greenberg Center for the Study of Religion in Public Life, which I direct, received a substantial grant from the Lilly Endowment to study religion and region in the United States. Although we considered incorporating Canada into the project, managing research groups for eight US regions seemed like the limit of our capacity. This decision, of course, meant that we were not able to speak to the ways in which some regions extended across international borders. The present volume addresses one of the most interesting instances of this phenomenon.

Our main concern in the earlier volumes was religion in public life, particularly the role of religion in shaping political cultures. Because of that, we did not permit the geography of religious adherence to split a state between (or among) regions. Louisiana, for example, might have been divided between a predominantly evangelical Protestant zone in the north and a predominantly

Catholic one in the South, each of which would be considered to belong to evangelical and Catholic regions extending into states to the east and west.[1] We were, however, not interested in identifying (relatively) religiously homogeneous territories but in exploring how the political life and public policy of a given state and region had been affected by whichever religious cultures happened to be there. It has been through the encounter of the evangelical north and the Catholic south that religion has shaped Louisiana politics.[2]

Of the eight regions, the Pacific Northwest posed the greatest challenge. As we defined it, the region included Alaska but not Montana or Idaho, which some geographers place in the region. Alaska proved a relatively easy fit with Washington and Oregon because, despite its very different current political culture, it shares with the two most recognizable Pacific Northwest states a history of the dominance of extractive industries. Like them, moreover, its level of religious adherence has always been low. As for Montana and Idaho, they became part of a Mountain West region, the former linked subregionally to the mining states of Wyoming and Colorado and the latter to Utah as the Mormon Corridor. The literature on religion in the United States had never conceived of Washington and Oregon (plus Alaska) as a distinct religious region, so we were required, in effect, to create a new subject of study. Fortunately, in Patricia O'Connell Killen we found a native daughter who was also a student of religion in the region and, as coeditor, she assembled an excellent group of scholars to take up the challenge. The volume that resulted, *Religion and Public Life in the Pacific Northwest* (Killen and Silk 2004), in hindsight, was the most successful and arguably the most important in the series.

Religion and Public Life in the Pacific Northwest: The None Zone

We subtitled the volume "the None Zone," because the Pacific Northwest region featured the highest proportion of Nones of all our regions.[3] The data for this came principally from the work of Barry Kosmin and his colleagues in two large studies, the 1990 National Survey of Religious Identification (Kosmin and Keysar 1991) and the 2001 American Religious Identification Survey (ARIS) (Kosmin, Mayer, and Keysar 2001). Both surveys asked respondents for their religious identity not, as is most commonly done, by providing a list of options to choose from but by letting them give whatever answers they wished. The 2001 ARIS signalled the rise of the Nones, finding that the proportion of Nones in the US adult population had risen from 8 percent to 14 percent since 1990 – a startling increase, but one that attracted little notice when it was first reported.[4] The survey showed Washington to have experienced the largest percentage-point increase of any state, from 15 percent to 25 percent of the adult population. Oregon's Nones grew more modestly, from 18 percent to 21 percent. Elsewhere in the country, the northern New England states came closest to the

Pacific Northwest, with Vermont, New Hampshire, and Maine registering Nones at 22 percent, 17 percent, and 16 percent, respectively, in 2001. In more populous southern New England, however, Nones were under 15 percent, bringing the region as a whole close to the US average.

Several themes emerged from our exploration of religion and public life in the region, particularly with respect to Oregon and Washington (as distinct from Alaska). These included the importance of interfaith cooperation and the prevalence of religious entrepreneurship. In a place where institutional religion for non-Indigenous people had never been strong, success required a high degree of enterprise, on the one hand, and, on the other, a pulling together on the part of religious communities that, elsewhere in the country, had historically kept their distance. To be sure, interfaith cooperation thrived nationally in the mid-twentieth century, but later, as it went into decline elsewhere, it persisted in the Pacific Northwest. The main avenue of common cause was environmentalism, which in our view had become the region's ethos – one so shaped by engagement with, and commitment to, nature that it amounted to the region's civil religion. A gospel of sustainability and biodiversity was strongly in evidence across the religious spectrum: in the Catholic and mainline Protestant churches, the non-Christian and New-Age faiths, and among the Nones themselves. Yet the Pacific Northwest also had its counterculture, located above all in its sizable evangelical community, where the region's religious entrepreneurship was especially on display. As one would expect, the region's evangelicals largely resisted the dominant culture on abortion and gay rights. Most strikingly, however, this was the one region where a majority of them took a negative view of environmentalism.[5] Clearly, in this regional version of the national culture war, environmentalism had become part of a spiritual ideology against which evangelicals felt obliged to set themselves.[6]

As well, and most importantly in the present context, the Pacific Northwest was distinct in including parts of two countries. One could, of course, point to other parts of the United States that maintain close ties across the southern or northern border. But Oregon and Washington understood themselves to be connected to British Columbia in a different way – in some respects connected more closely to that Canadian province than to the rest of the United States. On the religion front, British Columbia was Canada's None Zone just as the region was America's. And environmentalism was as much British Columbia's spiritual ideology as it was the Pacific Northwest's. All this was laid out at "Cascadia: Spirituality, Geography and Social Change," a conference organized by Douglas Todd at Simon Fraser University in 2006 that resulted in Todd's edited volume, *Cascadia: The Elusive Utopia*. Here was a region that stood apart – unreligious, possessed of an environmentalist culture all its own, transgressively transnational, the regional outlier of both countries (Todd 2008).

And yet, in this essay, I want to argue that in the decade and a half since the *None Zone* volume was published, Cascadia has proven to be not an outlier but the advance guard of religion in the public life of the two countries of which it is a part. This is most clearly indicated by trends in religious disaffiliation, which over the past two decades have made clear the extent to which the United States and Canada are following in Cascadia's footsteps. In the United States, the latest surveys show that 20 to 25 percent of the adult population identifies as None, where Oregon and Washington were two decades ago. In the meantime, the None population in Oregon and Washington has risen to 32 percent in the Pew Landscape Study of 2015 and to 44 percent in the 2017 Pacific Northwest Social Survey (PNSS), which was commissioned for this study and thus provides us with the most reliable figures (see Wilkins-Laflamme in this volume). In Canada, the last three decennial censuses show the proportion of adult Nones growing from 13 percent in 1991 to 17 percent in 2001 to 24 percent in 2011. In British Columbia, the growth was virtually identical in percentage-point terms, from 30 percent to 35 percent to 44 percent.[7] In our PNSS study, 49 percent of BC residents identified as having no religion.

To be sure, outside of Cascadia both countries show significant regional variation in the preponderance of Nones. In the United States, their percentage remains smallest across the southern Bible Belt and up through the Great Plains – what Philip Barlow calls the "Bible suspender" (Barlow 2004, 27). According to the Public Religion Research Institute's (PRRI) 2018 data, no religious identity is claimed by 15 percent of Louisianans, 17 percent of Mississippians, and 19 percent of North and South Dakotans. The proportion of Nones in northern New England is in the mid-thirties while in southern New England they check in at 29 percent (PRRI 2018). Notably, the American variation is smaller than the variation in Canada, which in the 2011 National Household Survey ranged from 44 percent Nones in British Columbia to 29 percent in the Prairie provinces, 23 percent in Ontario, 16 percent in the Atlantic provinces, and 12 percent in Quebec (Statistics Canada 2013).

US-Canadian Divergence

By almost any measure, Canada is a more secular country than the United States. Religion plays a smaller role in its national rhetoric, culture, politics, and by the numbers too. The last of these has not always been the case, however. In 1970, in fact, the proportion of Nones in the United States was slightly higher than it was in Canada – 5 percent versus 4 percent. But Canadian Nones pulled even in the mid-1970s and in the 1980s gained a small but significantly larger share of the adult population, even as American Nones showed no increase (Pew 2013).[8] With the proportion of Catholics in Canada remaining constant at 46 percent of the population in the 1980s (and giving up just one percentage point in the 1991 census and two more in 2001), it was clear that the rise of the Canadian Nones came largely at the expense of Protestants. Only in the first decade of the twenty-first century did the Catholic share of the population dip significantly, from 43 percent to 38 percent. Indeed, the absolute number of Catholics in Canada declined between censuses for the first time since record keeping began in 1881, from 12.9 million in 2001 to 12.8 million in 2011. Assuming (generously) that there is no further numerical decline in the next census, that would put the Catholic share of the Canadian population in 2021 at under 33 percent, based on the projected increase of the entire Canadian population to 39 million.

The rise of the Nones on the other side of the border has trailed Canada by approximately a decade. In the United States, the upward trajectory began in the 1990s, flattened out in the 2000s, and then bent sharply up in the 2010s. As in Canada, it was a decline in the Protestant population that led the way: the Catholic share of the US population remained stable at 25 percent through the first decade of the twenty-first century but in the second decade dropped below 20 percent, according to the PRRI American Values Atlas. The question to be answered is why, within Cascadia as well as nationally, the decline in religious identification has become more pronounced north of the border than south. In its 2013 report on religion in Canada, Pew points out that in both countries a major factor has been the gradual supplanting of more religious older generations by less religious newer ones (Pew 2013). This, of course, raises the question of why young Protestant adults in Canada should have turned away from religious identification sooner than their opposite numbers in the United States, as well as why Canada now displays an overall lower level of religious identification than the United States.

The answers, I would submit, have largely to do with the greater predominance of evangelical Protestants in the United States. In both countries, the rise of the Nones began with Protestants, and it remains the case that most Nones derive from the Protestant side of the ledger and mainline Protestantism in particular. In the United States, the mainline Protestant share of the population peaked in the late 1950s at 50 percent, beginning a steady decline such that now, six decades later, it accounts for only between 10 and 15 percent. Similarly, in Canada, the mainline share of the population dropped from 32 percent to 14 percent in the 1981 and 2011 Household Surveys.[9] Meanwhile, evangelicals were on the rise in the United States, while in Canada they were not. Today, they are much thinner on the ground, constituting, at most, 10 percent of the Canadian population compared with 25 percent in the United States (Reside 2018; Hiemstra and Stiller 2016). In Cascadia, Baptists and Pentecostals, the two largest evangelical communities, make up 3 percent of the BC population compared with 12 percent of the population of Oregon and Washington, according to the 2011 National Household Survey and the 2014 Pew Landscape Study, respectively (Pew Research Center 2015; Wilkins-Laflamme 2017). That nine-point differential amounts to two-thirds of the difference in the proportion of Nones, who at the time weighed in at 44 percent in British Columbia and 32 percent in the two US states. My argument, then, is that as the younger generation of mainline Protestants became Nones in both countries, the evangelical generational cohort tended to remain affiliated, thanks in no small measure to the strong emphasis placed on youth ministries by the evangelical churches. The larger growth in the proportion of evangelicals in the United States thus compensated to some extent for the decline of mainline Protestantism south of the border, thereby slowing the rate of religious disaffiliation nationally.

An additional factor likely relates to the relative size of the Black and Asian populations in the two countries and Cascadia. Black Americans are less and Asian Americans are more likely to be Nones than the rest of the US population. In the 2014 Pew Landscape Study, for example, the proportions were 18 percent for Blacks and 31 percent for Asians, as compared to 24 percent for whites (Pew Research Center 2015). While no comparable data are available for Canada, it is reasonable to assume that similar differences obtain. A lower proportion of Blacks and/or a higher proportion of Asians could thus be expected to push up the proportion of Nones in a given place. Oregon and Washington have a slightly smaller percentage of Asians than the United States as a whole (2 percent versus 2.8 percent) but a Black population less than half (under 4 percent versus 11.5 percent). British Columbia has fewer Blacks than Canada as a whole (1 percent versus 3.5 percent) and nearly twice as many Asians (27.5 percent versus 15 percent). In brief, these statistics provide a further explanation for the greater proportion of Nones in Oregon and Washington vis-à-vis the rest of the United States, in British Columbia vis-à-vis the rest of Canada, and in British Columbia vis-à-vis Oregon and Washington – as well as in Canada vis-à-vis the United States as a whole.

Finally, another possible factor is worth bearing in mind. In the United States, the rise of the Nones has to a significant degree not been about the abandonment of religious belief and practice but rather about a change in the way religious identity is understood. While religious identity was once taken as something inherited or ascribed, it has come to be seen as something one chooses for oneself. In the past, a person who was raised, say, as a Methodist but had not darkened the door of a church for decades would very likely continue to identify as a Methodist; now, that person is more likely to identify as having no religion. That this shift in understanding has been more pronounced in the United States than in Canada is, above all, indicated by the case of Quebec.

In what is known as the Quiet Revolution, the provincial government in the 1960s and 1970s effected a profound and rapid secularization in public life, taking control of the health and education systems from the Catholic Church. At the same time, French Canadians, hitherto one of the most religiously observant populations, began turning away from the beliefs and practices of their faith. Between 1968 and 2010, weekly Mass attendance in Quebec plunged from 80 percent to 10 percent, while the proportion of Catholic marriages in the province dropped from 90 percent to 30 percent (Nault and Meunier 2017). In 2020, 75 percent of Québécois said they thought abortion was acceptable, as compared to just 8 percent who said they thought it was not – the greatest differential in any Canadian province, including British Columbia (British Columbians split 75 percent to 9 percent) (Dart and Maru/Blue 2020). And in a 2017 Angus Reid survey, Quebec ranked second to British Columbia in irreligiosity among all regions of the country, with 18 percent "nonbelievers" (versus 27 percent in British Columbia) and 36 percent "spiritually uncertain" (versus 33 percent in British Columbia).

Despite these high levels of irreligiosity in Quebec, two-thirds of adult Québécois identified as Catholic in the 2011 census, and the province showed by far the lowest proportion of Nones in the country. That a large proportion of French Canadians consider Catholicism intrinsic to who they are is no doubt a legacy of their long struggle to keep their culture intact and separate from the anglophone Protestants who ran the country for so long. After Britain took control of French Canada in 1763, Catholicism became a strong marker of French Canadian identity. On the other side, a distinctive anti-Catholicism became engrained in English Canada during the Victorian period, persisting through the middle of the twentieth century as a feature of English Canadian nationalism (Miller 1987; Anderson 2013). Under the circumstances, we should not be surprised that a large portion of French Canadians identify as Catholics even as they have ceased to be practising (or believing) Catholics. Effectively, then, most Québécois are Nones and, in any meaningful religious sense, the number of Catholics in Canada is significantly lower than the decennial household surveys indicate. This helps explain why, although the proportion of Nones in Canada is only modestly greater than in the United States, Canadian society should be so much more secular.

Assisted Suicide

Nowhere has Cascadia's cultural coherence been more pronounced, and its influence beyond its borders more discernible, than in the matter of physician-assisted suicide. In 1991, Washington held a referendum that would have permitted the practice; it lost by a margin of 54 to 46 percent. The following year, Sue Rodriguez, a woman living in British Columbia who suffered from amyotrophic lateral sclerosis (Lou Gehrig's Disease), sought a legal exemption to be allowed to end her life with the aid of a doctor but was denied by the provincial authorities. The British Columbia Civil Liberties Association brought suit on her behalf, challenging the section of the Canadian Criminal Code making it a crime to assist someone in committing suicide.

The case gained widespread attention, not least thanks to a videotape played for the Canadian Parliament in which Rodriguez famously declared, "If I cannot give consent to my own death, whose body is this? Who owns my life?" In 1993, the case resulted in a five-to-four decision by the Canadian Supreme Court upholding the law. Ignoring the decision, Rodriguez went ahead and, with the help of a doctor, committed suicide on February 12, 1994. The following November, voters in Oregon narrowly passed a referendum creating the Death with Dignity Act, which (after unsuccessful litigation to stop it) went into effect in 1997. Then, after the law was upheld by a federal appeals court, the state legislature sponsored a second referendum to repeal the law. Evangelicals and Catholics organized a $4 million campaign on its behalf, while opponents spent $1 million as the Don't Let 'Em Shove Their Religion Down Your Throat Committee. Along with this libertarian message, Oregonians supporting assisted suicide were at pains to emphasize that theirs was a course in tune with nature. As one woman wrote on the Death with Dignity website, "I know the level of participation in life – mentally, spiritually, physically, emotionally – that I believe I need to continue as a valuable and contributing member of earth's family. I feel very strongly about preserving the right to make my final, very private choice of leaving this beautiful planet in peace, with dignity" (Killen and Silk 2004, 177). Although outspent, the opponents prevailed, and the law allowing assisted suicide was upheld by a wide margin of 60 percent to 40 percent.

Despite President Clinton's declared opposition to assisted suicide, his Justice Department chose not to contest the Oregon law. That position was reversed by President George W. Bush's attorney general, John Ashcroft, who directed agents of the Drug Enforcement Agency to investigate and prosecute doctors who prescribed federally controlled drugs to help terminally ill patients die. Oregon challenged the directive, and in 2006 the US Supreme Court, in a six-to-three decision, upheld Oregon's position that the federal government lacked the authority to punish doctors for assisting in suicides as authorized by state law. In 2008, voters in Washington again took up the issue, and this time, by a vote of 58 percent to 42 percent, approved medical aid in dying with certain restrictions. The following year, a court in nearby Montana found no public policy against assisted suicide, thus permitting the practice to be raised as a defence if a case in that state were to come to trial.

Then, in 2011, the BC Civil Liberties Association brought another assisted suicide case on behalf of a woman with ALS in an effort to overturn the *Rodriguez* decision. After a favourable ruling by the BC Supreme Court was overturned by the BC Court of Appeal in 2013, the Supreme Court of Canada took up the case and in 2015 reversed *Rodriguez*, making "medical assistance in dying" legal throughout Canada. Meanwhile, in 2013, Vermont became the first state in the United States to pass a Death with Dignity law by legislative act. Since then, Death with Dignity laws have gone into effect in California (2016), Colorado (2016), the District of Columbia (2017), Hawaii (2019), and New Jersey (2019) – all under Democratic control. Although it is unlikely that a national "right to die" will be established any time soon, there is good reason to think that within a few years a majority of the US population will live in jurisdictions that have legalized physician-assisted suicide. All in all, it is hard to avoid the conclusion that what enabled Cascadia to lead the way in both countries was its status as the advance guard of religious disaffiliation.

Civil Religion, Civil War

In 2007, when public opinion polls revealed that British Columbians had placed the environment ahead of the economy and health care as their number one issue, British Columbia became the first Canadian province to join the Western Climate Initiative, an effort to combat climate change begun by Oregon and Washington along with California, Arizona, and New Mexico. The next year, British Columbia enacted a carbon tax that many considered a model for dealing with climate change, and two years later, the tax was expanded.[10] Washington sought to follow suit with ballot initiatives in 2016 and 2018, both of which failed as a result of heavily funded campaigns by the fossil fuel industry. Undeterred, or perhaps redirected, the state's governor, Jay Inslee, in 2019 announced his bid for the 2020 Democratic presidential nomination based on making climate change his number one priority – the only would-be nominee in a very large field to do so. In the meantime, under the leadership of Prime Minister Justin Trudeau, the Canadian federal government passed a carbon tax into law in 2018, aided by economic data showing that British Columbia enjoyed the fastest economic growth of any Canadian province.

Under the spectre of the climate emergency, the environmentalism that serves as Cascadia's civil religion became, in the second decade of the twenty-first century, become the apocalyptic civil religion of the rising generation of American and Canadian adults – millennials. The extent to which this civil apocalypticism is linked to organized religion is not easily sorted out. In Cascadia itself, as noted above, environmental concern has long since been part of the self-understanding of all but the evangelical religious communities.[11] Such self-understanding is typified in Ecumenical Ministries of Oregon, an organization that defines itself as "bringing together Oregon's diverse faith community in service to God and Creation." In the wider world, too, expressing environmental concern has been a priority of many religious leaders, in some cases for decades.

In 1989, the Patriarch of Constantinople earned the sobriquet "green" by establishing September 1 as a World Day of Prayer for Creation for Orthodox Christians. In 1990, the Anglican Communion added to its four "marks of mission" a fifth: "to strive to safeguard the integrity of creation and sustain and renew the life of the earth." The same year, Pope John Paul II issued the first in a series of papal pronouncements on the environment that culminated, during the run-up to the Paris Agreement, in Pope Francis's climate change encyclical, *Laudato si.'* This was followed by strong statements from Buddhist, Hindu, Jewish, and Muslim leaders from around the world. Meanwhile, the clarion on climate change has for years been sounded by national faith-based organizations such as San Francisco–based Interfaith Power and Light, which, in 2020, said it "inspires and mobilizes people of faith and conscience to take bold and just action on climate change" (Interfaith Power and Light n.d.).

For all this, the degree to which the specifically religious sensibilities of the American and Canadian publics have been enlisted is open to question. Only 9 percent of Americans think climate change is a religious issue, according to a survey conducted in 2017 by the Yale Program on Climate Change Communication and the George Mason Center for Climate Change Communication. Seventy-seven percent think it is not (Leiserowitz et al. 2017). Moreover, in the United States, religion is a factor that tends to militate *against* concern for the climate. In an ABC News poll taken in the summer of 2018, just 32 percent of white evangelicals thought global warming was a serious problem for the United States, as opposed to 66 percent of Nones. Nonevangelical white Protestants and white Catholics fell precisely in the middle, at 46 percent. Notably, non-whites as a whole were much more likely than whites to see global warming as a serious problem, by a margin of 62 percent to 46 percent (ABC News/Stanford/Resources for the Future 2018). Notwithstanding evidence that resistance to the idea of anthropogenic climate change is shrinking, even among white evangelicals, the fact remains that it is among the younger, least religious segment of the population that concern about climate change is the greatest.

Altogether, after the election of Donald Trump, the culture war pitting Nones against white evangelicals became more intense than ever in the United States. In this respect, the long-standing contest of None culture and evangelical counter-culture in Washington and Oregon remained emblematic of the larger national contest. North of the border, there are religious right organizations with ideologies comparable to those in the United States; Canadian evangelicals have gravitated toward the Conservative Party and vote together on cultural issues of concern to them such as same-sex marriage. But the contest there has been far more muted. As Carleton University political scientist Jonathan Malloy has persuasively argued, evangelicals in Canadian politics should be seen "not as a monolithic ideological pressure group that may or may not control the government, but a broader social grouping that fits within a more traditional brokerage arrangement under the Conservative umbrella" (Malloy 2009, 1).

Until recently, American religious politics was not, in the final analysis, all that different from Canadian religious politics. Although Republican candidates for public office in the United States campaigned more overtly for evangelical votes, upon taking office, Republican presidents Ronald Reagan, George H.W. Bush, and even George W. Bush were very circumspect about advancing the evangelical agenda, contenting themselves largely with symbolic statements and acts. But with the Trump administration, the American religious right succeeded in establishing real power in federal policy-making. It is hard to imagine such a development taking place in Canada. As became evident between 2006 and 2015, when evangelical Stephen Harper served as prime minister, there simply are not enough evangelicals on the ground to make it worth a prime minister's while to kowtow to them. In this regard, it is telling that in the face of corruption and racism scandals, Prime Minister Justin Trudeau was able to form a minority government in 2019 by centring his campaign on an agenda to combat climate change – even as the Trump administration was doing everything in its power not to. On climate, in short, the None Zone that is Cascadia continued to lead the way in Canada, but in the United States, not so much.[12]

Spiritual but Not Religious – or Neither?

"In the Pacific Northwest, where the spiritual-but-not-religious reign demographically supreme" began an article by Douglas Todd in the *Vancouver Sun* in 2011 (Todd 2011). "The Northwest is filled with people who describe themselves as 'spiritual, but not religious,'" declared the blurb for a 2014 discussion at a Seattle church presented by Christ and Cascadia: "Most of them believe in some sort of spiritual reality or higher power but they would never darken the door of a religious institution" (Christ and Cascadia 2014).

If this widely held assessment is true, then one would expect non-Cascadian Americans and Canadians to be much less likely to call themselves "spiritual but not religious" than Oregonians, Washingtonians, and British Columbians. In 2015, an Angus Reid poll found fully 39 percent of Canadians describing themselves as "spiritual but not religious" (Angus Reid 2015). In 2017, Pew found 27 percent of all Americans describing themselves as "spiritual but not religious," up from 19 percent five years earlier (Lipka and Gecewicz 2017). The 2017 PNSS, however, found that just 17 percent of respondents in Oregon and Washington and 16 percent in British Columbia placed themselves in the category of "spiritual with no religion."[13]

How to account for this apparent anomaly? The simplest explanation is that "spiritual with no religion" does not mean the same thing to survey respondents as "spiritual but not religious." The former plainly excludes those who identify with a particular religion. The latter, evidently, includes those who *would* darken the door of a religious institution. In a word, just because you call yourself spiritual but not religious does not mean you do not also identify as a Christian, Jew, Muslim, Sikh, Hindu, Buddhist, or adherent of some other religious community. And, in fact, it turns out that most people who call themselves "spiritual but not religious" identify with a religion.

In Pew's 2017 survey, Lipka and Gecewicz found that alongside the 27 percent of Americans who considered themselves spiritual but not religious, 48 percent considered themselves "spiritual and religious"; 6 percent, "religious but not spiritual"; and 18 percent, "neither spiritual nor religious." For the sake of argument, let us assume that nearly all the people who put themselves in this last category are Nones. If so, then just 7 percent of the entire population is left to make up the full complement of American Nones (25 percent); call them the spiritual Nones. That means that three-quarters of the 27 percent in the "spiritual but not religious" category actually identify with a religion; call them the "spiritual but not religious adherents" (SBNRA). On the Canadian side, the Angus Reid (2017) survey registered the "neither religious nor spiritual" share of the population at 27 percent. That would include almost the entire body of Canadian Nones, leaving all but a few of the "spiritual but not religious" in the SBNRA category.

Instead of indicating a stable cohort of people who believe in some kind of higher power but want nothing to do with organized religion, "spiritual but not religious" may indicate a state of mind or posture toward religious belief and practice that is transitional – a way station on the road from religious adherence to unspiritual nonadherence (or possibly, for some, the other way around). In Canada and the United States as a whole, what we have seen is an increase in the number of both Nones and "spiritual but not religious" – the increase in the latter coming mostly among the religiously identified. And among the religiously identified, it is the "spiritual but not religious" who would seem to be most likely to become Nones. What the data from Cascadia imply is that, at a certain point, Nones cease considering themselves spiritual, such that when the proportion of Nones reaches a certain level, the proportion of "spiritual but not religious" in the entire population begins to decline.

According to the 2017 PNSS, 4 percent of British Columbian Nones and 9 percent of Oregonian and Washingtonian Nones consider themselves "very spiritual," and 23 percent of British Columbian, Oregonian, and Washingtonian Nones consider themselves "moderately spiritual." So the Nones of

Cascadia are not devoid of spirituality. Will they remain so? Pooled 2012–16 data from the General Social Survey indicate that young adults in the Pacific region of the United States (California, Oregon, and Washington) are half as likely to consider themselves "very spiritual" as older adult cohorts: 15 percent of eighteen-to-thirty-four-year-olds versus 26 percent, 30 percent, and 31 percent in the thirty-five to fifty-four, fifty-five to seventy-four, and seventy-five-and-older cohorts, respectively. Young adults are also less likely to be "moderately spiritual" and significantly more likely to be "slightly spiritual" and "not spiritual." Similarly, the middle-aged (thirty-five to fifty-four years old) rank lower on the spiritual scale than the two cohorts in front of them (Wilkins-Laflamme 2017).

It is hard to avoid the conclusion that just as young adults are moving the population of the United States and Canada as a whole away from religious identification, so they are leading it away from being spiritual.[14] One day, indeed, the religious may find themselves lamenting the disappearance of the "spiritual but not religious" – those marginally religious folks who, if they did not exactly keep the faith at least understood that the spirit bloweth where it listeth and maintained some kind of allegiance to a religious community. If that happens, we'll be able to say it happened first in Cascadia.

NOTES

1 The regional volumes, published by Rowman and Littlefield under its AltaMira Press imprint in 2004–06, are titled *Religion and Public Life* in, respectively, New England, the Middle Atlantic Region, the South, the Southern Crossroads, the Midwest, the Mountain West, the Pacific Region, and the Pacific Northwest. A ninth summary volume, *One Nation Divisible: How Regional Religious Differences Shape American Politics*, was published by Rowman and Littlefield in 2008, with an updated paperback edition in 2011.

2 For the project, we divided the United States into eight regions embracing every state of the union plus the District of Columbia (but not territories such as Puerto Rico). Some regions (New England, the Middle Atlantic) were familiar; others, less so. When a hard decision had to be made, we chose demographic throw-weight and sociocultural ties over geographic territory. Thus, we included Nevada in the Pacific region because most of its population is located near the California border and is most closely connected to the California economy. Missouri, which could plausibly have been made part of the Midwest, we grouped with Arkansas, Oklahoma, Texas, and Louisiana in a region we called the Southern Crossroads. The rationale for this had to do with the mixed ethnoreligious antecedents that Missouri shares with the other Crossroads states and that differentiates all five from both the South and the Midwest.

3 Alaska was completely aligned with Oregon and Washington with respect to the proportion of Nones.

4 Part of the reason the findings attracted little notice was that the report was released just weeks after the attacks of 9/11, when most public attention was focused on the number of Muslims in America. In addition, a shift in the wording of the questions (from "What is your religion?" to "What is your religion, if any?") made it possible for specialists to dismiss the reported increase in the proportion of Nones as an artifact of a question that opened a

door for respondents to answer "none." Subsequent surveys have, of course, proved that the 2001 ARIS was on to something.

5 Data on the attitudes of specific religious communities came from the National Surveys of Religion and Politics: survey data compiled in 1992, 1996, and 2000 at the Ray C. Bliss Institute of Applied Politics at the University of Akron.

6 For more on the perspectives of evangelicals in the region today, see Wilkinson's and Wellman and Corcoran's chapters in this volume.

7 For the United States, see Gallup (2019) and PRRI (2018). For Canada, see census data over time cited in the National Household Survey 2011 (Statistics Canada 2013). It is worth noting that a 2013 survey by Angus King put Canadian Nones at 36 percent (Hiemstra and Stiller 2016). It is worth bearing in mind that these surveys do not ask their "no religion" question(s) in precisely the same way, so the comparison of their results should be taken as approximate. More recent data on religion in Canada will have to wait for the 2021 census.

8 This report includes a comparison with the United States over time, with data drawn from the General Social Survey.

9 See Data Tables for the 2011 Canada National Household Survey: https://www12.statcan. gc.ca/nhs-enm/2011/dp-pd/dt-td/Rp-eng.cfm?LANG=E&APATH=3&DETAIL=0&DIM= 0&FL=A&FREE=0&GC=0&GID=0&GK=0&GRP=0&PID=105399&PRID=0&PTYPE =105277&S=0&SHOWALL=0&SUB=0&Temporal=2013&THEME=95&VID=0.

10 British Columbia was the second Canadian province to institute a carbon tax, following Quebec in doing so by one year.

11 Interviews conducted for the Cascadia Project offer scant evidence of a shift toward environmentalism on the part of Cascadian evangelicals. A long-time environmental activist who is now a pastor in Portland did say he thinks "the Bible puts a spotlight on our environment" and that "resources for true creation care that I have available to me through my relationship with Jesus, my understanding of who he is and what that means about all of this, is that He cares deeply." On the other hand, an evangelical in Seattle described his and his wife's circle of friends as follows: "I would say, very diverse group. So some people are contemplative orthodox, some people are probably hybrid Christian, environmentalist, ecologists." The implication is that being an environmentalist means embracing a worldview that is not Christian in the evangelical sense. See https://www.uvic.ca/research/centres/csrs/.

12 The extent to which Cascadia has actually led the way for Canadian national policy is, however, a matter of debate. Although Trudeau spoke loudly about fighting climate change, his government has steadfastly promoted expansion of the Trans Mountain oil pipeline from Alberta to British Columbia – much to the consternation of British Columbia's environmental and First Nations communities. See Paul Bramadat's chapter on reverential naturalism in this volume.

13 This is essentially the same breakdown the 2017 PNSS found in Cascadia: in Oregon and Washington, 36 percent of the Nones consider themselves spiritual with no religion; in British Columbia, one-third do.

14 Although space does not permit a thorough consideration of this issue, it is worthwhile to wonder about whether we are seeing a declining interest in being spiritual or (perhaps as well as) a declining commitment to the available *categories* (e.g., religious, spiritual, SBNR, irreligious) people might use to think about and convey these matters. The lack of interest in conventional ways of framing what used to be called spiritual beliefs, habits, practices, intuitions, and so on is quite clear in Cascadia.

REFERENCES

ABC News/Stanford/Resources for the Future. 2018. "Public Attitudes on Global Warming." ABC News/Stanford/Resources for the Future Poll: Public Attitudes on Global Warming, press release, July 16. https://www.langerresearch.com/wp-content/uploads/1198a1Global -Warming.pdf.

Anderson, Kevin. 2013. "This Typical Old Canadian Form of Racial and Religious Hate: Anti-Catholicism and English Canadian Nationalism, 1905–1965." PhD diss., McMaster University. https://macsphere.mcmaster.ca/bitstream/11375/13205/1/fulltext.pdf.

Angus Reid Institute. 2015. "Religion and Faith in Canada Today: Strong Belief, Ambivalence and Rejection Define Our Views." March 26. http://angusreid.org/faith-in-canada/.

—. 2017. "A Spectrum of Spirituality: Canadians Keep the Faith to Varying Degrees, but Few Reject It Entirely." April 13. http://angusreid.org/religion-in-canada-150/.

Barlow, Philip. 2004. "Religious Affiliation in the Midwest and the Nation." In *Religion and Public Life in the Midwest: America's Common Denominator?*, edited by Philip Barlow and Mark Silk, 17–20. Walnut Creek, CA: AltaMira Press.

Christ and Cascadia. 2014. "Spiritual but Not Religious: Seeking Transcendence in a Secular Age." Panel discussion, University Presbyterian Church, Seattle, Washington, May 2. http://www.journal.christandcascadia.com/spiritual-but-not-religious/.

Dart and Maru/Blue Voice Canada. 2020. *Abortion: A Canadian Public Perspective after Three Decades.* Poll, February 1. https://dartincom.ca/wp-content/uploads/2020/01/PostMedia -Abortion-Feb-F-1-2020.pdf.

Gallup. 2019. "Religion." https://news.gallup.com/poll/1690/religion.aspx.

Hiemstra, Rick, and Karen Stiller. 2016. "Religious Affiliation and Attendance in Canada." *In Trust: Center for Theological Schools,* New Year. https://www.intrust.org/Magazine/ Issues/New-Year-2016/Religious-affiliation-and-attendance-in-Canada.

Interfaith Power and Light. n.d. "Mission and History." https://www.interfaithpowerand light.org/about/mission-history/.

Killen, Patricia O'Connell, and Mark Silk, eds. 2004. *Religion and Public Life in the Pacific Northwest: The None Zone.* Walnut Creek, CA: AltaMira Press.

Kosmin, Barry A., and Ariela Keysar (principal investigators). 1991. *Research Report: The National Survey of Religious Identification, 1989–90.* https://commons.trincoll.edu/aris/ surveys/nsri-1990/.

Kosmin, Barry A., Egon Mayer, and Ariela Keysar (principal investigators). 2001. *American Religious Identification Survey, 2001.* New York: The Graduate Center of the City University of New York. https://commons.trincoll.edu/aris/files/2013/11/ARIS-2001-report -complete.pdf.

Leiserowitz, Anthony, Edward Maibach, Connie Roser-Renouf, Seth Rosenthal, Matthew Cutler, and John Kotcher. 2017. *Climate Change in the American Mind: October 2017.* Yale Program on Climate Change Communication/George Mason Center for Climate Change Communication. http://climatecommunication.yale.edu/wp-content/ uploads/2017/11/Climate-Change-American-Mind-October-2017.pdf.

Lipka, Michael, and Claire Gecewicz. 2017. "More Americans Now Say They Are Spiritual but Not Religious." *Pew Research Center,* September 6. https://www.pewresearch.org/ fact-tank/2017/09/06/more-americans-now-say-theyre-spiritual-but-not-religious/.

Malloy, Jonathan. 2009. "Stephen Harper, Evangelical Christians, and the Brokerage Tradition in Canadian Politics." Paper presented at the annual meeting of the American Political Science Association, Toronto. https://papers.ssrn.com/sol3/papers.cfm? abstract_id=1451718.

Miller, J.R. 1987. "Bigotry in the North Atlantic Triangle: Irish, British and American Influences on Canadian Anti-Catholicism, 1850–1900." *Studies in Religion/Sciences Religieuses* 16 (3): 289–301.

Nault, Jean-François, and Meunier, É.-Martin. 2017. "Is Quebec Still a Catholically Distinct Society within Canada? An Examination of Catholic Affiliation and Mass Attendance."

Studies in Religion/Sciences Religieuses 46 (2): 230–48. https://journals.sagepub.com/doi/abs/10.1177/0008429817696298?journalCode=sira.

Pew Research Center. 2013. "Canada's Changing Religious Landscape." *Pew Research Center,* June 27. https://www.pewforum.org/2013/06/27/canadas-changing-religious-landscape/.

—. 2015. "America's Changing Religious Landscape." *Pew Research Center,* May 12. https://www.pewforum.org/2015/05/12/americas-changing-religious-landscape/.

PRRI. 2018. "Religious Tradition." *The American Values Atlas.* http://ava.prri.org/home#religious/2018/Regions/religion/m/national.

Reside, Graham. 2018. "The State of Contemporary Mainline Protestantism." In *The Future of Mainline Protestantism in America,* edited by James Hudnut-Beumler and Mark Silk, 17–57. New York: Columbia University Press.

Silk, Mark, and Andrew Walsh. 2008. *One Nation Divisible: How Regional Religious Differences Shape American Politics.* Lanham, MD: Rowman and Littlefield.

Statistics Canada. 2013. "2011 National Household Survey: Immigration, Place of Birth, Citizenship, Ethnic Origin, Visible Minorities, Languages, and Religion." Statistics Canada release, May 8. https://www150.statcan.gc.ca/n1/daily-quotidien/130508/dq130508b-eng.htm?HPA.

Todd, Douglas, ed. 2008. *Cascadia: The Elusive Utopia: Exploring the Spirit of the Pacific Northwest.* Vancouver: Ronsdale Press.

—. 2011. "The Spiritual-but-Not-Religious: Arrogant?" *Vancouver Sun,* September 26. https://vancouversun.com/news/staff-blogs/the-spiritual-but-not-religious-arrogant-too.

Wilkins-Laflamme, Sarah. 2017. "The Religious, Spiritual, Secular and Social Landscapes of the Pacific Northwest: Part 1." *UWSpace.* http://hdl.handle.net/10012/12218.

7

Questing for Home: Place, Spirit, and Religious Community in the Pacific Northwest

PATRICIA O'CONNELL KILLEN

In 1881, Anglican bishop George Hills, after more than two decades toiling to replicate in the Crown colony of British Columbia the church he knew in England, bemoaned the "constitutional religious apathy" that marked "the people of the whole Pacific slope" (McNally 1990, 23; Marks 2017, 6). At the cusp of the twentieth century, a Presbyterian missionary wrote that "the great mass of the people care nothing for the gospel and treat all church organizations with supreme indifference" (Marks 2017, 29). These sentiments were echoed by institutional religious leaders south of the forty-ninth parallel. Oregon missionary Father James Croke, who regularly travelled by horseback and water from Portland south to Medford, west to the Pacific Ocean, north to Astoria, and east back to Portland, wrote to Archbishop Blanchet of Oregon City (Portland) in 1853 from southern Oregon: "The Catholics here are so few and in general so lukewarm that it requires some time for a priest to hunt them out, and even then it is not in one day that he can inspire them with the proper dispositions" (O'Hara 1939, 167). Father Peter Hylebos, pastor of St. Leo Parish in Tacoma, Washington, responded to the question "Number of Catholics in the parish?" for his 1898 annual diocesan report: "They come and go – impossible to keep track."[1] And Rev. David Gorsuch LeSourd, presiding Elder for the Methodists on Puget Sound in the 1880s, wrote of sending someone to find the Methodists in Snohomish, "only to have the person arrive to find the minister gone and no Methodists" (Howell 1966, 54). Making his first address to the Convention of the Episcopal Diocese of Olympia in February 1926, new bishop Simeon Arthur Huston noted that "In many communities the building which is known as the Episcopal Church could easily be lost in the private home of one of several communicants" (Jessett 1967, 40–41). In 1964, Methodist leaders expressed frustration that "more than one-half the Methodists who moved to the region dropped out of church altogether" (Howell

1966, 159–60). And a century after Hills's report, Catholic Church historian Jeffrey Burns summarized the history of Roman Catholicism in the Pacific states as "the difficult task of inspiring an indifferent people to devotion" (Burns 1987, 15).

The observations and judgments of these Anglican, Catholic, and Methodist pastors and institutional leaders are reflected in the histories of other religious groups in the region over the same period. Lutherans, Methodists, Presbyterians, and Congregationalists even share humour: the Rockies are white because so many people tossed their transfer papers when lightening the load in their wagons as they came across (Killen 1998).[2] Embedded in the lament, reports, and humour is a consistent theme: the fortunes of Christian communities are different here. Something happened to people who entered and remained in the Pacific Northwest, something that changed their relationship to inherited religious ideas, practices, and organizations.[3]

There is a clear indication that the region influenced the religious practices and sensibilities of those who enter it: since earliest Euro-American settlement, most people in the Pacific Northwest on both sides of the forty-ninth parallel have not participated regularly in local organized religious communities, which sets them apart from the population in the rest of the United States and Canada (Killen and Silk 2004, 10; Marks 2017, 29–36; Wilkins-Laflamme 2017, 6–7).[4] This pattern has persisted for more than a century and a half in the face of massive waves of in-migration and bursts of individual and institutional ecclesial creativity and entrepreneurship, much of it aimed at attracting people to congregations and retaining them (Killen and Silk 2004; Zelinsky 1961; Shortridge 1977).[5] To illustrate, between 1970 and 2000, the population of Oregon and Washington increased 66 percent while the percentage of the population that national religious bodies reported as adherents remained steady in the lower, mid-30 percent range (Killen and Silk, 2004; ASARB; United States Census Bureau n.d.).[6] So, while absolute numbers of people involved in religious organizations increased, the percentage of the population doing so did not. British Columbia during a comparable period (1971–2001) saw a population increase of 87 percent and a decrease in the percentage of religiously affiliated in the population from 87 percent to 62 percent (Statistics Canada n.d.; Pew Research Center 2013).[7] This data reveals a pattern of disconnection that has accelerated over the past two decades. Now, growing numbers not only do not participate in local organized religious communities, they also do not identify themselves with reference to any religious heritage. In Cascadia, Nones currently constitute "an estimated 49 percent of British Columbians and 44 percent of residents in the states of Washington and Oregon," making them "the largest (non)religious tradition in British Columbia and the second largest in Washington and Oregon (just below the 46 percent of residents affiliated with Christian traditions)," as Sarah Wilkins-Laflamme reports in her chapter in this volume, using 2017 Pacific Northwest Social Survey data.[8]

There is something about people's experience in the Pacific Northwest that upends the unstated assumption of the commentators whose quotes open this essay, an assumption shared by generations of institutional religious leaders since, namely, that regular participation in religious institutions is how religion "properly works" for individuals and society in Canada and the United States. In Cascadia, Christianity has not, if you will, functioned "properly" for the majority of the population.

To develop a more nuanced understanding of the dynamics of religion, spirituality, and secularization in the region, and what they might reveal about larger religious dynamics in the twenty-first century, this essay turns its attention to a regional minority: those who continue to identify with an historical Christian faith heritage and to participate on some kind of regular basis in local, organized religious communities.[9] It draws on the data gathered through the SSHRC-funded research project "Religion, Spirituality, Secularity and Society in the Pacific Northwest" and is anchored in family oral-history interviews of currently identified and practising Christians.[10] These interviews provide a snapshot of the religious experience and practices of families who have been resident in the region over three generations. My analysis and interpretation of their experience are supplemented, and at points contrasted, with the experience of interviewed religious leaders and focus-group participants, some of whom were born in the region and others who were in-migrants. The chapter explores three questions: What happens to people's relationship to inherited religious ideas, practices, and formal religious organizations over time? In what ways have people both adapted to and engaged with the regional context? What do their adaptions and practices of engagement tell us about the broader fortunes of religion in the region and about broader national and global processes of secularization and religious evolution in late modernity?

Christians in the Family Oral-History Interviews

Researchers gathered oral histories from individuals whose families had been in the region since before 1930, most since before 1920. The interviews contain unique information on the religious experiences and practices of families in the Pacific Northwest over time.[11] Within the body of family oral-history interviews, fourteen individuals still identified as Christian and participated in religious organizations to varying degrees. This subset included four Catholics, three evangelicals, one Pentecostal, the daughters of two of the evangelicals, and five liberal Protestants. Interviewees ranged in age from their mid-twenties to nineties, with the majority in the Boomer (born 1944–64) and Generation X (born 1965–80) age cohorts (Pew 2015).[12]

Religion in Families over Time in the Pacific Northwest

Since the earliest Euro-American settlement, the Pacific Northwest has lacked a dominant conventional religious referent group – whereas in other parts of the continent one or another Christian denomination, or cluster of denominations, has played this role – and so religion has not functioned as a form of social control to the degree that it has in other parts of Canada and the United States (Killen and Silk 2004, 10–11; Wilkins-Laflamme and Block and Marks, this volume).[13] The families that migrated into the region were influenced by this reality and responded to it. This combination of being influenced by a regional religious ethos and responding to it, sometimes self-consciously and sometimes not, has contributed to the fluid character of Cascadian religiosity. The majority of oral-history interviewees expressed a positive response to the region's more "open" religious environment (Killen and Silk 2004, 14), valuing the freedom it provided them and their children as individuals. Few, including parents who expressed regret about daughters and sons no longer participating in religious communities, recognized that the region's more open environment also contributed to an accelerated process of ceasing to participate in local religious communities, which in turn leads to subsequent "disaffiliation" (which includes no longer claiming a religious tradition as part of one's identity) that their families exemplify. Nor did they think that their religious environment had contributed to the intrafamilial conflict and individual spiritual seeking that some of their stories reveal. Only Virginia, a Pentecostal from Victoria, expressed unease with the regional context, highlighting the positive value of remaining within a tightly bounded religious community. Yet even she, from the time she returned to Victoria from Bible College in San Francisco, felt free to move from congregation to congregation within the Pentecostal world, searching for "a church that was cutting-edge, wanting to see the Kingdom of God come to the city of Victoria." She moved to a community of Christians, where she knew "there was a lot of power out there within the Kingdom of God because of the people who had a very strong commitment to the Lord, and they had been baptized with the Holy Spirit." To put it another way, from the family oral-history interview data it seems that most Cascadians remain unaware of the influence of the region's ethos on their lives and religious habits.

The pace at which Christians ceased to participate and then disaffiliated varied somewhat by denominational family, but both phenomena were present across all Christian groups represented in the family-history interviews. These patterns were consistent with those described in *Religion and Public Life in the Pacific Northwest: The None Zone*. However, the pattern was not unidirectional. In the case of Donald, an evangelical from Seattle, his persistence in the Christian faith set him apart from his father's abandonment of Christianity for agnosticism. In the case of Jane, another evangelical from Seattle, her daughter Heather opted for a narrower, more tightly bounded evangelicalism than she practised. In the focus groups, varied patterns of movement were also evident among adherents. In addition to reaffirming participation in the faith community in which they were raised or becoming a None, some had crossed from one Christian family to another, others from one world religious family to another.[14]

While the Cascadian religious environment supports fluidity and movement, it also works against religious stability. In an open religious environment, individuals must choose, which entails confronting questions of religious identity and belonging more directly than is the case in regions where more of the population participates in religious organizations (Killen and Silk 2004). Among them, the active Catholic, evangelical, and liberal Protestant interviewees had twenty-two living children. Of these, eleven, or half, were described as no longer involved with Christian religious institutions. Five were attached to the denominational family in which they had been raised, though not necessarily the exact denomination; evangelicals retained three and liberal Protestants two. None were active Catholics. The remaining six had either switched religious affiliation or their religious identity was not revealed during the interviews.

In the majority of families, one or more of the ancestors who came to the region set in motion the dynamics of ceasing to participate in a local religious community and then disaffiliating. Interviewees described their grandparents or great-grandparents as "getting away" (Betty), "doing a little bit of everything" (Seamus), "looking for something new" (Betty), and "suffering multiple failures in the gold rush and in business" (Henry). Their ancestors did not come to the region looking to replicate what they had left behind in Europe, Asia, or points east in Canada and the United States. The themes of escape from social constraint, aspiration to economic betterment, adventure and wanderlust, and fierce independence about religious ideas are woven throughout the stories (Donald's grandfather, for example, was called up on heresy charges by the Presbytery of Seattle for his views on universal salvation). The family narratives support the long-standing sociological and historical claim that the process of migration itself, which of necessity severs social ties and requires those who migrate to build new ones, contributes to the weakening of religious identification and participation (Killen and Silk 2004; Fink and Stark 2005; Stark 1984). Migration, for many, at least imaginatively, creates options. These options include a move away from religion, unfettered spiritual and religious searching, and affiliation with a religious congregation or heritage that fits one's needs.

For all but three of the family-history interviewees, ethnicity and social class evaporated rapidly as constraining forces on religious identification and participation. The connection between ethnicity and religion was most pronounced for Catholics. William, a Maronite Catholic from Portland in his seventies, was the son of a Syrian immigrant father and a first-generation Syrian American mother (both families hailed from a part of Syria that later would be included in Lebanon). His religious journey included helping to establish the first Lebanese Maronite Catholic parish in Portland – a sign of having achieved economic success and broader social acceptance – and being active as a coach at his daughters' Catholic elementary schools. His theological and political views were conservative. And William reported that he and his wife no longer attended the Lebanese Maronite Church in Portland, in part because of its distance from where they currently lived and in part because it was now home to "new immigrants" from Lebanon. I surmised from the interview that William and his wife did not have an affinity with the new immigrants, perhaps because of cultural differences between Syrian Lebanese and other Lebanese, perhaps because the newcomers were not advancing economically, as did William and his generation, or perhaps because the new immigrants did not embrace the assimilationist story that William narrated so proudly. Whatever the cause, William's Lebanese identity no longer seemed to carry the weight it once did in relation to his religious participation.

Seamus, also from Portland, who was eighty at the time of the interview, still identified with his Irish heritage and described being steeped in a Catholic sub-culture from elementary school through his university education. Still, he divorced, and his one living son, whom he raised, was no longer Catholic. In his very early years, sixty-year-old Matthew, from Portland, grew up in the farming community of Mount Angel, Oregon, surrounded by family in a German Catholic community. Attending mass was an "obligation" grudgingly met. His religious horizons expanded when his father moved the family to Portland for work and greater freedom. Matthew reported that, when he began attending Portland State University, rather than turn away from religion as many of his peers did, he became interested in "spirituality" and explored Christianity in groups of Protestant peers while continuing to attend his Catholic church. For these three interviewees, ethnicity played some role in their religiosity.

The erosion of ties between ethnic identity and institutional religious participation is also visible in the focus-group and religious leader interviews. For example, twenty-five-year-old Vancouver resident Daniel Mendoza, a Filipino Roman Catholic layman, worked professionally to keep Filipino ethnic organizations connected to the Roman Catholic Diocese. He reported that Filipinos made up 25 percent of the Catholic population of the diocese but 50 percent of those who attended church on Sunday. And yet Mendoza was uneasy with the trends he saw. On the one hand, he reported, there are Filipinos who attend Mass but "stay on their own," not registering with the parish or becoming involved in it. On the other hand, growing numbers of Filipinos are part of Filipino Catholic associations, such as Couples for Christ, which operate as small faith-based communities but entirely separate from the parish or diocese.

Mendoza knew that the diocese could not assume the continuing participation of Filipinos. Though Mendoza did not speak about Filipinos abandoning Catholicism entirely and joining the ranks of the Nones, data in Table 5.1 in Wilkins-Laflamme's chapter in this volume suggests that repudiation of ties to religious heritage occurs more slowly for visible-minority Christians, including African Americans, Latin Americans, and Filipinos.

Awareness of Regional Realities and Ethos

Those born and raised in the region who had lived elsewhere in the United States or Canada at some point spoke of regional differences and of how ethnic and religious populations being smaller here affected the region's religious behaviour and larger social life. Henry, a liberal Protestant from Portland, grew up in Oregon but attended Harvard as an undergraduate. In Massachusetts, he discovered whole towns that were "Irish Catholic, and Italian Catholic, and Jewish and Yankee." But growing up in Portland, he noted, "I had next-door neighbours that were Jewish, next-door neighbours that were Catholic, and Irish Catholic, and Italian Catholic. But they were just like us, you know." Henry noticed that religious and ethnic differences mattered in Massachusetts, where religious difference was essentialized and inflected into broader social life differently than had been the case in Portland. Except for Virginia, the Pentecostal from Victoria, all the other family interviewees proudly echoed the theme of having grown up with friends and neighbours who were of other religions or no religion. For these participants, religion was not, in their youth, a primary sorting category for social life, nor was it in adulthood. Still, Henry's "just like us" prompts the question: What were the identifying markers that categorized these families as being alike? The narratives shared by these interviewees foregrounded hard work, achievement, and freedom from any ties, including familial or ethnic ties, that might unduly constrain individual freedom. "Just like us" means families who participated in this narrative of self-reliance and individual achievement and often held it fiercely as a defence against painful memories of economic failure elsewhere.

Race is absent from the narratives of the Christian family-history interviewees and mostly absent in the other interviews. Henry did not include reference to his neighbours being overwhelmingly white, though race likely was one marker of "like us," given Portland's and Oregon's population demographics and history of racial discrimination. However, two pastoral leaders from Portland did address the invisible category. Reverend Richards, an African American in-migrant who at the time of the interview had led a predominantly white liberal congregation for eight years, reported experiencing Portland and the larger Pacific Northwest as inhospitable to African Americans. According to him, in every other city in the country that he visited, he could walk down the street and think to himself, "Oh, that is the way the world is supposed to look." He continued, "There is something fundamentally skewed about Portland," it being so overwhelmingly white. Pastor Armando, a life-long Portlander and convert from "None" to "evangelical" described the region as "brutal" for African Americans. In Oregon and Washington, the convergence of an embrace of the narrative of individual achievement (anything is possible here), smaller numbers of African Americans who live in concentrated urban neighbourhoods, and pride in the region's natural beauty have rendered structural forms of oppression less visible and so easier to ignore.

The religious leaders interviewed for this project also spoke about the region's distinctive religious ethos and sensibility. Father Biali, a Catholic priest in Portland, came from New England, where "90 percent of the people were Catholic" and ethnic Catholic parishes dotted cities and towns. But he said of coming to Portland, "So it was sort of a shock for me not to be in such a large Catholic population coming out here. It was just a very different feel ... New England was so settled and so old with regards to the life of the church. Out here, it was so new and so young and so very, very different."

The process of ceasing to participate in a local religious community and then disaffiliating was somewhat restrained by a set of factors, one of which, albeit rather weakly, was family. Take Matthew's situation. A Portland Catholic, Matthew stopped attending Mass at age thirty-seven when he and his wife encountered marital difficulties. He found an evangelical congregation in which he felt comfortable and raised his sons there. Later, he and his wife reunited. After a period of continued "shopping around" and "dabbling" in Buddhism and even atheism, he ended up back in a Catholic parish.[15] He was drawn to it by the choir's need for male voices and the opportunity to be active in the food bank. Matthew now serves on the parish council. He mused, "My son and my brain [were] telling me, future grandchildren are going to the [evangelical Church of God] church, so I considered that." He continued:

> Right now, I'm dealing with the sadness that my grandchildren will not be going to the same church as I do. Because I see, you know, grandpas and grandmas with their grandchildren. Now I will probably go over to [their church] or wherever they end up once in a while just to be around the grandchildren. But, you know, they've already, I'll be very involved in the grandchildren's lives whether it's in church or not.

Matthew poignantly felt one of the effects of a fluid context in which exploration is the norm. His searching brought him to living with irreconcilable values – sharing religious life with his descendants and responding to his own deep religious impulses, which, in the end, were rooted in the Catholic faith of his upbringing.

Other factors that retarded ending participation and disaffiliation were ongoing in-migration to the region; entrepreneurial religious ventures, especially those focused on young adults; and the function of churches as sites of community and civic engagement.[16] These restraining factors emerged more strongly in the religious leader interviews and the millennial and adherent focus groups than in the oral histories. In-migrants from locations where their religious and ethnic group was larger and more visible found themselves having to choose whether and how to be religious in Cascadia, something they did not have to do back home, where identity and participation were carried in the warp and woof of familial and social life. This was true for Christian, Jewish, and Islamic participants in the focus groups.

Both the oral-history interviewees and focus-group participants spoke about the importance of religious organizations as sites of gathering for young adults. Penny from Vancouver grew up in Penticton, British Columbia, about 400 kilometres (250 miles) east of Vancouver, the child of a United Church mother and an Anglican father. As she put it: "I always went to Sunday school and groups [at both the United Church and Anglican congregations] ... Like every small town, life revolved around the church. I mean ... there were movies once a week, that kind of thing. So, the life, everybody knew who belonged to what church, and actually there was no discrimination." Jessica, a Jewish millennial who had been in Portland for one month before the focus group gathered, noted: "While I was [in town for a job] interview ... I went to two young adult Jewish events. The day I got here after officially moving here, I went and met with young Jewish people. I was super comfortable, and I was like, 'Okay, I have friends,' basically." Fiona, a Chinese millennial Catholic from California, where she described herself as having been raised "culturally Buddhist" but converted to Catholicism in her freshman year at UCLA, had been in Seattle for four years. She said: "When I moved here, it was hard to find community, and the community I ended up in and really not branching out of is my church community." Fiona's comment echoed sentiments about the "Seattle freeze," the difficulty of building durable relationships in the city because of the economic pressure to work occasioned by the high cost of living, the prioritizing of career, and the privileging of the individual's privacy. Penny's description of religious participation and social life and those of Jessica and Fiona, while separated by seven decades, show that even in Cascadia, for some, religious congregations continue to be important sites of social life.

Whether in-migrants choose to embrace a religious congregation in negotiating a transition to the region depends, in part, on the narrative of the Pacific

Northwest that they choose to live. This is also true for in-migrants and life-long residents in groups that experience economic or racial discrimination. While these populations, if Christian, are more likely to remain connected to congregations, some individuals do embrace the options of unfettered religious exploration, "None" status, and nature that the region's more open religious environment provides (Wilkins-Laflamme, Chapter 5, this volume).[17]

The Primacy and Privacy of Individual Spiritual Journeys

The fact that no single Christian denomination has ever assumed a hegemonic position in the region does not mean that Cascadia lacks any kind of vestigial religious aura. Still, the lack of a single denominational reference group not only makes ending participation and disaffiliation easier, it also incubates two other pervasive characteristics of religion in Cascadia: the primacy and privacy of individual spiritual journeys. The family-history interviewees shared a pervasive and seemingly unquestioned valuing of the primacy of individual choice and individual privacy in relation to belief and spiritual practice. This came through in their accounts of spiritual searching, in their rejection of the religious coercion they remembered from childhood, in their own child-rearing practices, and in their reluctance to speak about religion. Vancouverite Penny converted to Catholicism in 1974 at the age of thirty-eight. She described herself as someone who believed and participated actively in Christian congregations all her life, but who, from early on, was still "spiritually searching" and wanting "that gut ... relationship with God." She found that relationship in 1971 while attending a women's retreat at a Catholic retreat house. The retreat began a nearly four-year journey during which "her desire never left" and that led to her joining the Roman Catholic Church. Penny's conversion created strains in her marriage. The family that once worshipped together as Anglicans no longer did so. Her husband ceased to participate in his church, though she reported that he did become actively involved again. Penny made it clear that her love for the Roman Catholic Church did not lead her to ignore the abuse that priests inflicted on children, particularly Indigenous children in church-run residential schools. Nor did she consider liturgical ritual to be central to her connection to Catholicism. She converted because the Catholic Church was, she said, "just a place where I felt at home." Penny continued to participate in her parish even while many of her friends no longer did so. And she remained part of the women's group that formed out of that 1971 retreat, meeting with the remaining living members every two weeks. For Penny, Catholicism, community, and gender relationships were intertwined.

The primacy of the individual in things religious was tempered in the case of Virginia, the Pentecostal from Victoria. While she felt free to seek a Christian community that, to her mind, was alive with the Spirit, her rebellion against her father's rules was more muted. Virginia secretly purchased her first record album, Barbara Streisand's *People,* while in high school but played it only after her father left the house for prayer meetings.

Henry, a liberal Protestant from Portland, described himself and his sister as childhood "church orphans" because of his parents' intense congregational involvement. When he began high school, Henry refused to attend his parents' church anymore. Their response: "'Well, you can stop going to our church, but you have to find another church to go to.'" He did: a liberal Protestant congregation with a better youth group. Henry continued this tradition with his own sons. He noted, "We never had discussions of beliefs; we had discussions of behaviour. We did go to church on Sunday. That wasn't an option. But as we said to the boys ... 'We don't care what you believe. We're not controlling your belief. But we are controlling your behaviour until you leave home.'"

The value of inherent respect for autonomy permeated many of the stories told during the focus groups as well. Nicole, a millennial university student in Portland, was raised Buddhist but converted to Reform Judaism. In her words: "I honestly hated going [to Nichiren Buddhist services], for the most part. I did try to dabble in it when I went to university because I was searching, spiritually, but it didn't really work for me. So then I started studying other religions and didn't really vibe with them. But I liked Judaism, so I decided to study that further. I converted here in Portland with [a Reform congregation]." At the time of the focus group, Nicole had not yet told her mother about her conversion.

The oral-history interviewees also disclosed a reluctance to speak to friends, coworkers, and even family members about their spiritual or religious journeys. William, the Maronite Catholic in Portland, sent his four daughters through Catholic K-12 and some of them to Catholic universities, but "like most kids today, they don't practice." Three of the four, said William, "still have it in their heart. They just don't go to church. The other one's kind of antireligion, anti-God." When asked if he knew why, William responded, "No, I never talked to her, you know. It's her business." He continued, "I'd kind of like to know why the three of them, you know, have fallen away." He also worries about his five grandchildren, none of whom has been baptized. Linda, now a liberal Protestant in Portland, says of her daughter who is antireligious, "She doesn't attend a church per se, or have a specific belief ... She may have something she could put down, but she hasn't shared that with me." Linda would like to understand, but will not ask, what led her daughter for a time to participate with her family in Druidism. Linda will listen, if her daughter speaks, but she will not pry.

Betty, a ninety-year-old liberal Protestant in Seattle said, "It's not up to me to tell everybody what they should be doing. They live their own lives and have, you know, good lives ... You just live your life and enjoy it and let them live theirs." In the Pacific Northwest, she continued, "everybody does what they want. I think it's good that some people can go to church, and some people don't. But I think that's their business."

Very few of those interviewed for the family oral histories mentioned theological ideas beyond the freedom of the individual to develop their own. Nor did most of the family histories explore how people understood the relationship between their spiritual experiences and religious ideas. Matthew, the Catholic from Portland, was an exception. He remained Catholic in part, he said, because of the Church's understanding of the Eucharist as the body of Christ. While the interview did not reveal why the doctrine compelled him, it is reasonable to infer that, for Matthew, it renders the divine more palpably experienced, another expression of Penny's hunger for a "gut" experience of God. Matthew also committed to the Church because "Catholicism is the biggest, or one of the biggest, charitable organizations in the world." He was clear on his call to serve the needy and proud of his parish council for having, in the face of complaints from neighbours about the people who come to the parish food bank, developed a statement on the parish being about caring for those less fortunate.

When the primacy and privacy of the individual prevails, talking about belief can be risky and may be perceived as coercive. That was certainly the case for the parents who worried about their children's and grandchildren's religiousness. As Vancouver evangelical Pastor Evan put it, "No proselytizing." Instead, he wanted people to see the integrity and coherence of the values being lived. Seeing that, he said, leads them to ask the questions that lead to Jesus. Jane, the evangelical originally from Seattle, shared a similar sentiment: believers must live their faith in visible ways if it is to make sense to others in the region.

The primacy of the individual's belief and practice prompted evangelical and liberal Protestant pastors to think creatively about the intelligibility and plausibility of the Christian message in the context of Cascadia, a place Portland evangelical Pastor Novak described as "the beginning of post-Christian America." This valuing of the individual's belief and practice, especially in a context where only a minority of the population participates regularly in organized religious communities, feeds a quite elastic religious environment. While characterized primarily by fluidity of belief and belonging, this environment also sustains smaller communities that maintain more rigid boundaries.[18] Religious ideas seem not to be central to religion in the region, or they are that piece of religion most out of bounds for conversation. The prevalent regional ethos – referred to in this book as the "Cascadia consensus" – erodes deference to the authority of historical faith traditions and the theological ideas they teach.

Christians and the Encounter with Nature in Cascadia

Christians in Cascadia live alongside persons of other religious persuasions, Indigenous peoples, and the now famous religious Nones. Cascadian Christians share with their neighbours the encounter with nature, both physical and imagined, that is an integral part of the region's ethos.[19] Most oral-history interviewees spoke warmly and positively about their encounter with the region's natural environment. As Betty, the elderly liberal Protestant in Seattle, put it, "I love this area. I love the lake, and I love the [Puget] Sound, and I love the water and the sunshine and the trees. And the churches." For Betty, there was no contradiction between loving nature and being religiously committed, but whether they are connected or simply parallel is unclear.

Betty's niece Jane, an evangelical Protestant who spent years abroad in social welfare mission work, saw nature as a defining category for people in the region. She said, "Real Northwesterners live outdoors. They don't even have an umbrella." When she was a child, "my father would find places for us to go into the mountains and fly fish where there was still fish. And he knew things that were not on maps, because his father had taken him there." For Jane, being out in nature – especially what she experienced as pristine nature – is significant. She shared with Abbot Drury, a Buddhist leader in Portland, a sense that the encounter with nature is "spiritual." But, Abbot Drury continued, "It's not just eye candy. It's like you have to breathe that air. You have to get dirt under your fingernails. It's important that you be with the natural world and feel your smallness." Abbot Drury's "eye candy" captures the connotation in Jane's comment that today "people are attracted to the beauty," which Jane does not equate with a deep encounter with nature.

North American Christians of all stripes run youth camps (McLoughlin 1978), an outgrowth of the revivalist tradition. Seattleite and evangelical Protestant Donald spoke of his profound religious experience while working for a summer on staff at Malibu, the premier Young Life camp north of Vancouver, British Columbia. He described the summer job as "in a sense, my call to ministry." Donald continued: "I was the garbage man and the groundskeeper, so I was around, meeting people everywhere. And that sense of *being with people, actively involved in a beautiful place,* was a significant life transition" (emphasis mine). His twenty-something daughter, Beatrice, now a post-Christian spiritual seeker, fondly remembered Tall Timbers family Christian camp, located in the Glacier Peak Wilderness near Leavenworth, Washington, for its beauty. For Betty, Jane, Donald, and others, being in nature and being in community are intertwined, though they did not discuss how the two are related.

For some, Cascadia's nature is explicitly a site of profound spiritual experience. This was the case for Roger, a Lutheran from Seattle and 1975 Midwest transplant to Cascadia. On his way to a ministry placement on Puget Sound, Roger spent time at his uncle's cabin in the Cascades. Recalling watching salmon spawn in the Methow River, he said, "That really was a conversion experience that has continued to ... drive a lot of the thinking that I do." He continued:

> All of a sudden, I saw these salmon, and it was like, "Woah." It just sort of took
> my breath away. I mean ... it made an impact on me at the time. But then ...
> what happens to those things is, in my experience ... they unfold over time,
> and layers of meaning get added onto 'em. And, you know ... the whole life
> and death thing ... made sense in a way. The whole thing about the death and
> resurrection of Christ made sense to me in a way that it hadn't before, so,
> through the salmon. Because I think ... for me, it's the same story ... I mean it
> really was in some ways a conversion to another way of looking at the world
> and thinking about life and spirituality. And ... I always was a little bit uneasy
> with orthodox Christianity. I mean ... I know that stuff. I've taught it and all
> that, but you know, it's like ... "Wow, wait a minute. Let's not be too dogmatic
> about some of this."

While Roger's experience of nature led him to a life of ongoing reflection on his Christian faith in light of a spiritual experience in nature that affected his thirty-five years of pastoring in the region, other religiously active participants from our study expressed uneasiness, even ambivalence, about the relationship between nature and faith. Henry's father relinquished mountain climbing and skiing with friends for a religious congregation in Portland once he had children. Reverend Olson, a liberal Protestant pastor in Portland, described a rub between sustained congregational involvement and being in nature:

> I have core families who think nothing of saying, "Oh, you won't see us next
> Sunday. We're going for a hike." Right? There's no embarrassment. There's ac-
> tually a little bit of pride around it. Like, "We're going to make the good choice
> next week. You won't see us. We'll be in nature." And that's interesting to me,
> that not only is there broad permission for that, but even a little bit of a, like,
> I feel like they think they're getting brownie points for it.

Vancouver millennial evangelical Cody was at pains to point out that nature is not "the main thing." While important, it is created, and so secondary to God. Cody thought God was revealed through nature, but nature is not suf-ficient in itself, not inherently spiritual. Pastors of evangelical, liberal, and Catholic stripe were aware of nature as a potential, if not actual, competitor to congregational membership and participation.

Beauty, pleasure, awe, a site of religious experience – nature is all of these things to the religious and irreligious alike in Cascadia. Roger's "Woah" upon viewing spawning salmon captures the awe in an experience of nature that disoriented him and compelled him to rethink what he believed. Jane's child-hood wilderness fishing trips with her father and siblings were journeys into a place of beauty and fecundity and of learning things that were "not on maps."

Most of the Nones in the focus groups, especially millennial Nones, also related experiences in nature that dislocated and decentred them in ways they found to be profoundly meaningful. Christians, Nones, and, as Rachel Brown points out in Chapter 10, persons who identify with other religious traditions all manifest the reverential naturalism that Paul Bramadat describes in Chapter 1.

The Tension between Freedom and Community

Musing about the endemic "mindset" of the Pacific Northwest and its influence on communal life, Rabbi Bauman offered that people "want meaning, but they want it with fewer obligations and [less] commitment." They "want the sense of purpose and fulfillment and connection that comes from committing oneself to a community, and to some degree subsuming one's sense of one's individual need to the larger need, but they're not willing to make the sacrifices and to search the communities and to make those commitments." The tension between freedom and community that the Rabbi framed as a matter of choice appeared in different ways in the family oral-history interviews and the focus groups. It emerged in expressions of loneliness, ambivalence about commitment, and the impulse to keep options open and, for some, in fierce expressions of their commitment to a particular faith heritage, religious community, or small group.

Linda, a liberal Protestant who with her husband, James, retired from Portland to a rural area near Vancouver, Washington, attended services far less frequently than when they were rearing their children and belonged to evangelical congregations. She said she missed her women's group. James noted that "the best part of my [previous] religious life was being involved in the community, times when you would take out turkey dinners to people." Yet they chose to live a far distance from any Christian community. In contrast, eighty-something Cascadian Vancouverite and Catholic convert Penny, still identified her primary community as the women's group that emerged out of the 1971 retreat that she attended. And Fiona, the millennial in-migrant to Seattle, remained committed to her Catholic parish as her primary community. Both invested in maintaining community connections.

Seattleite Stephanie, a thirty-two-year-old agnostic and former Episcopalian (Anglican), explained the tension between freedom and community in terms of loneliness and its consequences, "isolation and a little less inherent community." She reported having told her father:

> I feel like, compared to a lot of other people I know, I didn't really grow up with a sense of a larger community, as ... an inherent thing ... I had my friends, my sister had her friends, my parents had their friends. But they [her parents] had moved here far away from their families, and we didn't have [an] ... extended family that was a bigger community to kind of be, like, padding around us,

and have us grow up in a sense of, like, of having some people who you have fewer boundaries with. To me, there was a very isolated number of people in my whole lifetime that I feel like I have fewer boundaries with. Where I might feel comfortable in being, like, "Hey, you should come over here and do this thing that I think you should do."

Henry, the liberal Protestant from Portland, described a life-changing spiritual experience from his twenties when he found himself alone in a garden while he was travelling in Greece. The gist of the experience: religion is about "company ... 'That you're not alone. You're accompanied by other people, by plants, by animals, by God.' And that sense of not being alone is important." That experience preceded by some years his realization that he had "consciously avoided commitments of any kind," a realization that came to him when the pastor of a congregation he had been attending in Ashland, Oregon, asked him to join the church, which he did, moved by her personal invitation. He married the next year. Henry had "had spiritual moments and mystical experiences, but quite apart from Christianity." He returned "to a Christian church not thinking that Christian churches were the way." Portlander focus-group participant Stanley's journey took him from Catholicism to the Unification Church to Ignatian Catholic spirituality and Baha'i. He found that the last two, to his mind, shared a "not rule-based" affinity that resonates with him.

Pastor Richards, a liberal Protestant facing the demise of his denomination, saw a pervasive spiritual hunger in Cascadia:

> What I do believe, and I think I know, is that the yearning for both a spiritual community and for some connection to something beyond the individual personality is just as profound, maybe more so, than it was when I was growing up. The yearning is there. Whether or not institutions figure out how to respond to it, I think that's the question. And what it's going to look like, boy, I don't know.

Yearning for freedom and openness – the obverse of isolation, loneliness, longing, even rootlessness – came through in the interviews. Portland adherent and Lutheran pastor Tamara, a transplant to the region, spoke to this:

> One theological observation: something that happens to you really fast in the Pacific Northwest is that any idea that there's one way to God pretty much goes away, even if you promised it in your ordination vows [*laughs*]. You just can't live that anymore. You see, it's just in the water. And it's not that it waters down your own tradition, and I don't feel that it does. I think you can be just as self-differentiated and strong in your faith or in your piece of the truth and

acknowledge that there's a lot of truth out there. Maybe that's everywhere these days, but it's certainly true in the Pacific Northwest.

Her comments on self-differentiation were echoed by Matthew, the Portland Catholic interviewee: "I think people who are Christians in the Northwest are probably more committed for lack of a better phrase, or more understanding of what they're doing [than elsewhere in the United States]." Seattle millennial Michelle, raised evangelical but now Episcopalian (Anglican), agreed; "I think people who are committed are really, really committed." All three knew that it takes repeated, intentional choice to remain active in a congregation in Cascadia.

The religiously active interviewees offered community as the major rationale for their participation, but none criticized others for finding community elsewhere. In Cascadia, where individual freedom is highly valued and the longing for durable connections to others is palpable, finding and sustaining community of any kind is both prized and problematic.

Spirituality, Religious Organizations, and Wider Civic and Social Bonds

A pragmatic and private approach to religion dominated the family oral histories, which also reveal an awareness, often inchoate, of the fragility of religious organizations and social relationships in Cascadia. Henry's father swapped mountain climbing for congregational life while raising his family. Teaching children that belief is a private matter but that behaviour is not points to organized religion's function in establishing social mores and inculcating moral values. The stories of Portlanders Linda, her husband, James, and her sister, Barbara – who were raised as Pentecostals in poor, working-class contexts but migrated to liberal Protestantism as higher education improved their economic situations – illustrate religion's role as an indicator of social status.

Regional evangelical religious leaders said they were aware of the fragile social relationships, the personal challenges associated with the high cost of living in Cascadia's urban centres, and the hunger for community. Cognizant that evangelicalism is not the dominant religious path in the region, they prioritized building and strengthening community in their congregations. As Portland evangelical nondenominational Pastor Armando put it, for his church, "everything happens in the context of community."[20]

These pastors conserved resources of time, talent, and money when deciding how their congregations engaged with the wider community. Portland Pentecostal Pastor Novak noted that his members primarily serve the world through their employment and being good neighbours. Larger engagements with the community took place through collaboration with other local religious communities and focused primarily on assisting refugees. Vancouver, British Columbia, evangelical Pastor Evan strove to find ways for his congregation to give back to the larger community without it becoming "a burden thing for them to do" on top of all the rest of their responsibilities with families and jobs. His community settled on mentoring immigrants as its outreach (see Ammerman 1997, 2005).

Older, more established Christian and Jewish communities, as well as relatively recent immigrant communities such as the Sikhs in British Columbia, tend to collaborate through already established structures to engage in community service. Rabbi Levi's Portland synagogue engages through interfaith organizations. Pastor Olson sees his congregation as "a cathedral for the city of Portland" and aspires for it to become "a little bit more of the heart of the community, not so much as a worship centre or even an Anglican centre, but as a kind of civic, liturgical, artistic gathering place." The Sikh community in Richmond, British Columbia, is heavily involved in collaborating with a shrinking United Church on feeding the hungry in Vancouver.

Cascadian religious communities are engaged in social outreach. But as the family-history interviewees showed, there is unease about linking religion and politics. Only a minority associated service or justice work with their faith. Some took pains to make a distinction between service and faith. Vancouver Catholic Penny stated that one is obligated to contribute to the wider community and that she did not connect that obligation in any way to her religious practice or belief. Portland liberal Protestant Henry, on the other hand, subsumed any social service or political involvement under Jesus' command to love one's neighbour. He expressed frustration toward those who turn religion into nothing but a social justice campaign and those who reduce it to political ideology. Penny's and Henry's concern about how to express the relationship between religion and politics was shared by other interviewees. Underneath their expressions rests a sensitivity to the ideologically fraught character of some social issues in the US context – race, the rights of sexual minorities, women's role in society – and their potential to divide already fragile congregations. This concern was more pressing in the United States than in Canada, where, historically, residents presume that their government will be active in social justice endeavours.

In the interviews, social and political issues were topics where the border mattered. Generally, religious leaders tended to reflect national fault lines on contested social issues. Evangelicals emphasized matters of sex and gender, liberal Protestants freedoms and rights. As Chelsea Horton notes in Chapter 2, awareness and involvement in justice and reconciliation work with First Nations peoples characterized many (though not all) BC leaders, but were projects of only a few of the US leaders. Further, BC participants across age cohorts were more sensitive to issues of race and ethnicity than were US participants, among whom the US millennials showed greater awareness.[21]

***

The Christians interviewed exemplified the dynamics of individual and communal religion in Cascadia. Their stories disclosed a tendency to unfettered spiritual seeking; intense privatization of religion; highly personalized appropriations of theological teachings; and an emphasis on choice when it comes to religious affiliation and participation. Most took a socially pragmatic approach to religious participation. Their comments conveyed the fragility of social relationships and religious organizations and the weight of individual freedom, which was expressed both as isolating loneliness and boundless opportunity. In short, they provided fine-grained detail on religion and spirituality in an open religious environment where experience, belief, and belonging are fluid; where lived experience takes priority over assent to intellectual systems; where expressions of faith can alternate between continuous exploration and intense, bounded commitment; and where the encounter with nature dislocates and sometimes resituates the human.

In these ways, religious and nonreligious alike in the Pacific Northwest exemplify the possible future of spirituality, religion, and civic life in the United States and Canada. Here, we see simultaneous processes of religious decline or secularization, conservative reaction, adaption and reinterpretation, and innovation. While these might appear mutually exclusive, all are options that characterize religion globally in late modernity (Lambert 1999). Cascadia's distinctive religious environment has allowed all of them to develop freely and to become visible sooner here than in other parts of the United States and Canada.[22] For those charged with the care and feeding of religious communities, the data suggest that the particular and improvisational, more than the conventional and rote, characterize possible futures.

The project's data clearly reveal a decline of conventional religious institutions and the hold that inherited religious ideas have on people. The process of ceasing to participate and then disaffiliating from a religious community is persistent and pervasive, but so, too, is the impulse to explore, to seek a spiritual "home," as eighty-two-year-old Vancouverite Penny and twenty-five-year-old Portlander Nicole put it. For nearly all participants in the study, from across all religious traditions, including the nonreligious, this place and its nature has emerged as part of that home, a resource for grappling with significant questions about meaning, purpose, and connection in the lives of individuals and for confronting the massive environmental, economic, and social disruptions of our time.

NOTES

1 Archives of the Archdiocese of Seattle, annual reports, St. Leo Parish, Tacoma, Washington, 1898.

2   "Transfer papers" refers to formal documentation, normally a letter written by a pastor, that the named individual has been in good standing as a member of a religious congregation in the location from which they came. Any assessment of historical and contemporary writings from these groups has to take into account that these leaders expressed their thoughts in rhetorical tropes learned from the writings of Christian missionaries in other regions of the United States and Canada and wrote with multiple purposes: to raise funds, arouse the faithful, and explain the context in an effort to buffer results they felt did not meet the expectations of organizational leaders.

3   What changed, how, and at what pace varied. Factors influencing change included personal experiences; economic, educational, social, and religious group status; and race and ethnicity. But as this volume makes clear, change in relation to religious ideas, practices, and organizational participation crossed ethnic and racial groups.

4   "Participation" is defined by individual sociological studies, with "regular participation" most often understood to be attendance monthly or more frequently.

5   Beginning in the 1950's, cultural geographers have noted that when people move from one region to another they tend to adopt the religious practices of that region (see Zelinsky 1961).

6   "Adherents" is a sociological category used by religious statisticians in the United States. It includes "all members, including full members, their children and the estimated number of other participants who are not considered members; for example ... 'those regularly attending services'" (ASARB 2002, xv). It is calculated, in part, by religious institutions counting weekly attendance. The last is not data used in Canada, though Canada has survey-generated, self-reported data on attendance.

7   "Affiliation" refers to those who self-identify as belonging to a religious body and who may report participating in a local religious community. When we did *Religion and Public Life in the Pacific Northwest: The None Zone,* the percentage of the population that identified as being "an X" was slightly larger than the percentage of the population counted as "adherents" by religious statisticians. This finding aligns with Wilkins-Laflamme's (2017, 7) observation that in the US, individuals surveyed have tended to report attendance when they did not attend.

8   See Sarah Wilkins-Laflamme's and Mark Silk's chapters in this volume for discussion of Nones.

9   Following common practice, by "regular" I mean attendance monthly or more frequently.

10 This chapter focuses primarily on Christians. See Block and Marks, Chapter 4, on the irreligious; Horton, Chapter 2, and Crawford O'Brien, Chapter 3, on Indigenous and First Nations peoples; and Brown, Chapter 10, on communities from other world religious traditions.

11 While the number of interviews of current Christians is small, these interviews provide access to lived religion in the region over time at a more fine-grained level than has been available previously. Block and Marks address the limits of the oral histories as a data set in Chapter 4. See https://www.uvic.ca/research/centres/csrs/.

12 All but one of the still practising Christian family interviewees were of northern European descent. The religious leaders, adherent focus groups, and millennial focus groups were more ethnically and racially diverse.

13 While Christian denominations have not exercised social control to the degree they did elsewhere, they were influential. See Soden (2015). Brown, Chapter 10, this volume, presents a different take on Christianity and regional cultural norms.

14 Portland millennial Nicole, raised Buddhist, became Jewish. Seattle millennial Fiona, raised Buddhist, became Roman Catholic. Seattle millennial Michelle, raised evangelical, became liberal Episcopalian (Anglican). Victoria millennial Lindsay, raised None, became Christian. Portland adherent Dale, raised Protestant, became a Jodo Shinshu Buddhist. Seattleite

Stephanie, raised Episcopalian, became agnostic. Gloria, from Victoria and raised Anglican, became a None.

15 For an explanation of "shopping," see Cimino and Lattin (2002).

16 See Wellman and Corcoran, Chapter 8, and Wilkinson, Chapter 9, for discussions of these dynamics among evangelical Christians in the region; also Burkinshaw (1995) and Wellman (2008).

17 See Dale Soden's (2015, 96–100) discussion of the African American Church and Portland NAACP cofounder Beatrice Cannady, vocal critic of racism in Oregon and convert to the Baha'i faith. On racial dynamics involved in African Americans embracing the region's nature as a spiritual experience, see Evelyn C. White's classic "Black Women and the Wilderness" (1999).

18 For example, the Presbyterian Bible Church, independent conservative non-Charismatic churches, and Seventh-Day Adventists are overrepresented in the region. The region has also attracted sects such as the Doukhobors and utopian ventures such as the Aurora Colony and Rajneeshpuram, both in Oregon (see Killen and Silk 2004; Kopp 2009; and LeWarne 1995).

19 See Morrill, Chapter 11, on the theme of Christians and nature among nineteenth- and early twentieth-century writers in the region, as historical context for this section. See also Bramadat, Chapter 1, on reverential naturalism.

20 See Wellman and Corcoran, Chapter 8, and Wilkinson, Chapter 9, on evangelical Christians in the region.

21 The family oral-history interviews were largely mute on issues of ethnicity and race.

22 Silk, Chapter 6, argues that the region should be understood as the front wave in the growth of religious Nones.

References

Ammerman. Nancy. 1997. *Congregation and Community.* New Brunswick, NJ: Rutgers, 1997.
–. 2005. *Pillars of Faith: American Congregations and Their Partners.* Berkeley: University of California Press.
ASARB (Association of Statisticians of American Religious Bodies). 2002. *Religious Congregations and Membership in the United States 2000.* Nashville: Glenmary Research Center.
Burkinshaw, Robert K. 1995. *Pilgrims in Lotus Land: Conservative Protestantism in British Columbia, 1917–1981.* Montreal/Kingston: McGill-Queen's University Press.
Burns, Jeffrey M. 1987. "Building the Best: A History of Catholic Parish Life in the Pacific States." In *The American Catholic Parish: A History from 1850 to the Present.* Vol. 2, *The Pacific States, Intermountain West, and Midwest States,* edited by Jay P. Dolan, 7–135. New York: Paulist Press.
Cimino, Richard, and Don Lattin. 2002. *Shopping for Faith: American Religion in the New Millennium.* San Francisco: John Wiley and Sons.
Finke, Roger, and Rodney Stark. 1992. *The Churching of America, 1776–1990: Winners and Losers in Our Religious Economy.* New Brunswick, NJ: Rutgers University Press.
Howell, Erle. 1966. *Methodism in the Northwest.* Nashville, TN: Parthenon Press.
Jessett, Thomas E. 1967. *Pioneering God's Country: The History of the Diocese of Olympia, 1853–1967.* Seattle: Diocese of Olympia Press.
Killen, Patricia O'Connell. 1998. "Region and Religion: Interpreting Christianities in the Pacific Northwest." Paper delivered to the national meeting of Episcopal Archivists and Historians, Seattle, WA, June 25, 1998.
–. 2008. "Memory, Novelty and Possibility in This Place." In *Cascadia, the Elusive Utopia: Exploring the Spirit of the Pacific Northwest,* edited by Douglas Todd, 65–85. Vancouver: Ronsdale Press.

Killen, Patricia O'Connell, and Mark Silk. 2004. *Religion and Public Life in the Pacific Northwest: The None Zone.* Walnut Creek, CA: AltaMira Press.

Kopp, James J. 2009. *Eden within Eden: Oregon's Utopian Heritage.* Corvallis: Oregon State University Press.

Lambert, Yves. 1999. "Religion in Modernity as a New Axial Age: Secularization or New Religious Forms?" *Sociology of Religion* 60 (3): 303–33.

LeWarne, Charles. 1995. *Utopias of Puget Sound, 1885–1915.* Seattle: University of Washington Press.

Marks, Lynne. 2017. *Infidels and the Damn Churches: Irreligion and Religion in Settler British Columbia.* Vancouver: UBC Press.

McLoughlin, William G. 1978. *Revivals, Awakenings, and Reform: An Essay on Religion and Social Change in America, 1607–1977.* Chicago: University of Chicago Press.

McNally, Vincent J. 1990. "Victoria: An American Diocese in Canada." *Canadian Catholic Historical Association Historical Studies* 57: 7–28.

O'Hara, Edwin Vincent. 1939. *Pioneer Catholic History of Oregon.* Patterson, NJ: St. Anthony Guild Press.

Pew Research Center. 2013. "Canada's Changing Religious Landscape." *Pew Research Center,* June 27. https://www.pewforum.org/2013/06/27/canadas-changing-religious-landscape/.

–. 2015. "The Whys and Hows of Generation Research." *Pew Research Center,* September 3. https://www.people-press.org/2015/09/03/the-whys-and-hows-of-generations-research/.

Shortridge, James R. 1977. "A New Regionalisation of American Religion." *Journal for the Scientific Study of Religion* 16: 142–53.

Soden, Dale. 2015. *Outsiders in a Promised Land: Religious Activists in Pacific Northwest History.* Corvallis: Oregon State University Press.

Stark, Rodney. 1984. "Why Oregon; What Makes the State Attractive to New Religious Movements?" *Oregon Humanities:* 22–26.

Statistics Canada. n.d. "Table 17-10-0009-01: Population Estimates, Quarterly." https://doi.org/10.25318/1710000901-eng.

United States Census Bureau. n.d. "Population Estimates." www.census.gov/glossary/#term_Population.

Wellman, James K. Jr. 2008. *Evangelical vs. Liberal: The Clash of Christian Cultures in the Pacific Northwest.* New York: Oxford University Press.

White, Evelyn C. 1999. "Black Women and the Wilderness." In *Literature and the Environment: A Reader on Nature and Culture,* edited by Lorraine Anderson, Scott Slovic, and John P. O'Grady. New York: Addison, Wesley, Longman, 316–20.

Wilkins-Laflamme, Sarah. 2017. "The Religious, Spiritual, Secular and Social Landscapes of the Pacific Northwest: Part I." *UWSpace.* https://uwspace.uwaterloo.ca/handle/10012/12218.

Zelinsky, Wilbur. 1961. "An Approach to the Religious Geography of the United States: Patterns of Church Membership in 1952." *Annals of the Association of American Geographers* 51 (June): 139–93.

The Precarious Nature of Cascadia's Protestants: New Strategies for Evangelical and Liberal Christians in the Region

JAMES K. WELLMAN JR. AND KATIE E. CORCORAN

One of the challenges scholars face when working on religion in Cascadia is how to provide a dispassionate account of a geography that casts such a spell on those who live in it. Characteristically, explorers, settlers, and missionaries have sought to tame the West and to rebuild it in their own image – but this has never succeeded in the Pacific Northwest, or Cascadia, which is shaped more by the caprices of nature than the wants of humans. The story presented here is one of creative adaption but with recognition of a context that seems stacked against churched faith – liberal and evangelical Protestants struggle in this region, and their survival is in no way guaranteed. As we show, Cascadia has forced these religious groups to adapt: it has created opportunities for innovation, but it has also generated a sense of disappointment and failure. In response, liberal Christian communities in both the United States and Canada embody a growing libertarian moral ethic, a communitarian ethos, with just a dash of countercultural economics. In the case of evangelicals, whether in Canada or the United States, there is a moderate but changing conservative moral code that combines an entrepreneurial spirit with an occasional display of progressive politics – including environmentalism and forms of European evangelicalism with some experimenting with inclusive sexual ethics and others advocating for liberal immigration policies. Protestantism in Cascadia is, to a degree, insulated from conservative influences that are more evident elsewhere in the United States; it is also impacted by a more broad-minded Canadian and Northwest libertarian culture.

Cascadian libertarians are most often transplants from other regions of the country, quite often male (though not exclusively), who seek to do just what they want in work and play; who leave behind affiliations and institutional attachments, including religion; who think that nothing is impossible in work, love, and play; and who disdain religious structures, disciplines, and identities, often believing that they are spiritual but not religious. They want to become what and who they dream to be – independent, vital, free, and faithful to their dreams. They see the open nature of the West as their land of tomorrow and possibility. These values and beliefs have given rise to distinctive expressions of Christianity in response to a stubbornly secular regional culture.

Using data from previous research along with the data that forms the basis of this book, we argue that regional differences create powerful cultural flows that push against broader US trends. Indeed, in some ways, liberals and evangelicals in Oregon and Washington have more in common with Cascadians in Canada than they do with their coreligionists in the United States. As Mark Silk (2005, 265) discovered in his studies of regional religion in the United States, the type and manner of religion practised in the United States are "connected to the public cultures of different parts of the country; they shape and are shaped by them." In Cascadia, evangelicals, whether in Canada or the United States, are far more likely than evangelicals in other regions to affirm the value of immigration (Castleberry 2015) and, for some, to move in the direction of either partial or full acceptance of those in the LGBTQ+ community.[1] Thus, we argue that religious groups tend to reflect their local context more than religious groups within their own denomination. Moreover, we contend that the cosmopolitan nature of the Cascadia region leads to unique adaptions and innovations in these Cascadian religious groups.

The region of Cascadia – Oregon, Washington, and British Columbia – makes up its own religious ecosystem. This landscape features a largely unchurched population. According to the Cascadia research team's 2017 Pacific Northwest Social Survey, roughly 44 percent of those living in Washington and Oregon and 49 percent of British Columbians chose "no religion" in surveys, versus approximately 23 percent in the rest of the United States (Pew Research Center 2015) and 24 percent in the rest of Canada (Pew Research Center 2013).[2] Thus, in the United States, a nation known for its religious exceptionalism (Stark and Finke 2000), Cascadia is an exception unto itself. The region has appropriately been labelled the "None Zone." Canada embodies on its West Coast a region that is highly ambivalent toward religion – featuring a population that is even less religious than its US counterpart; this level of secularity led one Canadian informant to describe the country as "a pagan nation."

A region and culture where religiosity is neither assumed nor forced on anyone (Silk and Walsh 2008; Wellman 2008) presents particular challenges for a church-affiliated minority form of Christianity. This essay explains the precarious nature of Protestant communities of faith straining to adapt creatively to a culture that more often than not sees no purpose for institutional religion. It tells a story of the decline of liberal Protestant communities and the witness of evangelical Protestants that frequently mirrors the values of the region. In both cases, these communities are fragile and face a pronounced regional indifference to their existence. As one of the most effective evangelical megachurch pastors in the region explained in a sermon, "I fully expect that this church will die in the not-too-distant future." It was a remarkable confession from someone who has been able to succeed in this secular, unchurched region – underscoring the intense challenges that both liberal and evangelical Protestants face in the Cascadian context.

Data and Methodology

The analysis here combines two forms of data. The first is the Pacific Northwest Social Survey (PNSS) (see Paul Bramadat's Introduction for a description of the methodology) that was conducted for the "Religion, Spirituality, Secularity and Society in the Pacific Northwest" project. We present descriptive statistics for Cascadia South (Oregon and Washington) and Cascadia North (British Columbia) separately to show how the responses of evangelical and liberal Protestants are more similar to their Pacific Northwestern counterparts than they are to the general population in their respective countries. And, as we note below, this more recent statistical data confirms findings from our second data set.

The second data set consists of interviews conducted in 2003–05 for a project that examined (see Wellman and Corcoran 2013) twenty-four of the fastest-growing evangelical churches[3] and ten vital liberal mainline Protestant churches[4] in western Oregon and western Washington.[5] The findings from these interviews were confirmed by the more recent survey data on Oregon–Washington and may also reflect the experiences of evangelical and liberal Protestants in British Columbia. Our earlier interview data were collected from among US evangelical churches that had shown substantial growth in numbers (at least a 25 percent growth rate) and finances between 2000 and 2005. The vital liberal churches in our earlier study had maintained stable congregational numbers, finances, and church identity during a similar period. Both samples are fairly representative of the denominational distribution of churches in the US Cascadia region (Killen and Silk 2004). From December 2003 to August 2005, for each church, we observed church services, read church materials, visited church websites, interviewed the senior pastor, and conducted focus groups composed of lay leaders and new members (those who had been members for under two years). The interviews were semistructured and consisted of open-ended questions regarding faith, church, politics, and views regarding the region. There were 145 and 298 liberal and evangelical respondents, respectively, including both attendees and clergy. While this data goes back fifteen years, the PNSS survey and the qualitative data collected for the "Religion, Spirituality, Secularity and Society in the Pacific Northwest" project confirm and extend trends that we saw in our earlier research.[6]

Cascadian Civil Religion

Cascadia has the largest proportion of individuals with no religious affiliation relative to any other region of the United States and Canada (Silk and Walsh 2008), but among these so-called religious Nones, there is still a pervasive spirituality. A third of Nones in the 2017 PNSS believed that God or a higher power existed, suggesting a "secular but spiritual" ethos in the Pacific Northwest (see Wilkins-Laflamme, this volume; see Shibley 2004). Mark Shibley (2004) conceptualizes this spirituality as a form of "nature religion," and Paul Bramadat, in Chapter 1, describes the ethos of this regional culture as reverential naturalism. Either way, we argue that this is the dominant civil religion in Cascadia. That is, Cascadians view the beauty of the outdoors as their "sanctuary" and "chapel" and the wilderness as a place to experience spirituality or "the sacred" (Shibley 2004, 2011). Tellingly, 86 percent of Cascadians in the 2017 PNSS said they took part in outdoor activities at least once a year, and just over half of these residents described these activities as spiritual. Shibley argues that this alternative secular spirituality creates tension with the church-based population, but we suggest that reverential naturalism permeates the civil religion of Cascadia more broadly and therefore influences church-based populations as well. In this sense, participation in organized religious life is less important than the form of reverence for the place that is shared by both evangelicals and liberals. Both bow to the pervasive sense that what makes the region special is not a distant God who created it but the beauty that transfuses the environment, and so, even among evangelicals, nature takes on a sacramental ethos in which the divine can be present in the natural world.

The greater culture of Cascadia is often described as embodying a libertarian and secular ethos, in part because there is no dominant faith group and no established and pervasive ecclesiastical authority. In interviews with Cascadian evangelicals and liberals, we found that it is taken for granted that few participate in institutional religion. This was particularly true in the Canadian data, where, on occasion, the language of conventional Christianity was dismissed or publicly rejected. In contrast to the American South, for instance, where church going is assumed in public culture, quite the opposite is the case in Cascadia. People rarely talk about church in public venues, or even among acquaintances, making it difficult for individuals within specific Christian traditions to discuss their faith with others (Killen, this volume; Wellman 2008; Wellman and Corcoran 2013). Indeed, as we argued in 2013, claims about one's involvement in organized religion are typically met with indifference and occasionally with hostility, or with the same sort of curiosity one extends to a novelty item (see also Silk and Walsh 2008).

In interviews we conducted prior to our 2013 publication, we sensed among both evangelical and liberal Christian leaders a deep sense of anxiety and grief over the relative indifference that Cascadians exhibit toward their churches and organizations. This was voiced in particular by leaders in the downtown cathedrals, which have acted as stations of help and care for the vulnerable, including the homeless and hungry. One pastor remarked, "And [Protestant mainline volunteers] were really strong not that long ago. Unfortunately, now, spirituality has become more of a consumer good ... so it's more, like, me-centred rather than the other-centred." That is, without institutional commitment, volunteerism has decreased, and there are fewer interested in serving those in need. The same pastor goes on to say that this lack of interest and investment in the infrastructure of care has been devastating on the vulnerable: "So, overall, if we keep this trajectory going, if you say that, twenty years down the road, yeah, a lot of this stuff will be stopped." The pastor explained that there is a type of corporatization of community life, "To the point, to the extent that nobody wants to do anything unless there's a salary." We heard this from both Protestant and Catholic leaders: that the ethic of voluntarism is disappearing, replaced by a more utilitarian set of values that expects a return on any investment of time or effort.

Many who serve in these mainline and evangelical churches see a notable "de-Christianization" process underway, one that has real effects on the character and ethos of church life, and on the most vulnerable. In our research conducted during 2003–05, we found within the Portland communities that as volunteerism declined, so too did the capacity of religious organizations to offer care for the most vulnerable within their communities. With continuing secularization, pastors on the Canadian side of Cascadia have experienced a growing antagonism to faith and its expression. For example, Reverend Travis, a Roman Catholic clergy member in Victoria explained, "In fifteen years, [this] has gone to an open hostility, so that people of faith are saying, 'This is just getting really uncomfortable here because even if we raise our hand and ask a question, we are belittled and berated and ostracized.' So the Canadian fabric, which always prided itself on tolerance, is [now] completely intolerant of anything religious."

The US data reveals a similar and growing sense that in the Pacific Northwest faith-centred talk and actions are no longer assumed as necessary public goods – their public legitimacy is no longer self-evident. And so, while it is true that there is a growing proliferation of interest in spirituality, more generically understood, this has led to a decrease in interest and participation in conventional forms of Christianity with a concomitant decline in volunteerism to the poor and homeless in Cascadian cities. Indeed, clergy and those who attend churches reported a significant decline in volunteerism aimed at serving those who are most vulnerable in the region. As scholars in the study of religion, we would argue that this is surely an unintended effect of the dereligionization of a region. We are not suggesting that, by definition, the nonreligious spiritual residents are less compassionate, but we are pointing to what religious leaders observe: that the decline of churched religion in Cascadia has undercut care for those who are vulnerable, especially those living on the streets.

Interactions with evangelicals in higher education, business, and civic life reveal a "new cosmopolitanism" in Cascadian culture, which reflects the necessity to become more broad-minded in a culture that is thoroughly secular but also multicultural, multiethnic, and multireligious (Laird 2004). Evangelicals are shifting in the direction of a liberal orientation because they know that their ideas will otherwise be rejected by members of the dominant and increasingly secular culture. But they are shifting direction for two other reasons. First, they may very well have done missionary work in countries where they were minorities and thus learned the need to "earn the right to speak." Second, American Protestants privilege the right to be heard, not always because they think they know the truth but because they sincerely want to hear what the other has to say (Wellman 2008).

But again, these dynamics feed into a Cascadian region that is stubbornly libertarian, where there is more space – both actual and symbolic – to be and do what one wants than nearly anyplace else in North America. This notion of space deeply shapes the region's libertarian spirit and contributes to a respect for the natural world. This respect is manifested in the way so many speak of the region's beauty – as a kind of secular sacrament whereby meaning emerges in one's relationship to the natural world. This approach to nature is echoed in the volume's key theme of reverential naturalism – an orientation or meta-narrative that needs neither an organization nor a temple. It is no wonder, then, that Washington State's governor, Jay Inslee, has succeeded in passing some of the most stringent environmental policies in the nation. We see this value as well in the reverence that leading evangelicals show in tending the "earthly garden" of God's creation.

The regional emphasis on nature creates a problem for evangelical and liberal Protestantism. Evangelicals are challenged by the region's beauty, which is so inviting, and the opportunities for work and play, so abundant, that people do not have a reason to seek out faith for either consolation or inspiration. For liberals, the relative lack of social problems and the progressive nature of government reinforces the common notion that local social and political organizations are already filling the need for community care, reducing the motivation to serve through religious volunteerism. From a certain perspective, it is remarkable that anyone in the region attends church. And for many, that clearly is the question: Why would one need an organized religion in the first place? One can feel and hear a certain desperation in religious leaders' explanations of why it is important to be part of an organized religious faith system. Simply put, Cascadians do not consider organized religion a necessary part of their lives.

Trends in Cascadia's Demographics and Culture

Quantitative Data

The PNSS provides an up-to-date portrait of the behaviours and perceptions of Cascadia's residents. We use this data to provide a characterization of the religiosity and spirituality of the region, the cultural context in which Cascadian evangelical and liberal Protestants are embedded. Tables 8.1 and 8.2 provide descriptive statistics on identification as a spiritual person and various religious, spiritual, and/or secular activities. In response to the question "Do you consider yourself a spiritual person?," 22 percent of Oregon–Washington respondents said "very spiritual," and 35 percent said "moderately spiritual." Fewer BC respondents identified as "very spiritual," at 14 percent, but roughly the same proportion indicated that they were moderately spiritual, at 36 percent. Twenty-six percent reported that they were not spiritual at all.

Thus, the majority of Cascadian respondents considered themselves spiritual to some degree, and a majority considered themselves moderately or very spiritual. In terms of activities, respondents were asked: "In the past twelve months, how often on average did you practise or take part in the following activities, either in a group or on your own?" Comparing religious services,

TABLE 8.1   Spirituality and religious, spiritual, and secular activities/involvement, Oregon and Washington (%)

Do you consider yourself a spiritual person?		I want to become more involved with a religious group in the future.	
Very spiritual	22.29	Strongly agree	7.56
Moderately spiritual	34.64	Agree	16.79
Slightly spiritual	23.18	Neither agree or disagree	33.68
Not at all spiritual	19.89	Disagree	14.77
		Strongly disagree	27.20
N	757	N	758

In the past twelve months, how often on average did you practise or take part in the following activities, either in a group or on your own?	Religious services	Read sacred texts	Pray	Yoga/ meditation	Outdoor	Environmental
Once a day or more often/at least once a week	23.37	25.14	45.36	23.49	32.31	25.08
At least once a month but less than once a week	7.99	7.88	7.87	9.26	20.97	14.58
A few times a year but less than once a month	12.17	11.64	10.82	10.7	23.03	20.03
Once a year	8.57	7.14	4.84	4.79	5.21	8.67
Not at all	47.91	48.21	31.11	51.76	18.48	31.64
N	754	752	757	758	756	755

SOURCE: Data: PNSS, Oregon and Washington subsample, data is weighted.

TABLE 8.2   Spirituality and religious, spiritual, and secular activities/involvement, British Columbia (%)

Do you consider yourself a spiritual person?		*I want to become more involved with a religious group in the future.*	
Very spiritual	13.83	Strongly agree	4.24
Moderately spiritual	36.03	Agree	15.63
Slightly spiritual	24.19	Neither agree or disagree	26.48
Not at all spiritual	25.94	Disagree	19.96
		Strongly disagree	33.69
N	749	*N*	4.24

In the past twelve months, how often on average did you practise or take part in the following activities, either in a group or on your own?	Religious services	Read sacred texts	Pray	Yoga/ meditation	Outdoor	Environmental
Once a day or more often/at least once a week	15	14.77	30.6	21.35	40.29	23.53
At least once a month but less than once a week	4.47	5.27	7.62	9.36	22.47	16.66
A few times a year but less than once a month	15.34	13.56	14.41	12.99	19.41	20.34
Once a year	8.11	5.2	4.6	3.92	2.35	8.99
Not at all	57.08	61.2	42.76	52.38	15.38	30.49
N	746	748	750	748	750	749

SOURCE: PNSS, 2017, British Columbia subsample. Data is weighted.

48 percent (Oregon–Washington) and 57 percent (British Columbia) identified not attending them at all. Prayer, a more private form of religious and spiritual practice, had much higher participation rates, with 45 (Oregon–Washington) and 31 (British Columbia) percent of people indicating that they prayed at least once a week. Twenty-three percent (Oregon–Washington) and 21 percent (British Columbia) participated in yoga, meditation, or other mindfulness activities at least once a week. These rates are similar to those for religious service attendance.

Considerably more people engaged in outdoor activities in the two sub-samples; 32 percent (Oregon–Washington) and 40 percent (British Columbia) reported that they participated in them at least once a week. Roughly 76 (Oregon–Washington) and 82 (British Columbia) percent participated in outdoor activities at least a few times a year. Approximately 60 percent of respondents participated in activities to help the environment and the natural world at least a few times a year, and only 30 to 32 percent said they never engaged in such activities. Thus, activities that involved helping the environment were more frequent than attending religious services and meetings. When asked if they "want to become more involved with a religious group in the future," roughly 42 to 54 percent of respondents disagreed or strongly disagreed. Only a small percentage said they strongly agree (4–6 percent) and agree (14–16 percent). These results are consistent with previous research underlining the secular but spiritual nature of Cascadian culture, which values the environment over organized religion (Shibley 2011; Silk and Walsh 2008).

But do Cascadia's evangelical and liberal Protestants perceive the region in this way? Tables 8.3 and 8.4 provide descriptive statistics comparing the responses of the full regional subsamples to those of Cascadia's evangelical and liberal Protestants. Respondents were asked whether they "feel that the Cascadia/ Pacific Northwest region is a more spiritual place than other regions in North America." Twenty-two percent of the Oregon–Washington subsample and 30 percent of the BC subsample agreed or strongly agreed with this statement;

TABLE 8.3   Perception of the Pacific Northwest, Oregon and Washington (%)

I feel that the Cascadia/Pacific Northwest region is a more spiritual place than other regions in North America.	Entire sample	Evangelical	Liberal
Strongly agree or agree	22.29	14.01	27.22
Neither agree nor disagree	50.71	47.94	45.11
Strongly disagree or disagree	26.99	38.05	27.68
Total	100	100	100
N	758	109	75

I feel I have more in common with other American and Canadian residents of the Pacific Northwest than I do with people from elsewhere in my country.	Entire sample	Evangelical	Liberal
Strongly agree or agree	46.36	41.86	56.94
Neither agree or disagree	38.25	35.49	29.74
Strongly disagree or disagree	15.38	22.65	13.32
Total	100	100	100
N	755	110	75

I think that in the Cascadia/Pacific Northwest region people are freer to experiment with religion, nonreligion, and spirituality than in most other places in North America.	Entire sample	Evangelical	Liberal
Strongly agree or agree	43.63	34.43	46.57
Neither disagree or agree	44.38	46.98	41.86
Strongly disagree or disagree	11.99	18.59	11.57
Total	100	100	100
N	756	109	75

SOURCE: PNSS, 2017, Oregon and Washington subsample. Data is weighted.

TABLE 8.4 Perception of the Pacific Northwest, British Columbia (%)

I feel that the Cascadia/Pacific Northwest region is a more spiritual place than other regions in North America.	Entire sample	Evangelical	Liberal
Strongly agree or agree	29.79	16.36	29.39
Neither disagree or agree	48.02	52.15	53.33
Strongly disagree or disagree	22.18	31.49	17.29
Total	100	100	100
N	749	56	84

I feel I have more in common with other American and Canadian residents of the Pacific Northwest than I do with people from elsewhere in my country.	Entire sample	Evangelical	Liberal
Strongly agree or agree	43.03	34.06	21.29
Neither disagree or agree	39.77	53	60.35
Strongly disagree or disagree	17.20	12.94	18.36
Total	100	100	100
N	747	56	84

I think that in the Cascadia/Pacific Northwest region, people are freer to experiment with religion, nonreligion, and spirituality than in most other places in North America.	Entire sample	Evangelical	Liberal
Strongly agree or agree	38.98	30.56	41.08
Neither disagree or agree	49.43	47.9	46.28
Strongly disagree or disagree	11.6	21.54	12.64
Total	100	100	100
N	748	56	84

SOURCE: PNSS, 2017, British Columbia subsample. Data is weighted.

most neither agreed nor disagreed (51 percent and 48 percent), and 27 percent and 22 percent disagreed or strongly disagreed. Slightly more mainline Protestants in Oregon–Washington agreed or strongly agreed, at 27 percent. There was even less support for this statement among evangelical Protestants; only 14 percent of the Oregon–Washington subsample and 16 percent of the BC subsample agreed or strongly agreed, and 38 percent and 31 percent disagreed or strongly disagreed. These numbers suggest that the evangelicals associated spirituality with organized religion and understood they were in one of the most secular places in the continent.

To test whether evangelical and mainline Protestants were as connected to the Cascadian region as other residents, we examined responses to the following question: "I feel I have more in common with other American and Canadian residents of the Pacific Northwest than I do with people from elsewhere in my country." Roughly 47 percent of Oregon–Washington respondents and 43 percent of BC respondents agreed or strongly agreed with this statement. Compared to the entire sample, evangelical Protestants had lower levels of agreement (41 percent in Oregon–Washington, and 34 percent in British Columbia); there were higher levels of disagreement in the Oregon–Washington subsample (23 percent); and a higher percentage neither agreed or disagreed in the BC subsample (53 percent). Oregon–Washington liberal Protestants had higher levels of agreement (57 percent) and lower levels of disagreement (13 percent) compared to the entire Oregon–Washington subsample. BC liberal Protestants had the lowest levels of agreement (21 percent) and the highest percentage of those who neither agreed nor disagreed (18 percent). Although we argue that a regional identification is often more salient than a denominational one for Cascadian Christians, our data also suggest that evangelicals are somewhat less likely than their nonevangelical neighbours in the region to share this perspective. A possible explanation for this would be that the ambient secularity of the region tends to slightly depress evangelicals' identification with what we call the civil religion of the region.

In the PNSS, respondents were also asked if they "think that in the Cascadia/Pacific Northwest region people are freer to experiment with religion, nonreligion, and spirituality than in most other places in North America?" Approximately 44 percent of Oregon–Washington respondents and 39 percent of BC respondents agreed or strongly agreed with the statement. This is consistent with the characterization of Cascadia as an "open spiritual marketplace" (Laird 2004; Shibley 2004). Evangelical Protestants had a different pattern of response; 34 percent of Oregon–Washington respondents and 31 percent of BC respondents agreed or strongly agreed with this statement. Additionally, a higher percentage of evangelical Protestants (roughly 19 percent and 22 percent in both samples) reported that they strongly disagreed or disagreed with this statement. This might be explained by a perception among evangelicals that the bias against religion in the region means they are somewhat less free to practise their religion openly (Silk and Walsh 2008; Wellman 2008). We dig into this point more thoroughly below.

Qualitative Data: Pacific Northwest Evangelical Protestants

The interview responses from our 2003–05 (see Wellman and Corcoran 2013) research[7] on Oregon and Washington made it clear that evangelicals were aware of the region's secular culture. Respondents in twenty-two of the twenty-four churches (roughly 92 percent) used terms such as "unchurched or secular" (thirty-six respondents) and/or "liberal or libertarian" (thirty-two respondents) to describe the region's culture. A male respondent from a suburban megachurch in the greater Seattle area observed that Cascadia is "secular. It's unchurched. It's liberal. Washington State is either the number one or number two, depending on the statistics, between Washington and Oregon, as the most unchurched state in the nation."

When asked how their faith related to the Pacific Northwest, 93 percent of respondents identified feeling some form of tension or conflict, which ranged from merely feeling different to feeling persecuted. A male member of an urban Portland church identified a conflict between his conservative, religious values and the unchurched, liberal values of the surrounding culture. Similarly, a female respondent from an urban Seattle church described "feeling like a minority." She said, "I'm so different than everybody else, and I'm in conflict." One senior pastor at an urban Seattle church identified the liberal "unchurched climate" as a "cultural current" moving against evangelicals that felt "like a battle." A male attendee of a suburban Seattle church identified a "strong," "angry," "anti-Christian, anticonservative bias in Seattle." In general, participants observed that they had experienced a culture clash, to varying degrees, between evangelicals and the culture of the region. Michael Wilkinson's chapter in this volume also identifies a similar conviction among the evangelical pastors interviewed for the "Religion, Spirituality, Secularity and Society in the Pacific Northwest" project.

Many respondents identified prevalent secular activities that compete or conflict with religious practices. Sports and other outdoor recreational pursuits were the most commonly cited activities. This is consistent with the PNSS survey data, which revealed that outdoor and environmental activities were more prevalent than attending religious services or meetings. A statement by a male respondent from a suburban Seattle church exemplifies this sentiment: "I think part of it, especially in the Northwest, is liberalism has taken on a turn not only from the political views, but from everything we do. We [Pacific Northwesterners] are involved in sports ... We got recreation. Liberalism has been serving me first and doing what I want." Respondents from three churches noted that youth sporting events were often held on Sunday mornings with no consideration for church services. Three respondents in different churches mentioned that many families with children had to decide whether to miss church so that their children could participate in sports.

Respondents across multiple churches said the beauty of the Northwest environment competed with religious activities. A senior pastor from a suburban Portland megachurch noted that "competition is one of the greatest things here in the Northwest. There's always something else to do. You know, go to the mountains, go and ski, go to the coast, go camping. The list goes on and on." One male respondent from a suburban Seattle church said that Seattle had "a huge boating community, and you're boating on the weekend. You're not thinking about church as a part of the weekend. You're saying 'church,' that means I have to tie my boat back up." Respondents in these churches described Cascadians as "worshipping nature" and therefore feeling as though they had no need for church. For example, a man from a suburban Seattle church noted, "Their gods are their fields or going to the golf course or skiing." Many responses illustrated a "sacralization of nature" (Shibley 2004), which these evangelicals felt competed with religious institutions; in some cases, evangelicals condemned and criticized this behaviour.

Evangelicals experienced tension with what they identified as the overall spirit of Cascadia – independent, individualistic, and libertarian. The "I don't bother you, you don't bother me" spirit made it harder for evangelicals to discuss their faith and evangelize the population. One senior pastor of a rural Portland church identified this independent spirit as one of the reasons the Pacific Northwest is unchurched:

> There is a "give me my 640 acres [i.e., a section of farmland] and get out of my face" spirit here. And it's not a joining culture, in contrast to some of our friends who pastor churches in the Bible Belt or other places, where it's part of the culture that you belong, you participate. There is not that climate in the Northwest.

This goes along with what we saw in the PNSS interviews with Cascadians in British Columbia: conventional religion is not taken for granted. Further, there is an air of disdain for "joiners," and a sense that one should take care of things for oneself and not depend on the state or a community of faith.

At the same time, five respondents from different churches from our study (Wellman and Corcoran 2013) identified positive aspects of the region's "live and let live" mentality. For example, a female respondent from a suburban Seattle church said: "One of the things that is nice about the Northwest is that ... most people are content for me to be who I am, and I'm content for them to make their choices and be who they are. So, there's very much of a 'live and let live' philosophy that I think helps us." This aligns with the PNSS results, which showed that 34 percent of Oregon–Washington evangelicals and 31 percent of BC evangelicals strongly agreed or agreed that in the Pacific Northwest people are freer to experiment with religion, nonreligion, and spirituality than in most other places in North America. Michael Wilkinson's chapter in this volume, using interview data from the entire Cascadia region, also reveals that evangelical leaders in Cascadia viewed the region as more open to ideas and supportive of individual freedom. Thus, evangelicals expressed both an oppositional and an accepting relationship with this aspect of the Pacific Northwest.

While general feelings of tension with the region's culture permeated the interviews, only 15 percent of evangelicals indicated they were oppressed and persecuted by it. Instead, the majority of the churches saw the unchurched, open religious market of Cascadia as an opportunity for evangelism (respondents in fourteen churches mentioned this). Over and over again, ministers and lay people observed that Cascadia was a "mission field." A female from a suburban Seattle church said, "As believers, we have to look at this whole liberal community here in Seattle more as an opportunity than as a hardship." As a senior pastor from an urban Seattle megachurch said, "If you wanted to encapsulate what this church wants to be about, it's making God famous in the city of Seattle." In fact, seven senior pastors mentioned that they chose to pastor a church in the Pacific Northwest specifically because they saw it as a mission field (see Michael Wilkinson's chapter, this volume).

One of these pastors compared evangelizing to selling products; just as a salesperson does not want to sell products in a saturated area but rather in an untapped market, so too evangelicals should want to missionize in unchurched areas. In the fourteen US churches we studied in our earlier project (Wellman and Corcoran 2013), evangelicals enthusiastically discussed their ambition to "win" the Pacific Northwest for Christ. For example, a female from a suburban Portland church said, "It's kind of fun in a sense, in that, as a Christian, you have a neat opportunity to share with those other people too." Consistently, they spoke of evangelizing the "unsaved" and churching the "unchurched." In this way, the evangelicals' reaction to the distinctiveness of the Pacific Northwest culture was less about conflict than indicated by Rodney Stark and Roger Finke (2000) and more about viewing it as a challenge and an opportunity to evangelize, that is, more of a cooperative than oppositional relationship.

In pursuit of this aim, churches strategically engaged the culture to attract new people. One senior pastor of an urban Portland church said:

> When you're in [an] urban, highly unchurched context ... people don't have to go to church. And they're definitely not going to go to hear an infomercial about Jesus. So, either it's real and they see it happening, or they sleep in. We engage the culture of today, and we contextualize the gospel to today's culture, which means everything from dress to music to issues and style.

Their services included contemporary worship, an invitation for individuals to come to services "as they are," and an informal dress code. However, sixteen of the churches from which we collected interview data distinguished themselves by making church *not feel like church* – that is, by creating venues that looked like secular sites and services that read like community gatherings rather than church services.

The eight churches that described Cascadia as having an "independent spirit" all identified specific ways they were seeking to work with this spirit to appeal to Pacific Northwesterners. In particular, they noted that their free-thinking spirit made it such that religion could not be "forced down anybody's throat." Respondents observed and contended that direct witnessing typically did not work in the region; instead, they had to evangelize through their behaviour, by going out into the community and forming relationships. A male from a suburban Seattle church said, "And I think because [of] the liberalness of this culture, it has forced us to change how we interact with it by doing community, by doing relationship." One urban Seattle church specifically teaches individuals in its new-member class how to "interact with the Northwest, which is probably the most liberal of the liberal [areas]."

The sentiment expressed by the eight churches was that to evangelize Pacific Northwesterners meant to "walk the walk" (female, Portland suburban megachurch) by going out into the community and helping people. One male respondent from an urban Seattle church summed up this sentiment: "[Church name] is not very evangelical in the general sense of evangelicals. They are a church that just wants to reach out and bring people in, not by telling them about Jesus and going out and whacking them over the head with the Bible, but just by going out and helping the school next door build their new playground." Across these eight churches, the respondents highlighted how this nontraditional, indirect evangelism strategy was contributing to their success in this region.

Qualitative Data: Pacific Northwest Liberal Protestants

Like the evangelicals we studied in 2003–05 (Wellman and Corcoran 2013), the liberal Protestants also identified the Pacific Northwest as secular, unchurched, and/or liberal; these terms were used in all ten of the liberal churches. When the respondents used the term "liberal" to describe the region, it was typically used positively as a reflection of what the respondents themselves believed. For example, a female attendee of a suburban Portland church said: "Being a liberal Christian in Portland or the Northwest is much easier. You connect with people much more easily than you do in some of [the] other parts of the country. We have a lot of friends who are not church people, and we can talk about [political] issues." Although the respondent was Christian, she felt that the liberal nature of her religiosity meant that she had a great deal "in common with the unchurched" population of the region, which she viewed as sharing her liberal views. This is consistent with the PNSS data: 57 percent of Oregon–Washington mainline Protestants agreed or strongly agreed that they had more in common with other American and Canadian residents of the region than they did with people from elsewhere in their country. Respondents across all the liberal churches felt a positive affinity for and cooperative relationship with the liberal environment of the region.

According to many scholars, the beliefs of liberal Protestant churches are found in institutionally embedded cultural, legal, and political norms related to egalitarianism and inclusiveness; because of this, scholars assume that liberal religious communities do not experience a significant degree of tension with the surrounding culture (Stark and Finke 2000; Evans 2003; Wellman 2002). However, while the liberal Protestants in this study did tend to agree with the liberal and political values evident in the region, they also experienced tension with the regional culture as well.

Like the evangelicals, liberal Protestants were in tension with the independent spirit of the Pacific Northwest, the lack of institutional or cultural support for religion, and competition with recreational activities. Respondents in five churches described an individualistic, independent, libertarian spirit in the region. The senior pastor of a Seattle Church described it as "the last bit of the West and 'we don't need you to tell us what to do' kind of thing." Another described it as "very libertarian." According to a senior pastor of an urban Portland church, Pacific Northwesterners "will say, I'm spiritual without being religious, and what they mean is, I'm spiritual, but I don't like all that communal stuff." This aligns with the PNSS data, which shows that the vast majority of Cascadian respondents considered themselves spiritual to some degree and that the majority of Cascadians were not interested in becoming more involved with a religious group in the future. Respondents in these five churches discussed an incongruity between the individualistic Pacific Northwest culture and the communal spirit of liberal churches. The senior pastor of an urban Portland church suggested that churches thrive in the Bible Belt and other places because there is a sense of community there, which does not exist in the Pacific Northwest: "[The] biggest cultural idol that we have to fight is individualism. The church is imbued with community ... And you can't be individual and be a Christian; you have to be part of a community of faith."

The question then for these churches is how to reach out to Pacific Northwesterners seeking spiritual experiences but not within religious institutions. The senior pastor of an urban Portland church said that "what the church needs to do is use the libertarian spirit to invite people in." One way her congregation did this was by having an interfaith ministry for spiritual development directed toward those who say they are spiritual but not religious. She noted that this draws people who otherwise would have "never, ever entertained the notion of being part of the church." Fifty percent of the liberal churches offered some form of interfaith or spiritual (but not religious) ministry, including specific centres, retreats, groups, seminars, and even Buddhist meditation classes.

Other liberal Protestants complained that residents simply avoided formal, institutionalized sacred spaces and that many considered religious services either anachronistic or a waste of time. Respondents across five churches identified the lack of institutional and cultural support for religion in the region as a deterrent that often drove liberal Protestant leaders out of the ministry. For example, one female interviewee from Portland compared the Pacific Northwest to the South and noted that the latter supports going to church on Sundays: "In the south ... you were supposed to go to church, so you went. I think this is a whole different place. I was shocked when we moved here, and I found out that the Boy Scouts held their Christmas tree pickup on a Sunday morning. That never would have happened in the South. They were at church."

The lack of institutional support for religion was also expressed by two liberal pastors who mentioned that there were no special "perks" from the community for clergy, such as automatic memberships in athletic or entertainment clubs, as there were in other regions. Instead, clergy were met with indifference. Evangelicals sensed the same lack of interest but saw it either as an opportunity to evangelize or as the fault of leaders who did not know how to better present the gospel in ways that would engage secular Pacific Northwesterners.

Liberal Protestants also mentioned the pervasive "nature religion" of Cascadia as a challenge. Respondents in 50 percent of the liberal churches in our earlier study (Wellman and Corcoran 2013) expressed some frustration about this, as though they were competing with nature for members. For example, a male respondent from a Seattle church said, "Some people I have invited [to come to church] said that they go hiking in the mountains, and the trees are their religion and their God ... Here, one might say, Gore-Tex is a religion." Again, this mirrors the PNSS survey data, which shows that more Pacific Northwesterners participate in outdoor and environmental activities than religious services. In our earlier study (Wellman and Corcoran 2013), the senior pastor of a Seattle church described this as a type of "personal spirituality," in which individuals experience God "in creation," "the mountains," or "on the water." Yet these respondents (Wellman and Corcoran 2013) also shared the same affinity with the environment. They contended that although nature was a site where one could experience the presence of God, a religious community was important as well. The liberal churches in our earlier work reflected the Pacific Northwest's commitment to the environment – nearly all had created some form of ecojustice ministry or group.

Four Observations on the Precarious Nature of Cascadian Christianity

Cascadia Is Adamantly Secular but Spiritual

While many Cascadians are nonreligious, the region has produced a "reverential naturalism" that moves with and is in some tension with its entrepreneurial spirit, which, while producing innovation and wealth, also threatens the very environment that so many cherish. In that sense, even secularists have a tough time not bowing to the mystery, beauty, and power of Cascadia's ecology. Many who come here already shared or had adopted the libertarian spirit of the region, which is often antagonistic toward those who espouse a need for organized religion. To be sure, most Christian lay people and leaders recognize the spirituality of the natural world, but the churches' identification of nature with the Christian narrative is unlikely to slow the progress of secularization. In particular, there is resistance to religious representatives who tell their fellow Cascadians how to live, much less what to live for. In both our earlier work and the PNSS, many Christians not only were indifferent to conventional religious institutions but in one instance forced a religious leader at a funeral for a loved one "not to use present-tense language about their dead relative." As our project data and previous work confirm, for the majority of Cascadians, the very idea of religion is neither plausible nor practical. Nonetheless, the region enchants many with its beauty and mystery.

Evangelicals Must Prove Their Words in Deeds

In Cascadia, if organized religious faiths are going to be taken seriously, they cannot depend on any established religious institution or broad set of assumptions about the obvious appeal of religion. There is no sacred canopy that contains and sustains faith; if faith is to exist, the canopy must be built in ways that appeal to Cascadia's spiritual-but-not-religious spirit. This challenge forces evangelicals to adjust and innovate. For example, some Cascadian evangelicals have taken on a European type of evangelicalism that is traditional in belief but often radical on issues of the environment and immigration. In that sense, the region is the ultimate baptism by fire for evangelicals – they know that they must have a faith that creates a more humane world, including the passionate need for ecological justice to recognize and preserve the beauty of the world.

Liberal Christians Face a Dilemma

For liberal Christians, there are no simple answers. The question is stark: Should churches simply mimic the secular and progressive values of the moral and cultural landscape of Cascadia? This was a real concern for many of the

Christians involved in the earlier study (Wellman and Corcoran 2013) and those interviewed for this volume. Liberal Protestantism may be the toughest sell in a generally secular and liberal region. Liberal Protestants, in some sense, naturally feel at home in the surrounding society, but they must also differentiate themselves from it. A handful of leaders assumed "that in ten years we will no longer exist." There are, of course, predictable consequences of these shifts. Downtown churches in Cascadia have been known to be sources of care to the "least and last" in these cities, but there are fewer donors and volunteers to show hospitality or care to those in deep need. But for some, the prophetic Christian message creates opportunities to understand and undo the privileges enjoyed by middle-class, white liberals and to become active on issues of immigration, social inequality, and the dangers of modern economies to the environment. Moreover, among liberal Christians – first in Canada, but increasingly in the United States – there is a growing consensus that all settlers in this region live on land stolen from Indigenous peoples. For some, and perhaps many, the knowledge of this cultural displacement haunts an uneasy liberal conscience.

Cascadia Will Not Be Conquered

Chief Seattle knew this best. A Homeric figure, Seattle, whose tribe, the Duwamish, are still not recognized, became Catholic. He did so to save his people; he knew the European colonizers had won the day. But the ultimate irony is that this triumph made the very environment, which serves so many so well, suffer. Residents of Cascadia South and North grapple with different challenges, but a concern for the environment unites settlers and Indigenous peoples alike. Even though the stakes are high, perhaps these shared interests are being expressed too late; perhaps settlers will fail to learn from Indigenous peoples, especially those in Canada, who are forging ahead with spiritual traditions that embody more respectful approaches to the natural world. All of this remains to be seen; the region's destiny has yet to be determined.

Notes

Acknowledgment: Part of this chapter is reprinted and adapted with permission. It appeared in James K. Wellman Jr. and Katie E. Corcoran, "Religion and Regional Culture: Embedding Religious Commitment within Place," *Sociology of Religion* 74, 4 (2013): 496–520, courtesy Oxford University Press.

1   This is based on James Wellman's research on local Seattle evangelical churches, where he has found that some accept and sometimes affirm the LGBTQ+ community, in partial and sometimes full inclusion.

2   For a rich description of the Nones in this region, see Sarah Wilkins-Laflamme's chapter in this volume.
3   Following Bebbington (1989) and Noll (2001), we define "evangelical" as the umbrella term for conservative Christians in American culture.
4   We define liberal Protestant congregations according to a distinct set of ideological characteristics. They generally propose that Jesus is a model of radical inclusiveness, justify themselves by reason as well as by tradition or scripture, and leave decision making about faith or personal morality to the individual. They also have a liberal theology that advocates for the concerns and rights of the LGBTQ+ community and supports justice causes such as peace, ending homelessness, and ecological stewardship (Ammerman 1997, 2005; Wellman 1999, 2002).
5   This data is not publicly available.
6   For archival and interview data, see https://www.uvic.ca/research/centres/csrs/.
7   This data is not publicly available.

REFERENCES

Ammerman, Nancy. 1997. *Congregation and Community.* New Brunswick, NJ: Rutgers University Press.
—. 2005. *Pillars of Faith: American Congregations and Their Partners.* Berkeley: University of California Press.
Bebbington, David W. 1989. *Evangelicalism in Modern Britain: A History from the 1730s to the 1980s.* London: Routledge.
Castleberry, Joseph. 2015. *The New Pilgrims: How Immigrants Are Renewing America's Faith and Values.* Franklin, TN: Worthy Books.
Evans, John H. 2003. "The Creation of a Distinct Subcultural Identity and Denominational Growth." *Journal for the Scientific Study of Religion* 42 (3): 467–77.
Killen, Patricia O'Connell, and Mark Silk, eds. 2004. *Religion and Public Life in the Pacific Northwest: The None Zone.* Walnut Creek, CA: AltaMira Press.
Laird, Lance D. 2004. "Religions of the Pacific Rim in the Pacific Northwest." In *Religion and Public Life in the Pacific Northwest: The None Zone,* edited by Patricia O'Connell Killen and Mark Silk, 107–37. Walnut Creek, CA: AltaMira Press.
Noll, Mark A. 2001. *American Evangelical Christianity: An Introduction.* Oxford: Blackwell.
Pew Research Center. 2013. *Canada's Changing Religious Landscape.* https://www.pewforum.org/2013/06/27/canadas-changing-religious-landscape/.
—. 2015. *America's Changing Religious Landscape.* https://www.pewforum.org/2015/05/12/americas-changing-religious-landscape/.
Shibley, Mark A. 2004. "Secular, but Spiritual in the Pacific Northwest." In *Religion and Public Life in the Pacific Northwest: The None Zone,* edited by Patricia O'Connell Killen and Mark Silk, 139–68. Walnut Creek, CA: AltaMira Press.
—. 2011. "Sacred Nature: Earth-Based Spirituality as Popular Religion in the Pacific Northwest." *Journal for the Study of Religion, Nature and Culture* 5 (2): 164–85.
Silk, Mark. 2005. "Religion and Region in American Public Life." *Journal for the Scientific Study of Religion* 44 (3): 265–70.
Silk, Mark, and Andrew Walsh. 2008. *One Nation Divisible: How Regional Religious Differences Shape American Politics.* Lanham, MD: Rowman and Littlefield.
Stark, Rodney, and Roger Finke. 2000. *Acts of Faith: Explaining the Human Side of Religion.* Berkeley: University of California Press.
Wellman, James K. Jr. 1999. *The Gold Coast Church and the Ghetto: Christ and Culture in Mainline Protestantism.* Chicago: University of Illinois Press.

—. 2002. "Religion without a Net: Strictness in the Religious Practices of West Coast Urban Liberal Christian Congregations." *Review of Religious Research* 42 (2): 184–99.

—. 2008. *Evangelical vs. Liberal: The Clash of Christian Cultures in the Pacific Northwest.* New York: Oxford University Press.

Wellman, James, and Katie Corcoran. 2013. "Religion and Regional Culture: Embedding Religious Commitment within Place." *Sociology of Religion* 74: 496–520.

9 Evangelicals in the Pacific Northwest: Navigating the "None Zone"

Michael Wilkinson

For evangelical Christians, Cascadia is a mission field, and numerous conferences, podcasts, theological journals, and books have attempted to help evangelicals understand the region, engage with it culturally, and plant churches. The term "mission field" carries significant valence for evangelicals as a place of both opportunity and risk. It is a bounded space where the commitment to the gospel expressed in evangelical belief and practice is often in tension with the dominant ethos (Edgell 2012). In this essay, I discuss the distinctive ways evangelicals have come to articulate their religious lives in the "None Zone." To create a sense of community not only with other Christians but also with members of groups they have not engaged with much in the past – such as LGBTQ+ advocacy groups, environmental movements, and refugee and immigrant organizations – the evangelical communities of Cascadia North and Cascadia South are in the process of expressing a regionally specific form of Christianity. This form of evangelicalism is one strand in a worldwide Christian family and therefore part of evangelicalism's ongoing change and development. Whether the Cascadian form of evangelicalism will influence the movement in Canada and the United States more broadly, or even globally, remains to be seen.

Evangelicalism has been defined in various ways but, traditionally, the scholarly literature focuses on evangelicalism as a subculture within Protestantism and refers to qualities that are oriented around renewal, revival, or reform of some kind (Balmer 2006). Evangelicalism has also been defined according to a range of characteristics that reflect essential beliefs and practices, including crucicentrism (the centrality of salvation gained through the death of Jesus Christ), biblicism (the authority of the Bible), conversionism (the importance of an individual transformative experience), and activism (an emphasis on spreading this form of Christianity through evangelism and congregational participation) (Bebbington 1989). Scholarly research often focuses on the political dimensions of evangelicalism, highlighting its conservative political and social alliances and commitments that put the movement in conflict with dominant social trends (Smith 1998). While evangelicalism is mostly known for this conservative trend, there is a small progressive and socially engaged form that goes back to the nineteenth century. This more progressive or "left"-leaning evangelicalism is drawing the attention of scholars such as Joseph O. Baker and Gerardo Marti (2020), who examine how widespread it is and whether there is a resurgence of social concern and political activity centred on social issues such as immigration and the environment. They also examine voting behaviour, noting that these evangelicals did not support Trump. Baker and Marti offer context for making sense of the evangelicals interviewed in this study who hold progressive social and political views in line with the evangelical left in the United States. While the evangelical left has declined in the United States from 15.1 percent in 1998 to 11.9 percent in 2018 (Baker and Marti 2020, 132), about 20 percent of evangelicals in the western states can be identified as liberal or left-leaning in their social and political views.[1] While the evangelical left is declining throughout the United States, there is a considerable group of progressive evangelicals in Cascadia.

Scholars have also shown that evangelicals share a common subculture in Canada and the United States; they have theological similarities but social and political differences. For example, Sam Reimer (2003) has demonstrated that while there are some regional differences in Canada and the United States (e.g., evangelicals are more conservative in the South than in the western states), similarities among evangelicals across all regions in Canada and the United States reveal a high level of consistency for religious identity, practices, beliefs, moral boundaries, and social attitudes. However, regional variation within Canada or the United States is not as significant as the variation between the two countries: Canadian evangelicals are more irenic (i.e., less combative, inclined to use reason to reconcile theological differences), less nationalistic, less aligned with a political ideology, and more inclined to practise what they believe (Reimer 2003, 118–42). Irenicism, argues Reimer, is the key characteristic that differentiates the two countries, and Canadian evangelicals demonstrate higher levels of tolerance and higher levels of comfort with nonevangelicals than their American counterparts. Reimer's conclusions are supported in our project data, which shows that the Pacific Northwest region, in general, is more progressive than other regions in Canada and the United States. However, the border that separates the two countries also shows that evangelicals in Canada are more progressive than their counterparts in the United States. What Reimer's research does not examine, however, are the social and cultural processes that illustrate how evangelicals negotiate boundaries and borders, reconsider theological beliefs, and attempt to "live" or practise evangelicalism, which this essay addresses (see Edgell 2012). More specifically, evangelicals in Cascadia are negotiating new boundaries of belief and practice within the context of the increasingly secular backdrop of what some of my colleagues in this volume call the "Cascadia consensus." For evangelicals, engaging nonevangelicals raises questions about the nature of evangelicalism, prompting the development of new forms of community and propelling them to consider issues of diversity.

This essay draws on extensive discussions among team members about a large data set of archival material, survey data, oral histories, focus groups, and interviews on Cascadia.[2] More specifically, it draws on insights from key interviews with leaders of churches and directors of ministries in Portland, Oregon; Seattle, Washington; Vancouver, British Columbia; and Victoria, British Columbia. These interviews were conducted in 2017 as part of the "Religion, Spirituality, Secularity and Society in the Pacific Northwest" project. Interviews with evangelical leaders, as key informants, offer us insight into the region, the congregations and ministries they direct, and the types of issues Cascadian evangelicals generally face in ministry.[3]

Pastor Smith of Victoria, British Columbia, in his late fifties, was raised in the Roman Catholic tradition but disaffiliated as a teenager only to return to Christianity later. He was pastoring an evangelical congregation seeking to leave its denomination. The origins of the initiative to separate were rooted in the issue of women in leadership but increasingly became focused on his (comparatively progressive) view of the Bible and LGBTQ+ people.

Pastor Evan, from Vancouver, British Columbia, pastored a predominately Chinese congregation. He lived his entire life in the Pacific Northwest and likewise directed a ministry attempting to promote human flourishing in the city through a variety of activities that he understood to be rooted in Christianity but not overtly oriented around specific missions or belief statements.

Jason worked in Portland with a parachurch organization that began in the 1960s as a traditional evangelistic ministry but has transitioned into an organization that works across church traditions to create networks and a sense of community that is part of the cultural ethos of the city.

Pastor Shannon, originally from Florida, regularly preached in a large congregation in Portland. She discussed how her work as a pastor was at odds with more conservative evangelical churches and yet was situated in a cultural context where women's roles were central to the church.

Pastor Armando was in his late thirties and part of a large, multistaff nondenominational congregation. His work was primarily to build community in the city of Portland, working with individuals who were not affiliated with any church and with groups that were marginalized in some way because of race or social class. Building community meant developing new networks and partners, including other faith-based organizations, congregations, and civic organizations.

Pastor Novak, also in his late thirties, led a Pentecostal congregation in Portland. He clearly articulated the challenges of being a Christian in Cascadia but also the ways ministry is redefined to fit the context.

Finally, Donald, from Seattle, worked with evangelicals and had lived in the Pacific Northwest for sixty years. He worked as director of a parachurch organization that focused on theological education. He also spoke regularly in churches throughout the region.

To develop my interpretation of the distinctive ways that these evangelicals articulated their religious lives in the "None Zone," I use a grounded-theory approach described by Kathy Charmaz (2006). My interpretation of the experiences of these pastors and their communities is guided by the following questions: How did the interviewees describe sources or points of actual or potential contention for evangelical self-understanding, practices, and self-definition? What activities, processes, or contextual factors have led to the emergence of these issues as points of contention and reflection for evangelicals? How has their approach to these issues changed over time? What are the implications of these issues for Cascadian evangelicalism? I read each interview to understand the social conditions of Cascadia, how the participants responded or acted in response to a range of often controversial issues, and the implications of those actions. My reading of the interviews is informed by the research questions of the "Religion, Spirituality, Secularity and Society in the Pacific Northwest" project and the findings from the data. Hence, I wanted to know how Cascadian evangelicals imagined Cascadia as a distinct geographical and perhaps religious zone. I also reflect on how evangelicals interpreted and responded to this cultural context and to what extent these movements and participants are embedded within the larger evangelical world in the region, the United States, and Canada.

I have chosen to use a grounded-theory approach because it allows me not only to attend to the pastors' interpretation of their experience of the region, through what they say, but also allows me to get at the "lived religion" of Cascadian evangelicalism. Lived religion is a theoretical orientation that focuses on the cultural qualities of everyday religious experience, including the contested qualities of religion across a number of borders and boundaries of social life (Edgell 2012; see also Block and Marks, in this volume). The participants' responses were rooted in the everyday interactions of evangelicals, their churches, beliefs, practices, and sentiments, or what can be understood as "lived religion." In this essay, I use comments from the interviewees to develop an argument about their definition of and response to the themes of the None Zone, evangelicalism, community, and diversity.

Defining the None Zone

Throughout the interviews, Cascadia was described and discussed in multiple ways, including as a secular place, a spiritual place, a naturally beautiful area, a place to make money, and a place where people are lonely, looking for friends, and seeking community. It was also referred to as a region that was different from the rest of the country, whether that country is the United States or Canada. As several other authors in this book observe, participants consistently framed the region as being unlike anywhere else. That difference was often attributed to the region's relation to the mountains and the coast but also to its being a diverse and not overly religious region, at least when it comes to Christian identification and participation in congregations. While phrases such as "post-Christian" and "secular" were used, there was also reference to the Pacific Northwest as the "None Zone," a phrase that entered the public discourse in the region (among evangelicals and others) after the publication of *Religion and Public Life in the Pacific Northwest: The None Zone* (Killen and Silk 2004; see Mark Silk's chapter in this volume, in which he reflects on the implications of new data for the ways he and Killen framed the region in 2004). Interviewees used the "None Zone" and terms captured in Christopher B. James's *Church Planting in Post-Christian Soil* (2017). James's book is based on his research in Seattle on different models of churches seeking to be "mission churches" and how evangelical churches and leaders are trying to convey their religious convictions in ways that have affinities with the cultural ethos. In particular, using the language of the frontier,[4] James explores how the region is a mission outpost for evangelicals. What is of interest here is the theological justifications the seven evangelicals used for planting churches and practising ministry in a secular region that is unlike anywhere else. Their rationale, according to James, was that, if they were going to be effective, they could not simply provide a conventional evangelical message. Because the Cascadia consensus is increasingly identified with a certain kind of secular spirit, they had to think about the theological reasons behind what they were doing; this forced them to reflect on their understanding of the region's Nones, and their own minority status, in ways that would not have been common before (see Chapter 8, this volume).

Each of the interviewees emphasized the beauty of the natural environment, especially the mountains and the water. Donald said of the people who lived there: "Many of them say, 'I love the beauty of this place.' Mount Rainier on a sunny day is kind of hard to beat, and Puget Sound is pretty incredible, and you can live on an island, take a ferry, and be at work. So, there is a mystery that's there. A mystique, so to speak." Pastor Shannon said: "I think, of course, you can't talk about the Pacific Northwest without talking about its unique, majestic beauty as well. Just how gorgeous it is, how green it is, how lush it is, how huge the mountains are." Linked with the natural beauty is a broad openness to working for the common good, being open-minded and tolerant, key qualities of an irenic evangelicalism. Jason said: "I love living in Portland. I think there's a willingness to work for the common good ... They [people in the region generally] came here from other parts of the country for the natural beauty and to be in a place that's pretty open-minded, and tolerant." Speaking about the beauty of the region is one way that evangelicals identify with Cascadia and its inhabitants.

There were various ways in which the interviewees described the region as unique. For example, Pastor Smith said: "The sense of being out here in the West, being somewhat alienated, somewhat ignored, somewhat underappreciated, somewhat not treated like we really are Canada ... that hurts our pride because Canada thinks it's Ontario and Quebec." Pastor Shannon said:

> There's a different spirit on the West Coast that is, it's an adventure, pioneering spirit that I think, at least as someone who's been a transplant, is evident to me. People are independent. So, there's independent thinking, there's deep thoughtfulness, there's less tribal mentality, and more, you know, just independent thought, which is cultivated in different spaces, and I just think there's also space and freedom for that to happen.

Donald said: "The nature of the West Coast – it's a highly transitional place that has weak roots, in a sense, that have not allowed the kind of stability that you find in other parts of the United States, and that is its weakness, but it's also its strength because it has high adaptability inclinations to move with where the seasons take it." Pastor Novak described Cascadia as a place different from the rest of America, but he also thought the future of the country would look more like Cascadia (see Silk, this volume): "I would say that Portland represents (and Cascadia) the beginning of post-Christian America. So, it's just the front end of the post-Christian story in America. America in fifty years is going to be completely different than it is now, and whatever you're seeing here now will be in Kansas in ten years." This is one way that evangelicals speak about regional differences, as noted above by Sam Reimer (2003). The view that evangelicalism in Cascadia is the direction that all evangelicalism will go is still to be determined. However, if evangelicalism follows previous trends, it is likely that it will remain a regionalized form that is characteristic of the Pacific Northwest.

There is also a sense that Cascadia is notoriously nonreligious. Sometimes "spirituality" is identified as a replacement for religion, but just as often, one encounters a strong antireligious sensibility. Pastor Evan said, "You know that a lot of the Pacific Northwest or Cascadia is very vehemently against religion."

The interviewees were, however, mostly positive about this quality, believing that it was evidence of an openness to what they were doing; they often described antireligious sentiment as being open to spirituality but closed to organized religion. As Pastor Armando said: "What I've experienced is that we're a highly religious region; that our primary religion is our humanity; that we believe that if you can create the right structures, if we are more generous and more patient and more loving, we could create a true Cascadia." Pastor Armando believed the spirituality of the region was in line with his understanding of evangelicalism and that there were opportunities to work together to make Cascadia a more generous and loving place for the people who live there.

Participants also noted that evangelicals were politically similar to others in the region in that they did not support President Trump. American evangelicals in our study distanced themselves from the view that "evangelical" means "Republican." Pastor Novak said: "Evangelicalism in the States is more diverse than our media outlets have portrayed them. There are progressive evangelicals and conservative evangelicals. The assumption that all evangelicals voted for Trump is not correct." Pastor Shannon said:

> Obviously, institutions [evangelical churches] like ours are not able to politically express our views or anything like that from the pulpit. But I would say, at least for those of us who are hopefully thoughtful followers of the teachings of Jesus and the way of Jesus, that in this cultural moment, we're looking at what people are calling Christianity and what they're calling evangelicalism, especially by way of Trump and his whole administration, and we're saying, "That doesn't represent anything that we would see, understand, or have studied in the scriptures. It's nothing that we understand of the way or the life of Jesus." So, in this cultural moment, we are looking at our political climate and the language that's now been woven into this and saying, "That's not who we are."

Jason said: "I can't think of one of the larger evangelical churches in Portland that are out there rallying the vote for Trump." It also shows how evangelicals are attuned to the political views of the people of Cascadia generally.

Redefining Evangelicalism

As noted earlier, Sam Reimer (2003) argues that evangelicalism is a subculture shared between Canada and the United States. However, as others argue, evangelicalism is also a worldwide movement (Hutchinson and Wolffe 2012). As such, the tradition is neither monolithic nor homogenous. It shares similarities when it comes to core beliefs, but there are also differences between evangelicals when you look at their histories and theologies. For example, Baptists, Pentecostals, Mennonites, and Wesleyans all self-identify with the evangelical movement, and yet they have very different histories and theologies. Evangelicalism varies from region to region and country to country as well.

Much of the concern about evangelicalism revolves around the broader cultural and political understanding of the movement. In a slightly cheeky way, Pastor Novak said: "You know, I'm not an evangelical. That's the great thing about being a Pentecostal; you get to sidestep that word a lot." Although this is not the place to explore in detail the relationship between Pentecostals, fundamentalists, and evangelicals (see Wacker 2001; Hutchinson and Wolf 2012), Pastor Novak's words demonstrate the tension, if not pain, of association experienced by some evangelicals. Self-identifying as Pentecostal might not get Novak out of the conundrum of association with evangelicalism, especially when the differences are lost among the public. Nonetheless, Novak's strategy of self-identifying as a Pentecostal, a particular type of evangelical, is one way of attempting to address the problem he identified with evangelicalism in the region. Whether it has implications for the rest of the country or throughout the region is unknown.

Pastor Novak contended that work among immigrants and refugees differentiated evangelicalism in Cascadia from the rest of America. He also discussed his work on environmental issues, or what he called "creation care," as an important theological and ecclesiological practice. He argued that these types of activities aligned him with what he called a "socially progressive evangelicalism." He said: "The kingdom of God is not coming on the back of donkeys or the back of elephants. It's not going to come because somebody has the right politics. Politics can never bring about the fullness of the Kingdom of God. And our church is radically diverse when it comes to politics." For Novak, evangelicalism could be progressive on a range of issues without aligning itself to any political party. Jason said something similar when he described his work with immigrants and refugees; he made the point that to be progressive does not mean you have to give up traditional interpretations of Christianity: "Evangelical churches in Portland are conservative theologically when it comes to a view of scripture, but not so much politically."

However, it appears that evangelicals in other parts of the United States are not so sure that a progressive stance on issues about the environment or immigrants is possible without giving up on traditional evangelical beliefs. Donald said one implication of evangelicals holding progressive social views on immigration and the environment is abandonment by other evangelicals, including denominational organizations in the rest of the country. This has led to many new nondenominational congregations in the region, according to Donald. More specifically, there has been an attempt by evangelicals in the region to distance themselves from the wider and largely negative public perception of evangelicalism, while not abandoning the core of evangelical theology. Of course, the need to distance the evangelical movement from Trump and a particular political party is not so urgent in Canada, where evangelicals have demonstrated a more irenic and less ideological approach to politics (see Reimer 2003).

There are evangelicals, however, who are questioning the traditional beliefs of evangelical theology, especially how some evangelicals interpret the Bible and apply it to issues like the role of women in the ministry and marriage. Pastor Smith discussed how the congregation he now leads initially left the denomination over the issue of women in leadership. The origin of that schism was based on an interpretation of the Bible that he and members of his congregation found indefensible. Increasingly, Smith and his congregation are questioning the theology of their denomination, which does not allow LGBTQ+ people to participate in the congregation. Smith said:

> But these things are all theological at the core. The core pure-theory beliefs that make us what we are and also that would have us say, "We're going to part company," the core issue of parting company at [the other evangelical church] was not women in ministry, and it was not the question of gay membership or anything like that. It is an actual deeper issue on what we think the Bible is, what we think revelation is.

Smith went on to critique the way evangelicals understand the Bible as some type of revelation that is simply to be read and understood, not realizing that it is always interpreted: "And that's the dividing line. That's the core of what we're backing away from, which is what I call Bible worship."

Whether the move to redefine evangelicalism is mostly in response to the political and cultural context of Cascadia or a shift among evangelicals to rethink what it means to be a practising Christian in the region is difficult to assess. While the public criticism of US evangelicals' support for Trump may have played a role, it was most likely the impact of a tendency within evangelicalism to contextualize beliefs and practices in local regions such as Cascadia. However, theological debates cannot be separated from material interests, and it is important to remember that denominations also have buildings, programs, staff, and budgets to consider. Evangelicalism and its subcultural repertoire create boundaries that protect both the theological and the material.

Viewing Cascadia as a "mission field" includes a process of theological reflection, ministry evaluation, and contextualization of practice in relation to the predominantly nonreligious population. Pastor Shannon said:

> I think it's a hard moment, because, you know, in the theological framework, evangelical is what we are. There is an expression of that, which is true. But it's

been so distorted by people, which is what always happens – distorted by agenda, by the political climate, by all these things – that now ["evangelical"] feels like a cheap, ineffective word to use when you're trying to express what it actually meant. Yes, it's cringeworthy because I think those who are bearing the name "evangelical" ... we don't even know that you believe the same thing, even remotely. You're not reading the same book.

Here, we get a sense of how evangelicals are thinking about the cultural and political context but also how it is tied to a particular interpretation of the Bible. Evangelicals living in Cascadia are engaging in theological reflection and contextualization of belief and practice, and they're thinking of the place as a mission field.

Creating Community

Brian Steensland and Philip Goff argue in *The New Evangelical Social Engagement* (2014) that evangelicals in the United States have increasingly become concerned about a range of issues on the environment, economic development, urban renewal, racial reconciliation, and human rights. Drawing on primarily historical and sociological case studies, Steensland and Goff's edited volume brings together a series of articles that show how evangelicalism is changing and what the implications of that change are for religion, politics, and civic engagement. The interviews here echo some of the claims made by Steensland and Goff, especially the way evangelicals want to create a sense of community with the people of the region. According to Steensland and Goff, left-leaning evangelicals believe that a stronger community is good for everyone, not just for evangelicals. However, evangelicals not only believe they can play an important role in bringing people together to serve the needs of the region; they are also taking steps to build community relations, networks, and programs in conjunction with existing faith-based groups and new initiatives. Jason said, "What if we tried to build a greater sense of trust and camaraderie between the evangelical community and the community as a whole?" He went on to discuss how important it is for evangelicals and religious Nones to work together in ways that can contribute to stronger communities.

Pastor Shannon described three ministries her church was involved in that were attempting to make Portland a better place. First, she described the work initiated by a woman in the church who had created a nonprofit organization that became well known for its work with refugees. The organization drew on the congregation for volunteers, who put together supply kits for refugees that included everything from kitchen supplies to bedding and furniture. The organization then worked with refugees to facilitate their transition to Portland. Pastor Shannon also talked about the congregation's work in foster care, helping children find homes where they can be cared for but also working with foster parents to support them. She said: "One of our pastors leads a ministry called Foster Parent's Night Out where we give the foster parents once a month a night of rest, where they take the kids, work with them. They do crafts and all that crazy stuff." The work with foster care included educating, funding, volunteering, and training. The third ministry revolved around supporting sustainable projects throughout the world like fish farms, schooling, and development.

The work with immigrants and refugees may be regional in the United States as Cascadian evangelicals develop new programs and activities to support immigrants and refugees. However, in Canada, evangelicals supported the national government's response to the Syrian refugee crisis in 2015 by taking in a large number of Syrian refugees. On occasion, there are conservative voices in Canada who disagree with immigration policies, but those views are not widely shared among evangelicals in Canada (Reimer 2003; Bean 2014).

Donald talked about how he had worked to facilitate community building through practices such as prison reform and urban renewal. For Donald, the work flowed from what he described as his "relational" theological orientation, which guided him to ask, How can we come together to create a neighbourhood? He said:

> As the outwork of my theology – the nature of neighborhood and community and knowing and being known, and that people who are different – getting together is better than [being with] people who are the same. So, to have very different people sitting at the table generally is quite an exciting thing. And people end up learning from each other and walking out, saying, "we should do something together," and they actually do that.

Working together is also important. Pastor Novak said:

> We really are intentional in trying to work alongside other churches that are attempting to bear the witness of Jesus in our world. In that sense, [we're] a very ecumenically minded church ... There's a number of churches here in Portland who work a lot together that are rooted in that kind of evangelical tradition but have some elasticity outside of that.

Jason saw the work he does as an extension of his evangelical commitment, but he made it clear that he did not see what he did as somehow distinct from evangelism or, traditionally, what is referred to as "sharing the gospel" with others. In other words, for Jason, "good works" or acts of serving others were not separate from what it means to be an evangelical. Nor did he prioritize "preaching" or "telling people about Jesus" over any social action. Cascadian evangelicals do not want to be known as the kind of Christians who are simply interested in "saving" people for the afterlife and are not concerned about "this world" and how people can live and flourish. Jason said:

> Clearly, we're called to love our neighbour as yourself, to work for justice and common good kind of issues. So, can we do all those things without abandoning our understanding of scripture and our desire to share what we would believe is a life-changing message about Jesus Christ? Can we, though, throw our lot in with the City of Portland, can we build trust with our LGBTQ+ community, can we repent of and acknowledge huge weaknesses and apologize for all kinds of things that we've done and not done, and yet maintain our distinctiveness? ... We don't want to be known so much for what we're against, but rather what we're for.

Pastor Evan was even more upfront: "No proselytization. You can't just drop an Alpha course [a program that introduces non-Christians to the basics of Christian belief and practice] on them, right? I think that's mean. That's nasty."

As evangelicals, they wanted to see their communities become good places for all people to live. Pastor Armando said: "Let's invite new people who don't know the gospel, who don't know Jesus, to be a part of a family and a community that's about love and about new life and is centred around Jesus." This is considered "good news" by evangelicals for the people of Cascadia. Evangelicals want to be known for providing care for the people who live there. Proselytization, for these evangelicals, is not "good news" if it only means "saving souls" for the next life and not working to make this life better. This approach means making the region a more hospitable place for all inhabitants, regardless of whether they attend their church.

Diversity

When interviewees brought up the topic of diversity, their concerns revealed that racial and ethnic differences, women in ministry, world religions, Indigenous peoples, and members of LGBTQ+ communities were contested among evangelicals. Many scholars have explored evangelical approaches to these areas. For example, Gerardo Marti and Michael O. Emerson (2014) note that evangelicals are polarized about race or, in many cases, largely ignore it. Gender and women in evangelical ministry are explored in the work of R. Marie Griffith (2000). Robert Wuthnow (2005) pays attention to how the churches have responded to immigrants with a range of responses, from embracing them to rejecting them. Some current research is examining the relationship between evangelicals and Indigenous peoples, from how they were evangelized by settlers (Tarango 2014) to the ways evangelicalism has taken root among Indigenous groups (Clatterbuck 2017). LGBTQ+ issues are divisive among evangelicals, among whom there is much debate and discussion, especially over appropriate responses. Responses range along a continuum from outright rejection of LGBTQ+ people to "welcome but do not affirm" to "welcome and affirm" (Jennings 2017). These issues are polarizing among evangelicals with some differences between regions and between Canada and the United States (Reimer 2011; Bean 2014). Responses to diversity highlight differences among evangelicals in Cascadia North and Cascadia South, where Canadians consistently adopt a more progressive approach.

When asked questions about race and ethnicity, the interviewees responded in ways that suggested they were aware that these issues needed to be addressed but were often at a loss as to how to offer what they thought were adequate solutions. For example, Portland was described in the interviews and focus groups as a white city, which was reflected in the churches. It was clear during the interviews that the assumption was that to be white was to be affluent. Portland continues to reflect its early history of racial divisions. Pastor Novak said:

> If you drive through my zip code, it is the whitest, most affluent, progressive neighbourhood that you will ever go through. And you will see more Black Lives Matter signs than anywhere else you go. And when you talk to African American communities in our city, there is profound resentment toward white progressivism, for naming Black Lives Matter, but "Man, we could never live in your neighbourhood."

Pastor Novak described his own church as a predominately white church; nonetheless, he talked about race and invited members of the Black community to come and worship with them.

Pastor Armando discussed the long history of racism in Oregon and the difficulties for all non-white people in the state. He said:

> Yeah, I mean, the history of Oregon is pretty ugly. We were founded as a white utopia. It was illegal to really even live here as [a] person of colour until the railroad was coming through, and we changed the laws for Chinese workers. I mean, this area is just brutal. African Americans weren't allowed to cross Martin Luther King Boulevard until after the Vanport flood.

Pastor Shannon talked about the difficulties of trying to respond to racial differences and working together. She said: "We're actually growing in diversity, which is really odd. And that's been a newer thing, and it's our desire. It's just been a really slow boat, because you know Portland's predominantly white. It's hypersegregated in so many ways; it's operating just so individualistically, too. So that's been pretty difficult." The strong emphasis in public and political discourse on fraught interactions between African American and white communities leaves other racial minorities – especially people of Asian descent – feeling they are not part of the discussion. Pastor Novak said: "If you want to talk about people that feel really marginalized, the Asian communities here in Portland feel like they've been completely forgotten in the diversity conversation. Which they have. I know a guy who left Portland because, in his own words, he was the wrong kind of minority."

It does not appear to be any better for Indigenous people. Most of the interviewees were aware of some Indigenous Christians in the United States who were trying to raise awareness of problems within Indigenous communities or engage in theological discussions about what it means to be Indigenous and evangelical. However, none of the evangelical interviewees – in Canada or the United States – were themselves involved with any Indigenous groups. Most were aware of the settler history and its impact on Indigenous peoples (see chapters by Chelsea Horton and Suzanne Crawford O'Brien, this volume). Most of our interviewees commented that they had been in a setting of some kind where a local welcome or prayer was offered that recognized the land as historically associated with Indigenous peoples. Jason talked about someone he knew who had converted to evangelical Christianity and along the way experienced tension about his identity as an Indigenous person and evangelical Christian. The man said, "Wow, in doing so, unintentionally I lost my Native culture; and what does it mean for me to fully embrace my Native culture? Can I do that and still be a follower of Jesus?"

Evangelical engagement with people who identify as Muslim, Hindu, Buddhist, or any other non-Christian religion seemed to occur infrequently, and when it did, it took the form of individual rather than congregational interactions. Pastor Novak, for example, said he often worked alongside people of other religions on environmental issues but not with his congregation. He noted that it was easy for him as an individual, but for his congregation to partner with another group would be more difficult because, he believed, the two groups did not share the same mission. As a result, he said, from "a missional approach, we're trying to help people experience and encounter the life of Jesus, and so we partner with other communities that have the same orientation." On the other hand, Pastor Armando talked about the way his congregation worked alongside Muslims, especially in organizations that bring them together to support refugees and resettlement. He said: "So, we do a lot of work with them, and a lot of our friends who are Muslim coming from other places ... We'll do, like, [another evangelical church in town just did] an ecumenical thing with Muslim neighbours. We got to be a part of that. It was pretty cool." These examples illustrate the ways Cascadian evangelicals were crossing borders and creating new boundaries between themselves and nonevangelicals in the region. Crossing borders and boundary making reveal the social and cultural processes evangelicals are engaging in.

Gender issues such as equality for women in ministry are still problematic among evangelicals. Indeed, in some cases, the problem has led congregations to leave a denomination and become independent; in others, it has led congregations to seek out a female pastor or staff member. All seven of the interviewees held views that women on staff should also be able to preach publicly. Pastor Shannon described in some detail her experience when she was part of a conservative evangelical church in the US South in which women pastors were not allowed to preach. In Portland, she regularly preached in a rotation with other staff. She said: "It's only been in the last couple years that I've started preaching. I feel like, at least the culture of our church is hyper-responsive to me, as a woman, in a way that's just like a no-brainer to them. It's not an odd thing." She spent considerable time working with women in the church, offering pastoral care, leadership development for women, crisis care, and hospital visitation. The executive leadership team of the congregation, however, was all men. They would consult with her on occasion about new developments, seeking her opinion regarding the possible impact on her ministry.

Sexual diversity for evangelicals in Cascadia is still controversial, and while the interviewees, with one exception, expressed a desire to build better relationships with LGBTQ+ people, the churches took a "welcome but not affirm" position, meaning that LGBTQ+ people were welcome to attend their congregations, but pastors were not allowed to preside at same-sex marriages, if asked, and leadership positions were restricted to heterosexual and celibate LGBTQ+ members. Pastor Shannon said: "We do teach with conviction that we believe marriage is [between] one man, one woman, for life." Jason said:

> The fact that we maybe wouldn't feel comfortable performing a gay or lesbian wedding doesn't mean that we're going to be talking about it from the pulpit and making it a big deal. It just means that we're going to quietly, humbly, say: "You know what? Our view of scripture doesn't let us go there." But it doesn't mean that we are anti-LGBTQ+.

Some of the interviewees believed that changing their view would mean adopting a theologically liberal position that would lead to congregational decline. Pastor Novak, for example, said: "I've had three or four friends who have become open and affirming theologically and practically, and interestingly enough, the church dies pretty quick after that. The theme of theological liberalism has generally been accommodation to culture." He went on to say that if "we have no theological reason to actually be a community of faith, the church just becomes an enemy to getting my mimosa and brunch on Sunday."

Pastor Novak placed a line in the sand on LGBTQ+ issues, reflecting the historical patriarchal ordering of men and women along with Christianity's traditional definition of marriage between one man and one woman. However, his view stood in contrast with that of Pastor Smith, who was moving toward a "welcome and affirm" position with his congregation. Adopting this position meant they would most likely separate from the denomination and become independent. As with his position on women in ministry, Pastor Smith had shifted to what he argued was a more evangelical and Wesleyan biblical view that considers the authority of scripture, tradition, reason, and experience. In the end, said Pastor Smith, "Gay marriage is very conservative. You know you're not questioning the institution of marriage when you're endorsing that, right?" Clearly, these two interviewees represented different views about marriage, sexuality, and what it means to be evangelical.

The Meaning of "Evangelical"

Evangelicalism in Cascadia is changing as evangelical leaders engage with the shifting cultural landscape. As a subculture of Protestant Christianity in the United States and Canada, evangelicalism is, in many ways, marginalized further in a generally liberal Cascadia. As evangelicals reflect on their place in an increasingly secular or post-Christian region, they have been forced to consider important questions about how they define themselves. While evangelicals in the Pacific Northwest appear to be relatively traditional and conservative compared to liberal churches and secular advocacy groups, their approach to engaging with refugees, immigrants, and LGBTQ+ communities distinguishes them from conservative evangelicals elsewhere in the United States, but not in Canada (Reimer 2003). Some evangelicals in Cascadia believe they are at the leading edge of change and that what happens in the Pacific Northwest will eventually occur in their religious tradition and other regions on the rest of the continent. Still, questions about evangelicals in Cascadia remain to be explored, questions that have some implications for understanding the changing nature of religion in a secular or post-Christian society.

James Bielo's (2011) three-year ethnographic study of what he calls emerging evangelicals – or those who are starting a range of ministries, mission work, practices, and theological explorations – offers some insight into the shifting landscape of evangelicals. Bielo's study focused on young pastors from largely white, urban, and middle-class evangelical congregations in the United States who were dissatisfied with the conservative subculture. These young evangelical pastors were also at odds with the growing numbers of megachurches modelled after corporations and with a consumer approach to faith. Not only did these young pastors challenge the megachurch, they considered ways to plant new churches among people who did not fit within the megachurch model. They understood that what they were doing was a new approach to mission, one that sought to connect with postmodern or post-Christian culture. For Bielo (2011, 20–21), these evangelicals offer important insights into how religious groups negotiate social and cultural tensions in times of social change, leading to new practices and ways of living.

Bielo (2011, 28–31, 62–27) identifies two important processes that are instructive for interpreting what is happening among evangelicals in Cascadia. The first is a process of "deconversion," whereby evangelicals construct new personal stories or narratives about what it means to be an evangelical. The deconversion narrative, however, is not about losing faith or adopting another religion. Rather, it is about movement away from a current expression, or what is perceived to be an incorrect account of the faith. For Bielo, the second phase of the process is seeking an authentic expression of faith that includes self-reflection, irony, and humour to deal with cultural shifts.

The interviews with evangelical religious leaders in Cascadia certainly reflected both the prominence of irony and a shared conviction that these leaders had found an authentic form of Christianity. Bielo (2011, 70) also describes how these evangelicals drew on what he calls "ancient-future faith," whereby the faithful become practitioners of Christianity through regular participation with the non-Christian community. This, too, is highly valued among Cascadian evangelicals; the interviewees spoke of the importance of living in the community. These evangelicals contended that they ought not to live in isolation but in relationship with those around them. Cascadian evangelicals are not simply seeking to find Christians to fill their pews. Instead, they practise their Christianity every day in practical ways and view themselves as missionaries in a cultural context that is unlike their own subculture and in need of transformation (Bielo 2011, 118). Evangelicals in Cascadia recognize that the number of Christians has declined dramatically in Canada and the United States (see Thiessen and Wilkins-Laflamme 2020), and they no longer assume they are serving a nominally Christian society. Instead, they focus on a population that is not churched or, in Cascadia, one that is spiritual but not religious. This is an important marker for Cascadian evangelicals who find in the spiritual language and practices of the region a common point of reference with people who live in the None Zone. However, engaging with people in Cascadia requires new churches to accommodate the people who join them. A small industry of speakers, books, and conferences has emerged to support evangelicals who are trying to engage religious Nones (Bielo 2011, 157). However, to use a theological phrase, Cascadia does not allow "new wine to be poured into old wineskins" –

hence (see James 2017) the many new evangelical congregations that have been planted and those that have started as independent congregations from older churches or denominations with head offices in other regions of the country.

While discussion about evangelicalism tends to revolve around what evangelicals believe, another option is to consider how evangelicalism is "lived" in a specific place or region such as Cascadia. The concept of lived religion does not ignore beliefs but takes into account how they are negotiated in everyday life and held in tension with everyday practices. Such a focus emphasizes the ways a given religious community situates itself within a region's natural environment, the material practices that come to be associated with it, the ways it attempts to create community, and the ways it engages with the diverse views and cultural practices of that place. The questions raised by the interviewees may not be unique to Cascadia; nonetheless, evangelicals in the Cascadia region are clearly grappling with these questions in ways that reflect the political, historical, and geographical realities of Oregon, Washington, and British Columbia.

NOTES

1   There is no comparable study for Canada. The figure of 20 percent for liberal evangelicals in the western states includes California, Oregon, Washington, Hawaii, and Alaska and represents a considerable constituency (Joseph O. Baker, correspondence with author, April 14, 2020).

2   For archival and interview data, see https://www.uvic.ca/research/centres/csrs/.

3   Research in the United States and Canada with key informants in leadership positions, such as clergy, are considered highly accurate and important sources of data for the congregations and ministries they lead (see Chaves 2004; Reimer and Wilkinson 2015). Other strategies include interviews with individual participants and selected case studies of congregations. Each of these strategies have limitations. In this chapter, we hear from evangelical leaders who work with the broader evangelical world, including networks, congregations, theological schools, denominations, and other activities with evangelicals in the pews. Their perspective, while limited to their leadership position, is highly important for the broad overview they offer through their active participation among evangelicals. The interviewees are identified with pseudonyms, and their ministries are not named.

4   For more on the problematic nature of using "frontier language" see Chelsea Horton's chapter, this volume.

REFERENCES

Baker, Joseph O., and Gerardo Marti. 2020. "Is the Religious Left Resurgent?" *Sociology of Religion* 81 (2): 131–41.

Balmer, Randall. 2006. *Mine Eyes Have Seen the Glory.* 4th ed. New York: Oxford University Press.

Bean, Lydia. 2014. *The Politics of Evangelical Identity: Local Churches and Partisan Divides in the United States and Canada.* Princeton, NJ: Princeton University Press.

Bebbington, D.W. 1989. *Evangelicalism in Modern Britain.* New York: Routledge.

Bielo, James S. 2011. *Emerging Evangelicals: Faith, Modernity, and the Desire for Authenticity.* New York: New York University Press.

Charmaz, Kathy. 2006. *Constructing Grounded Theory: A Practical Guide through Qualitative Analysis.* Los Angeles: Sage.

Chaves, Mark. 2004. *Congregations in America.* Cambridge, MA: Harvard University Press.

Clatterbuck, Mark, ed. 2017. *Crow Jesus: Personal Stories of Native Religious Belonging.* Norman: University of Oklahoma.

Edgell, Penny. 2012. "A Cultural Sociology of Religion: New Directions." *Annual Review of Sociology* 38: 247–65.

Griffith, R. Marie. 2000. *God's Daughters: Evangelical Women and the Power of Submission.* Berkeley: University of California Press.

Hutchinson, Mark, and J. Wolffe. 2012. *A Short History of Global Evangelicalism.* Cambridge: Cambridge University Press.

James, Christopher B. 2017. *Church Planting in Post-Christian Soil: Theology and Practice.* New York: Oxford University Press.

Jennings, Mark. 2017. "A Silence Like Thunder: Pastoral and Theological Responses of Australian Pentecostal-Charismatic Churches to LGBTQ Individuals." In *Pentecostals and the Body,* edited by Michael Wilkinson and Peter Althouse, 217–38. Leiden: Brill.

Killen, Patricia O'Connell, and Mark Silk. 2004. *Religion and Public Life in the Pacific Northwest: The None Zone.* Walnut Creek, CA: AltaMira Press.

Marti, Gerardo, and Michael O. Emerson. 2014. "The Rise of the Diversity Expert: How American Evangelicals Simultaneously Accentuate and Ignore Race." In *The New Evangelical Social Engagement,* edited by Brian Steensland and Philip Goff, 179–99. New York: Oxford University Press.

Reimer, Sam. 2003. *Evangelicals and the Continental Divide: The Conservative Protestant Subculture in Canada and the United States.* Montreal/Kingston: McGill-Queen's University Press.

–. 2011. "'Civility without Compromise': Evangelical Attitudes toward Same-Sex Issues in Comparative Context." In *Faith, Politics, and Sexual Diversity in Canada and the United States,* edited by David Rayside and Clyde Wilcox, 71–86. Vancouver: UBC Press.

Reimer, Sam, and Michael Wilkinson. 2015. *A Culture of Faith: Evangelical Congregations in Canada.* Montreal/Kingston: McGill-Queen's University Press.

Smith, Christian. 1998. *American Evangelicalism: Embattled and Thriving.* Chicago: University of Chicago Press.

Steensland, Brian, and Philip Goff, eds. 2014. *The New Evangelical Social Engagement.* New York: Oxford University Press.

Tarango, Angela. 2014. *Choosing the Jesus Way: American Indian Pentecostals and the Fight for the Indigenous Principle.* Chapel Hill: University of North Carolina Press.

Thiessen, Joel, and Sarah Wilkins-Laflamme. 2020. *None of the Above: Nonreligious Identity in the US and Canada.* New York: New York University Press.

Wacker, Grant. 2001. *Heaven Below: Early Pentecostals and American Culture.* Cambridge, MA: Harvard University Press.

Wuthnow, Robert. 2005. *America and the Challenges of Religious Diversity.* Princeton, NJ: Princeton University Press.

10   "To Be or Not to Be" Religious: Minority Religions in a Region of Nones

RACHEL D. BROWN

What is it like to identify with a minority religious tradition in a region where nearly half of the population identify as religious Nones and where Christianity has a significant cultural footprint? Does it change how members of non-Christian minority communities imagine themselves as religious? Does it impact the kinds of religious communities that individuals feel comfortable being a part of, or the kinds of religious communities that religious leaders from minority religions create or lead? Drawing on qualitative data from this project, this essay explores how the distinctive approach to religion, secularism, and the region itself affected the lives of non-Christian participants. I argue that the experiences of individuals from minority religious communities reveal the possible barriers facing those who are rooted in traditional and typically conservative communities but also part of a postinstitutional liberal environment; they provide insight into the differences between what we sometimes call Cascadia North and South; and, they offer a valuable window into the social implications of secularization, as it exists in the region. I show how the individuals we interviewed who identified as Baha'i, Buddhist, Jewish, Muslim, and Sikh engaged with their religious, spiritual, and/or cultural identities in potentially regionally specific ways.

Demographics and the Problem of Categorization

Pollsters, journalists, and scholars tend to look for and write about formal religious affiliation or disaffiliation. Studies are usually set up to look only at groups or individuals who identify with well-defined "world" religious traditions.[1] As Bruce, a Baha'i participant in Portland said, "I feel like when I see these checkmark surveys, I feel like I would end up looking more like an atheist than a believer."[2] It can be difficult for individuals who do not align with the way religions are understood by survey companies and the public to determine which box to

TABLE 10.1   Religious affiliation, British Columbia, 2011, and Washington and Oregon, 2014

	British Columbia, 2011 (%)	Washington and Oregon, 2014 (%)
Anglican (and Episcopalian in US)	5.0	1.3
Baptist	2.1	6.4
Christian Orthodox	0.9	0.8
Lutheran	1.5	3.8
Methodist	–	1.4
Mormon	–	3.5
Pentecostal	1.2	5.2
Presbyterian	1.0	2.2
Roman Catholic	15.0	15.0
United Church	5.1	–
Other Christian	12.9	22.3
Indigenous	0.2	0.2
Buddhist	2.1	0.7
Hindu	1.0	0.6
Jewish	0.5	1.2
Muslim	1.8	0.6
Sikh	4.7	0.0
Other non-Christian	0.8	2.8
No religion	44.3	32.0
Total	100	100

NOTES: N (BC) = 116,750; N (Washington and Oregon) = 1,130. A dash indicates that data were not provided for the group in question: affiliates for these groups can be found in the "other Christian" category.
SOURCES: Statistics Canada (2011); Pew Research Center (2014); Wilkins-Laflamme (2017).

check. Surveys may not capture the full picture of minority religious identification in the region; the major surveys conducted indicate that non-Christians represent just under 11 percent of the population of British Columbia and 6 percent of the population in Washington and Oregon (Statistics Canada 2011; Pew Research Center 2014).

Although many of these non-Christian religions are growing (whereas forms of Christianity are generally contracting in British Columbia, Cascadia, and North America),[3] they are still much smaller, in terms of population, than Christian groups. Table 10.1 presents the statistics available on religious populations in Cascadia North and South.

Religions are often organized into broad categories such as Christian and non-Christian, as they are in Table 10.1 It is important to pause to think about this categorization. The idea that minority groups must always define themselves against the largest population around them is not new, but it does potentially have the effect of cementing definitions of religion, tradition, spirituality, and so forth, at a time when scholars are demonstrating that religious phenomena are always tied up with – in fact, dialectically related to – powerful political, ethnic, national, racial, class, and gender dynamics. The "non-Christian" label, therefore, both underlines and inadvertently naturalizes the dominance of Christianity (see Killen, this volume) and the subaltern nature of non-Christians in North America. Given the high numbers and consistent expansion of the Nones in the Pacific Northwest, it might be equally valid to refer to conventionally religious people as non-Nones in surveys. If this seems absurd, it is important to stop and wonder why labelling people as non-Christian does not seem equally inappropriate.

I should note that none of the available categories – religious, irreligious, Christian, secular, non-Christian – is perfect. However, we can choose metaphors and categories that do not perpetuate problematic norms. The point here is to give voice to individuals who identify with religious, spiritual, or ethnic communities that are statistically small. I want to reflect on what might be the experience of being, or living lives as, Buddhist, Sikh, Muslim, Baha'i, or Jewish people in the region.[4] So rather than using the term "non-Christian," I refer to these traditions, and the people who identify with them, as minority religions and traditions. I use "minority" in a strictly statistical manner.

Although the five minority traditions I focus on account for an estimated 9 percent of British Columbia's population and 3 percent of Washington's and Oregon's,[5] these Cascadians made up 30 percent of our qualitative data set.[6] In particular, our focus-group and interview respondents were approximately 11 percent Jewish, 8 percent Buddhist, 7 percent Muslim, 3 percent Sikh, and 1 percent Baha'i. There are a few interesting things to note here. First, the over-representation of Jewish participants (11 percent in our qualitative data versus 0.5–2 percent in the general population) was the inevitable result of qualitative research that relies on volunteer engagement. While this may seem somewhat unbalanced, considering the relative dearth of research on Jewish communities and practices in the Pacific Northwest, this over-representation is a welcome accident (Brym, Neuman, and Lenton 2019; Cone, Doker, and Williams 2003; Killen and Silk 2004; Marks 2014). The second notable feature of the minority participants in our qualitative data pool was their geographical location. Muslim and Sikh participants resided on the Canadian side of the border, Jewish and Baha'i participants were on the American side, and Buddhists were split (two thirds in Canada, one-third in the United States). Since Sikhs make up less than 1 percent of the Washington and Oregon population yet 5 percent of the population of British Columbia, this makes sense. In fact, our research team, wanting to reflect forms of diversity on the ground in the four research locations, attempted to invite and interview individuals who reflected the profiles of religious, spiritual, and secular diversity found in each location.

While these traditions are minority religions in other regions of the continent, their minority status is particularly clear to newcomers to the Pacific Northwest. As Rachel, a Jewish participant in Portland, described it: "Moving to Portland was a huge culture shock because there are no Jews here [laughs]. There's a few thousand. So, it was very interesting coming from DC, where you literally can't walk down the street without seeing ten Jews that you know, and then you move here and you're like, 'Where are they?'"

Not All Things Are Equal
Members of minority religious traditions did not share the same experiences when it came to living in the region, beyond being members of minority religious traditions. In fact, no one was defined by just one feature of their personal history or convictions – rather, their identities were intersectional in the sense that we are all characterized by a number of overlapping, socially constructed realities (ethnicity, race, age, gender, education, social class, etc.) (Crenshaw 1989; Guittar and Guittar 2015; hooks 1994). Hence, the members of minority religions in our study were shaped by many overlapping identities that made each person's experience distinctive.

For example, the combination of racial politics and religious identification added to the complexity of lived experience for some. Participants in the Seattle millennial focus group discussed in depth the nineteenth- and early twentieth-century history of state-wide exclusion of all nonwhite people in the Cascadia South region, and a Sikh leader in Vancouver echoed his group's history of exclusion in British Columbia.[7] Our data suggest that the physical representation of religion on racialized bodies only increased the taboo around certain religions. For example, Gianmeet, a Sikh participant in Vancouver, explained that "our religion is very physical. Outwardly, you can tell right away whether someone is a practising Sikh or not [by his or her uncut hair, turban, or metal bracelet, for example]. And that, I guess, is the number one issue, because then you stand out. You become different from everybody else." For Gianmeet, there was a cost associated with standing out as religious. While this was not true for many of our participants, Gianmeet, in a broader conversation about the general taboo around religion in the region, explained that he faced more discrimination living in Vancouver, just by being religious at all, than he did when he lived for seven years in the Bible Belt of the United States.

Because of concerns in both Canada and the United States about the integration of newcomers, migration status is another feature of identity that may impact the way a particular religious community is viewed by people in the host context. The majority of people who identify with minority religious communities are born outside of Canada and the United States (Statistics Canada

2011; Wilkins-Laflamme 2017). One of our participants linked the rate of migration to attitudes toward certain religious minorities in the region. Muhammad explained,

> I would say that immigration was happening at a pace that was allowing it to be diluted by whatever the norms are here. And I think now it's happening at a pace and with enough numbers that the reality is that there are many more people with faith and religion than there used to be, and that number is growing relative to those who don't.

In fact, while Nones have been increasing since the 1970s in both Cascadia North and South, in both absolute and proportionate terms (see Bramadat and Seljak 2005; Laird 2004; Ravvin 2005; Thiessen 2015; Theissen and Wilkins-Laflamme 2020), what is interesting to note is that Muhammad *thinks* that the rate at which migrants, and their religious traditions, are entering the region directly impacts how they might be "diluted" by, or adapt to, the cultural milieu.

Race and migration are just two factors that impact the experience of religious-minority individuals and groups. It is important to note that because of the complex interaction of a low level of religious literacy, media interests (in sensational narratives), and a long history of prejudice against minorities, certain religions in the region are viewed as more problematic than others. In fact, Sophie, a Buddhist participant, asked a Muslim participant the following: "I guess my question is, Do you really believe that religion is taboo, or are only certain religions taboo?" Muhammad responded,

> I think it's probably easier to talk about more New Age kinds of spirituality, nature-based spirituality, talking about regional approaches ... But I think it's very different when it comes to, particularly, Christianity and Islam ... And Islam, of course, we have all sorts of deep injustices carried out in the name of Islam ... So that all gives rise to a very unfriendly environment toward religion.

Research has shown that, in North America, traditions such as Buddhism are looked on with more curiosity and patience than other non-Christian religions (Borup 2016; Moore 2008; Tweed 2008). Dale, a Buddhist participant in Portland, highlighted this when he said, "Buddhism is still kind of exotic in a lot of people's minds, which is why they want to come here [to the temple]." Sophie agreed and explained that because of the "good perception of Buddhism ... the response is quite positive when I identify as belonging to a religious community." Muhammad's picture of Buddhism was similar: "Buddhism has a reputation for being very peace-minded and loving, so there is kind of a rational justification for why some religions seem to be abhorrent and others don't." I provide these examples to show that not all things are equal for members of minority religions in Cascadia and to highlight the difficulty of trying to speak broadly about an incredibly diverse group of individuals.

Religion in an Irreligious Region

Kamal, a Muslim participant in Vancouver, told us that he engaged in the "deeply political project" of exerting "my Islamic identity in a public space to change the cultural perception of what it is to be a Muslim and how that's perceived." This is a political project because religion is rarely a key topic of discussion in Cascadia. Muhammad explained that people

> have to learn that here, religion is taboo. This is one of the things you don't talk about, that people coming from different parts of the world are okay with expressing themselves ... in a very interfaith way ... It's just that that's part of their reality ... But all of a sudden, here, it becomes almost a rude thing to bring up. It's not a safe topic.

A strong feature of Cascadia is the norm that one simply does not talk about religion (see Killen, this volume), which is viewed as something from "over there" or far away in the "Old World." Muhammad explained, "I think a degree of protectionism [exists] that makes people feel like it's a big deal to break that barrier and to actually bring religion into this otherwise serene part of the world. Like, don't clutter it with that baggage that the rest of the world has been afflicted with." According to Rachel, while everyone was religious on the East Coast, "out here, it's like everyone is nothing unless you're forced to be something." Because of this broad discomfort with religion, some minority communities come together to combat this impression. For example, Ahmed Bashir, a Muslim leader in Victoria, explained that he and the rabbi in town "actually meet quite frequently. So, we're just trying to make people understand the greater purpose and idea behind religion, that it is supposed to improve people's lives and not necessarily be a barrier to interaction and so on."

According to several members of minority religions, religion was an unfamiliar concept to many in Cascadia.[8] It was often presented as an interloper within a highly secular context. As Bruce, a Baha'i participant in Portland, explained, "Here, we are facing similar challenges as any other religious group would, of maintaining identity in the face of a counter tide that sees the world fundamentally through a secular lens." In a context where religion is often viewed by the majority of the population as unknown, strange, or simply private, one can see why religious minorities might feel as though extra effort is required to maintain their identity. In fact, Rabbi Bauman joked that "Seattle is the 'New York, New York' of faith: 'If you can make it here, you can make it anywhere.'"

While some of our participants explained that religion is viewed as unknown, or strange, others observed that the region was characteristically accepting of difference (Rabbi Levi, Portland; Abbot Drury, Portland; Rashid Tahan, Vancouver; Akal Singh, Vancouver; Ahmed Bashir, Victoria). To put it another way, the taboo might not be against religion as such, but rather a certain kind of religion. Specifically, the ideal form of religion fits with the anti-institutional approach of Cascadia. Here, one may be religious, but the preference is for personal, private, and noncoercive forms.

Anti-institutionalism

In his introduction to this volume, Bramadat suggests that the "Pacific Northwest is almost famously secular or postinstitutional." This postinstitutional approach showed up often and in interesting ways in our interviews. A common theme was that deinstitutionalized forms of minority religion – "do it yourself" or "you do you" forms – would be popular in Cascadia. This theme related to the general and common disdain among participants toward the structures and institutions that people had left behind in the "east" of North America. This trope is evident in the literature on religion in the Pacific Northwest (Marks 2017; Killen and Silk 2004; Todd 2008) and throughout our data pool. Indeed, one might say that people here are not just postinstitutional but often anti-institutional. This sentiment is especially common in the younger generation's (millennial and younger) comments about the racism and anti-LGBTQ2S+ perspectives they believe are historically built into many institutions, religious or otherwise. Abbot Drury, a Buddhist leader, spoke of these sentiments:

> Most of the people that come to us either grew up with no religion or they grew up with some form of Protestant [or] Catholic Christianity. And most of them are mad at their origins. Some because they're gay and their church of origin was really hard on that. Some because they're feminist and felt excluded or put down in their origins. Some because they ran into some hypocrisy in their church.

Anti-institutionalism can lead to a heightened focus on the self and on individual expressions of religiosity, often understood to be linked intractably with the natural world, as well as a rejection of discriminatory institutional religious affiliation. For example, Rabbi Bauman explained that "there's something inherent in the Pacific Northwest that both attracts people with a certain nonconforming mindset or nurtures people into a certain more individualistic nonconforming mindset, and I think that clearly has ... an impact on the classic model of religious communities." Andrew, a Jewish participant in Seattle, explained that it is not a matter of Cascadia being nonspiritual or nonreligious; instead, "there's been this idea of institutions, usually institutions, which are associated with East Coast life, or anything outside of the Northwest are suspect." This anti-institutionalism gets worked out in concrete ways, as Andrea, another Jewish participant in Portland, articulated, "There is a lot of focus on the self, which can be very good and inclusive, but I think sometimes, getting them to be, like, 'Shabbat starts at this time. It does not start when you feel like it starts. It starts now.' You know what I mean?"

Bruce explained it as follows: "It's that quest for, 'How do I find meaning in my life' that is much more DIY in the West? I think here we do look to ourselves ... whereas on the East Coast there was more the sense that there are important predecessors who have set up frameworks." This rejection of the institutions and the authority figures who represent them is the difficult background against which all religious communities – minority traditions included – in the region must attempt to find and keep members. Because of this, even if the number of religious-minority communities is growing, affiliation with religious organizations does not necessarily follow suit. Rabbi Levi explained: "You know, everybody wants to talk about how 'unchurched' Oregon is. Yes, and the evangelicals are doing very well. And the Jewish community is doing well, in the sense of not shrinking. The Jewish community is certainly growing, [but] the affiliation rates aren't growing. That's where the challenge is right now."

While this may be a challenge, it is not a new challenge for religious-minority communities in Cascadia. Rabbi Bauman explained that "we are in the third or fourth iteration of people who work in faith communities of dealing with this and of finding ways of engaging people within that [cultural] climate." He explained that even if this is not a new challenge, "there is something about the mindset of this area in terms of its endemic mindset and the kinds of people it attracts who are more intensively resistant to communal affiliation and connection than [are people in] other parts of the country," making it much more difficult to convince people to stay affiliated or to become affiliated in the first place. Rashid Tahan, a Muslim leader in Vancouver, thought another reason for the lack of affiliation was the acceptance of diversity in the region: "Life here is more open than other societies," and because of this acceptance of difference, there is a sense of safety that arises for minority individuals that potentially leads to less need for security: "They don't have the fear ... There is no push to go into your enclave and seek security." This lack of drive for communal affiliation and the creation of enclaves (a historically significant aspect of religious communities), then, might pressure religious groups to adapt by providing something more.

Creative Adaptation

Leonard spoke of the process of adaptation and living as a Jewish person in Portland:

> My sense of living as a Jew on the West Coast: there's a phrase "galuta ti galuta," which is, "the exile of the exile." America is already not Israel, and then this place out here is so far from Jewish consciousness that it's up to us to reconstruct or construct what it means to be a Jew in this location ... So that leaves a space for us to *create things*. There's a huge number of unaffiliated Jews in Portland, [so there's an interest among some] to try to reconstruct something that feels indigenous to the region ... There is an opportunity to construct a Jewish myth of the West Coast on the West Coast that doesn't exist.

The opportunity to be innovative, mixed with pressure to not look like the religious institutions of "over there," means not only that religious-minority communities can adapt but, in some cases, they might feel as though they must adapt. Here, I use the term "adapt" to refer mainly to the creative engagement of minority individuals with the dominant physical and sociocultural characteristics of the region; it is also true that the region has adapted to the presence and influence of religious groups (Soden 2015).

Adaptation and creativity were obvious in the physical worship space of minority traditions in the region. According to participants, religious spaces were often adapted to reflect regional influences. Muhammad described how mosques had "a regional interpretation of the requirements of a prayer space, as opposed to anything imported. So, there's a strong connection to the region, however you define it ... kind of a regional approach to Muslim architecture." Rabbi Bauman emphasized that the current synagogue "was built to incorporate nature. It was built for the Pacific Northwest." This incorporation of nature into the built environment points to one of the most significant characteristics of Cascadian minority religiosity.

There is no question that the beautiful, and inescapable, natural environment of the Pacific Northwest is one of the region's most influential characteristics. Todd Ferguson and Jeffrey Tamburello (2015) suggest that in naturally beautiful regions, religious affiliation is much lower, in part because being in nature is a spiritual competitor to religion. It is not a zero-sum game, though: it is not simply that people only have time to hike or go to a religious service but that hiking and other activities in nature are framed as spiritual activities. In Chapter 1 of this volume, Paul Bramadat uses the term "reverential naturalism" to refer to an orientation that is "inclined to perceive and imagine the natural world in ways that are redolent (from the Latin *olere*, 'to smell') of mysticism, panentheism, animism, pantheism, and inclusive forms of theism."

He reveals that many of the region's residents speak about being in nature as "their church," for example.

If reverential naturalism is part of the default orienting schema of the region (Bramadat, in this volume; see also Ferguson and Tamburello 2015), conventional religious groups might frame nature as a potential competitor. We asked members of religious-minority groups about this, and while they affirmed the existence of reverential naturalism, they did not see it as a threat. Rather, they experienced nature as an influence on the kind of religious community they would need to create in the region. For example, Rabbi Levi responded:

> I don't see it as a threat; I see it as an opportunity. I think we need to be smarter ... So, one answer that we've had has been an outdoor service during the summer. There's nothing better than summer in Portland. And so we have this beautiful space right in front of the gorgeous facade of our synagogue, and we set up on a Friday night. We do services out of doors ... It's one of the more popular things we do.

Other members of minority religious traditions also expressed the importance of bringing nature into their communities and ritual practices. Ahmed described how nature has become an essential part of the potential spiritual and religious activities of the community and how the leadership team attempted to facilitate this aspect of people's lives: "So I'm not sure if they think about [nature] in a spiritual/religious way ... Before, they might never have actually been out hiking, but once they move here, it becomes part of that. At the mosque, we try to facilitate that and take them for different activities, swimming and hiking and just outdoor activities." When asked whether he had been engaged in the outdoor activities common in Cascadia when he lived and worked in Toronto or the United Kingdom, he responded with a hearty laugh and resolute no.

Rabbi Bauman took the importance of engaging with the natural environment a step further; he suggested that it is not just about the enjoyment that nature brings, or something one does "just because," but that it is an important step in adjusting to the mindset and attitude of Cascadia:

> I gave a high holiday sermon about spirituality I found walking in the woods. That's something that I think in Pittsburgh might be a little woo-woo and out there, but for Seattle, I think it resonates. People get it. And I think it's important that people see that the established figurehead rabbi gets it, more, even more than gets it. My job is to span the chasm between where they're at and what's meaningful to them and how Judaism can be a part of that.

While nature is a part of people's lives in the Pacific Northwest, the significance of nature is still restricted to certain circles. Gianmeet made this point clearly when he said, "In Surrey, you talk about nature, and they're, like, 'Where are you from?' Vancouver is different." Gianmeet's comment reveals how engagement with nature varies depending on where one lives in the region, the size and character of the ethnoreligious community one calls home, and even economic circumstances.

While many of our minority religious participants discussed the incorporation of nature into their religious practice and traditions, Shirin, an Ismaili Muslim participant in Victoria, observed that the two categories were inevitably different:

> When we were younger, we grew up on [the] coastal area. My mom would and I would always go sit by the water, and just listening to the waves was just so calming and so peaceful, but it's never associated with religion. Like, I don't associate the two together. It's calming and it's peaceful, but it's not, like ... Transcendence for me only comes or has always been tied to religion.

For many, adjusting to the None Zone (Killen and Silk 2004) by creatively engaging with nature was not a problem, for them or their friends, family, and communities. For some, adjustment was even an inevitable part of one's religious tradition. Ai, a Buddhist participant in Vancouver, stated with confidence that, for Buddhists, place did not matter since "we adapt [to] the place we are in." Andrea similarly described the ease with which Jewish institutions and communities could adapt: "I know especially from my understanding and my experience with the Jewish community always moving; there's always a way to pack up whatever traditions there are and put them someplace else." However, not all our participants felt this way. In response to a question about whether it is easy to thrive in a region where very few people hold religion and religious ways of life as a central value, Kamal replied: "I would say every orthodox Muslim that I know is compromising in some way, that they would prefer not to."

These kinds of reflections, and these kinds of engagements with nature, are also highly impacted by social class and generation. Since it is exorbitantly expensive to live in the four main urban centres of the Pacific Northwest, a few participants – especially millennials and working-class individuals – argued that only the privileged could make the time to integrate their religious perspectives with their relationship with the natural world. Some residents were constantly working just to make ends meet. Individuals who identified with religious traditions with obligatory practices (e.g., the five daily prayers of

Islam) had to adapt to the fast pace of the environment. As Kamal explained, "I don't have time for certain spiritual practice. I just don't. I'm up. I'm working. I'm trying to work my second job. I'm trying to create opportunities for my third job ... just so I can afford to live here. I don't have time for spiritual practice."

Stepping Up and Stepping into Social Justice

If people are not able, or do not want, to take the time to practise any kind of religion, will the social services that religious institutions provide continue to be offered? With the decline of mainline Christianity, and a significant increase in Nones, one might wonder who will provide the labour that Christian organizations have long contributed to society, such as refugee resettlement, English as a second language training, and food-security initiatives. Dale Soden (2015) posits that evangelical churches and Mormons may take up this role but does not consider the possibility that religious minorities may as well. When we asked members of religious minorities if they thought their communities would step into this role, Ahmed said he thought the labour shortage would probably be short-lived: "I do feel that there's a lot more people coming over here, either with Muslim background or any other faith group. So it could be that decline is just for a short period of time, and it might change."

Although, historically, Christian organizations were the principal organizers and supporters of food banks and soup kitchens in the region (Soden 2015), some participants suggested that this work was being taken up by religious-minority groups. As Rabbi Levi observed, "In the Jewish community, food's a big issue. So there's a lot of those kinds of things. A lot of people work with the food bank in town as well." Similarly, within Sikh communities, Guru Nanak's Free Kitchen was a significant movement in the provision of food services.[9] Gianmeet explained, "I've come to understand that with the migration of Sikhs into this part of the country, a lot of people actually like and admire what is being done. We feed between 900 and 1,200 people every Sunday, about 50,000 – sometimes we do it twice a week – about 50,000 meals a year." Similarly, Lily, a Buddhist from Vancouver, provided examples of people from her community "giving out the sandwiches," and Rashid, a Muslim from Vancouver, commented that his community distributed "food to those in need."

Even if people are not necessarily active with a religious group, they are often still interested in community service. In Statistics Canada's 2013 General Social Survey, for example, 46 percent of BC respondents who did not attend religious services regularly (less than once a month) had nevertheless volunteered in the year prior to the survey, and 75 percent had given to charity. Shirin noted that in her faith community, people might not be "strictly practising," and many young Ismailis will not attend prayer at the Jamatkhana (the place of worship in Ismaili Islam), but they will be "very active when it comes to volunteer work" (an essential aspect of the Ismaili tradition). She explained:

> I think what's kind of really nice is that the religion, I guess, kind of provides that framework through which people can do that, and it does ... ignite that spiritual component in them as well. And I think that's sort of part of most faith communities, is giving and charitable work and things like that, and I think for the younger members, that is something that I think resonates with them quite a bit more so than actual reciting a chant, or whatever.

In a North American context, where youth engagement with traditional forms of religiosity is declining, and especially in Cascadia, where anti-institutionalism is strong among the younger generations, being able to engage religious youth in these ways can be an effective means both to maintain some level of affiliation and to inculcate a sense of responsibility for the welfare of others.

While many minority religious communities engaged in this work within their communities, there was also collaboration between religious minorities and between religious minorities and Christian communities to address social needs (see also Wilkinson, this volume). As Rabbi Levi said, "there's so much that can be done in interfaith coalitions around social activism." He explained that members of his community were working with a church and with other Jewish organizations to build tiny-home communities to help contribute to affordable housing initiatives; the synagogue was also working with Catholic charities to deal with the refugee crisis. Rashid also emphasized the importance of cooperation between Muslim, Christian, and Jewish organizations in Vancouver on refugee settlement, among other social issues. Although, at this point, we can neither confirm nor quantify the scale of these collaborations, several participants confirmed their interest and involvement in such endeavours.

However, it is not certain that minorities will pick up the slack created by the declining institutional capacities of Christian groups in the region. As Kamal explained, "I see groups like [the] Muslim food bank picking up that slack and definitely growing, but I also see a state-sponsored Islamophobia, anti-Muslim racism, which means very few Muslim people trust the state enough to work with them to solve these social issues, and that's a real concern for me." Beyond this, there is also a class dimension. Although some minorities have wealth in their communities – Gianmeet described getting an entire train car of chickpeas donated by a Sikh farmer and businessman – other minority communities may not be able to make similar contributions or may not feel they have the capacity to do so. Muhammad described the situation:

> There's definitely not a surplus in the Muslim community, not in the way that you're describing [referring to the chickpea story], I think, particularly because of the waves – Somali refugees, Iraqi refugees, Syrian refugees now. There's been layers of need, and it is not traditionally a high-income population ... There's a lot of institutional networks that are a part of the old infrastructure that don't easily translate, meaning the upper-middle class with their connections and their religious affiliations. The different nonprofits had a way of delivering and channelling and so forth. As you transition from a different set of networks, from a different set of infrastructures, I don't see it being as smooth.

So, while some religious-minority communities might fill the gap (since most of these traditions emphasize the value of community service), this transition might not be simple or smooth. How easily a community can work with government agencies, or feel comfortable fulfilling these needs, or afford to live in the region are factors that are often dependent on which side of the Canada-US border they live on.

What Difference Does the Border Make?

Although the themes I cover above relate to what Paul Bramadat describes as a "Cascadian imagined community," there are some differences between the experience of being a religious minority in Cascadia North and Cascadia South. First, the border matters organizationally – that is, there are different governing bodies and structures in place. Rabbi Levi told us that Reform Judaism in Canada and the United States is quite different:

> The border kind of ends at Seattle, and a little bit north. Our camp is ... just a little bit north of Seattle. But it's kind of in that region. The Jewish community beyond that we sometimes have some interaction with through our youth group, and that region is larger; that would definitely, like, go up to the Canadian border, but not past ... I don't think NFTY or the NFTY Northwest region [a Reform Jewish Youth movement], I don't think it formally encompasses Canada.

Similarly, Ahmed agreed that in terms of organizational connections, Muslim communities were connected to national and provincial/state bodies but not regional ones.

For the Sikh community in the region, things were somewhat different. Akal explained that there are growing communities of Sikhs in British Columbia, Washington, and Oregon but that, regionally, the Sikh community is bound together by the *Komagata Maru* incident of 1914.[10] Although many see it as a dark moment in Canada's history, Akal noted that this event created solidarity among the Sikhs of the Pacific Northwest. US Sikhs, particularly farmers in Portland, brought potatoes to feed the people on the ship.

The border also significantly impacted the engagement of religious minorities with Indigenous communities. As Chelsea Horton describes in Chapter 2, participants from Cascadia South tended to be less aware of and have less · involvement with Indigenous communities than participants from Cascadia North. The same pattern is true of religious minorities. Rabbi Bauman described a general lack of knowledge about Indigenous issues, but he did describe a feeling of understanding, or commiseration, for the shared "experiences of oppression and annihilation at the hands of the majority culture ... But I have not really explored that. I probably should, especially in Seattle. It would make sense to do so." These examples highlight what was common among participants in Cascadia South: they virtually all suggested that they *should* know more about and perhaps do more with Indigenous peoples but that it was not something that was naturally in the forefront of their thoughts. They noted that they knew less than their Canadian regional counterparts but understood that these issues were more prominent in the Pacific Northwest of the United States than in other regions. For example, participants in Washington and Oregon emphasized that their knowledge of and interaction with Indigenous communities was very slight, but at the same time, said Rabbi Levi, "there's much more acknowledgment, there's much more inclusion on the political level, and on the interfaith level. It's not much, but in comparison to what I experienced on the East Coast, it's a huge difference." The only participant in our US sample who did bring up the subject, and who spoke quite eloquently about Indigenous peoples' experience, was Andrew, who grew up in Canada and was far more familiar with the kinds of conversations underway in the public arena in Canada around indigeneity and First Nations history and rights than were others in the United States.

Although the awareness was greater in Cascadia North, many religious-minority participants also described a lack of actual interaction with First Nations communities. Akal said: "We support them, and we respect them, but in Richmond there is not much of an Indigenous community, and, you know, we have very little connection with them, to be honest with you." Three Buddhist participants in Vancouver stated that they knew little about the Indigenous communities and had almost no contact with them. However, Lily noted,

> we already destroy so much their land, their culture, the way they survive for generations. And they try to survive in this society. I think this society, they really, really, they didn't treat the Indigenous people fairly, right? And so that's why I really have sympathy for them. And then I really support their choices.

Even if not much contact had yet been initiated, the desire to make connections with Indigenous communities was present for many participants. Rashid was the only religious-minority participant who described a real, concrete interaction and collaboration with Indigenous communities:

> I wanted, when I was in the prison [as a chaplain], I wanted to reach the community so bad, because I thought from commercial benefits. Because the Muslims eat halal food, and the Aboriginal[s] have the land, and instead of importing the halal from the United States, I was telling the guys in the prison to start raising cattle in the reservations. And you can make millions of dollars because the Muslims need the halal food, and we started a bit talking, but it didn't materialize. Now we started talking ... [a month ago] about maybe reaching the Aboriginals, and ... we started a connection. You have the land, and then we buy everything you raise.

This anecdote highlights the kinds of collaborations possible for minority religious communities and Indigenous communities in Cascadia; no comparable possibilities were identified by individuals in Cascadia South.

***

Religious minorities live within the "Cascadian consensus." Although the interview and focus-group subjects belonged to different ethnic, national, and religious-minority communities, they shared some experiences: 1) the need to respond to anti-institutionalism, which is part and parcel of the Cascadian approach to religion; 2) the drive to adapt to and live out a regional interpretation of their tradition; and 3) an interest in addressing the social services gap created by the rise of Nones and the decline of most forms of Christianity. The fact that many religious-minority participants felt like outsiders, despite having a long historical presence in the region, deserves closer examination. What does this feeling indicate about the religious landscape in Cascadia? Many of these groups have been present, at least in small numbers, since the beginning of colonial settlement in the region and were integral in establishing the settler societies. And yet, like the experience of many minorities elsewhere, so many of them have a sense of being outside of the dominant culture and in need of adapting to it. Does this speak to a sense of historical amnesia within these groups? While some participants described their religious group's long histories within Cascadia, complicating the idea that these traditions are foreign or recent arrivals, many, and especially younger, participants seemed to accept the rhetoric of religion as unusual – both religion in general, and their specific religion in particular – and therefore storied their experiences accordingly, emphasizing the need to adapt and take on post- or anti-institutional forms.

In fact, for religious minorities, there was almost a double adaptation at work: one to the dominant (albeit increasingly vestigial) Christian culture of the region and the other to the ascendant None culture, both of which have shaped the region's sociocultural characteristics.

Religious minorities are growing in Cascadia, in numbers and influence. Their innovative adaptations to the dominant religious and cultural forms demonstrate the complex ways religions can and do endure in predominantly secular settings. Like Soden's (2015, xiii) religious activists, religious minorities in Cascadia continue to exercise "influence beyond their numbers on the cultural and public life of the region." Ultimately, as we see here and throughout this volume, if religious minorities can "make it" in Cascadia, a region with the largest population of Nones alongside an ethos still shaped by Christian traditions, then religion can "make it" almost anywhere. What their institutions, and their individual expressions of their religious lives, look like, however, might not resemble anything we have seen before.

Notes

Acknowledgments: I'd like to thank Paul Bramadat and Patricia O'Connell Killen for their incredibly helpful feedback and insightful comments and questions. I feel lucky that I was able to engage deeply with them both on this topic and am appreciative of their editorial touch. I would also like to thank Sarah Wilkins-Laflamme for her help with the statistics in this chapter, and for her encouragement throughout the writing process.

1 Although a full discussion of this matter is beyond the scope of this chapter, it is important to point out that many scholars in our field are critical of the "world religions" paradigm. This approach focuses on the "big five" traditions – Judaism, Christianity, Islam, Hinduism, and Buddhism – and sometimes neglects smaller traditions such as Sikhism, to name just one. Moreover, the term "religion" is a Western conceptual tool that often fails to convey the complexity and variation of religiosities and spiritualities in the world; Chinese religions and many Indigenous or new religious movements also sometimes fall outside of the expectations of the category. In addition, when we use one term – religion – to refer to cultural realities as diverse as urban Pentecostalism in Victoria, rural expressions of divination in the Philippines, the Catholic Church in Italy, and politically engaged Hinduism in India, we miss the ways in which several of these "religions" are simultaneously also forms of ethnicity and nationalism (to name just two of the other equally useful categories at work).

2 For archival and interview data, see https://www.uvic.ca/research/centres/csrs/.

3 For example, in British Columbia, religious traditions grew or shrunk at the following rates between 2001 and 2011: Sikhism, 49 percent; Hinduism, 45 percent; Islam, 41 percent; no religion, 38 percent; other, 36 percent; Jewish, 9 percent; Buddhist, 6 percent; Christian, -9 percent (Statistics Canada 2011).

4 Although Hinduism is the religious tradition of approximately 1 percent of the population in British Columbia, Washington and Oregon, we do not have any Hindu participants in our qualitative data. Furthermore, while Indigenous traditions are often included in both the "non-Christian" and "minority" religious traditions' category, two other chapters in this book address the experience of Indigenous religion and spirituality in the region (see Horton's and Crawford O'Brien's chapters in this volume).

5   It is important to note that Statistics Canada and PEW data do not have specific percent-
     ages for Baha'i communities in the region. "Baha'i" is usually lumped into the "other non-
     Christian religions" category. It is safe to estimate that Baha'i make up less than 1 percent of
     the overall population of British Columbia or Washington and Oregon.
6   Minority religious traditions made up 14 percent of the BC data and 9 percent of the
     Washington and Oregon data (Wilkins-Laflamme 2018).
7   See Paul Bramadat's introduction to this volume for a discussion of moments of state-wide
     exclusion of minorities in the region. See also the discussion of reconciliation and racism in
     the conclusion to this volume.
8   Since the region is famous for its strong tradition of irreligion, there is a good chance that
     mainline Christians might recognize themselves in some of the broader observations I make
     here. See Killen's, Wellman and Corcoran's, and Wilkinson's chapters in this volume.
9   Guru Nanak's Free Kitchen is a Sikh-led volunteer organization, based in Vancouver, that
     provides food for all. Its slogan is "Love All, Feed All." It uses the concept of *langar,* the
     communal kitchen and meal, as a means of enacting *seva* (selfless service) in the real world,
     "regardless of caste, colour, creed, and economic status." For more information see the group's
     website.
10 The Continuous Passage law of the early twentieth century stipulated that one must arrive
     by continuous passage to be admitted into Canada. Since no ship at the time was able to
     sail continuously from India, this policy effectively froze the immigration of Indians to
     Canada. When the *Komagata Maru* arrived (through a continuous passage) from Hong
     Kong, the ship was prevented from docking, and passengers were prevented from dis-
     embarking for two months. During this time, local Sikh communities worked together to
     support those passengers. Eventually, only twenty-four passengers were allowed to disembark
     and the remaining passengers were sent back to India. When the ship arrived in India, a riot
     broke out, and twenty Sikhs were killed by police.

REFERENCES

Borup, Jørn. 2016. "Branding Buddha-Mediatized and Commodified Buddhism as Cul-
     tural Narrative." *Journal of Global Buddhism* 17: 41–55.
Bramadat, Paul, and David Seljak, eds. 2005. *Religion and Ethnicity in Canada.* Toronto:
     University of Toronto Press.
Brym, Robert, Keith Neuman, and Rhonda Lenton. 2019. *2018 Survey of Jews in Canada:
     Final Report.* Environics Institute, March 11. https://www.environicsinstitute.org/docs/
     default-source/project-documents/2018-survey-of-jews-in-canada/2018-survey-of-jews
     -in-canada---final-report.pdf?sfvrsn=2994ef6_2.
Cone, Molly, Howard Droker, and Jacqueline B. Williams. 2003. *Family of Strangers: Building
     a Jewish Community in Washington State.* Seattle: Washington State Jewish Historical
     Society/University of Washington Press.
Crenshaw, Kimberlé. 1989. "Demarginalizing the Intersection of Race and Sex: A Black
     Feminist Critique of Antidiscrimination Doctrine, Feminist Theory and Antiracist
     Politics." *University of Chicago Legal Forum:* 139–67.
Ferguson, Todd W., and Jeffrey A. Tamburello. 2015. "The Natural Environment as a Spirit-
     ual Resource: A Theory of Regional Variation in Religious Adherence." *Sociology of
     Religion* 76 (3): 295–314.
Guittar, Stephanie G., and Nicholas A. Guittar. 2015. "Intersectionality." In *International
     Encyclopedia of the Social and Behavioral Sciences,* 2nd ed., Vol. 12, edited by James D.
     Wright, 657–62. Amsterdam, London, New York: Elsevier.
hooks, bell. 1994. *Teaching to Transgress.* New York: Routledge.

Killen, Patricia O'Connell, and Mark Silk, eds. 2004. *Religion and Public Life in the Pacific Northwest: The None Zone.* Walnut Creek, CA: AltaMira Press.

Laird, Lance. 2004. "Religions of the Pacific Rim in the Pacific Northwest." In *Religion and Public Life in the Pacific Northwest: The None Zone,* edited by Patricia O'Connell Killen and Mark Silk, 107–37. Walnut Creek, CA: AltaMira Press.

Marks, Lynne. 2014. "'Not Being Religious Didn't Take Away from Their Jewishness': The Complexities of Lived Religion among Late 19th- and Early 20th-Century B.C. Jews." *BC Studies* 181 (Spring): 63–82.

—. 2017. *Infidels and the Damn Churches: Irreligion and Religion in Settler British Columbia.* Vancouver: UBC Press.

Moore, Rick C. 2008. "Secular Spirituality/Mundane Media: One Newspaper's In-Depth Coverage of Buddhism." *Journal of Media and Religion* 7 (4): 231–55.

Pew Research Center. 2014. *Religious Landscape Study.* Accessed July 2, 2017. https://www.pewforum.org/religious-landscape-study/.

Ravvin, Norman. 2005. "Jews in Canada: A Travelling Cantor on the Prairie, and Other Pictures of Canadian Jewish Life." In *Religion and Ethnicity in Canada,* edited by Paul Bramadat and David Seljak, 111–32. Toronto: University of Toronto Press.

Soden, Dale E. 2004. "Contesting the Soul of an Unlikely Land: Mainline Protestants, Catholics, and Reform and Conservative Jews in the Pacific Northwest." In *Religion and Public Life in the Pacific Northwest: The None Zone,* edited by Patricia O'Connell Killen and Mark Silk, 51–77. Walnut Creek, CA: AltaMira Press.

—. 2015. *Outsiders in a Promised Land: Religious Activists in Pacific Northwest History.* Corvallis: Oregon State University Press.

Statistics Canada. 2011. *NHS Profile, 2011.* Catalogue no. 99-0004-XWE. https://www12.statcan.gc.ca/nhs-enm/2011/dp-pd/prof/index.cfm?Lang=E.

Thiessen, Joel. 2015. *The Meaning of Sunday: The Practice of Belief in a Secular Age.* Montreal/Kingston: McGill-Queen's University Press.

Thiessen, Joel, and Sarah Wilkins-Laflamme. 2020. *None of the Above: Nonreligious Identity in the US and Canada.* New York: New York University Press.

Todd, Douglas, ed. 2008. *Cascadia: The Elusive Utopia: Exploring the Spirit of the Pacific Northwest.* Vancouver: Ronsdale Press.

Tweed, Thomas. 2008. "Why Are Buddhists So Nice? Media Representations of Buddhism and Islam in the United States since 1945." *Material Religion* 4 (1): 91–93.

Wilkins-Laflamme, Sarah. 2017. "The Religious, Spiritual, Secular and Social Landscapes of the Pacific Northwest: Part 1." *UWSpace.* https://uwspace.uwaterloo.ca/handle/10012/12218.

—. 2018. "The Religious, Spiritual, Secular and Social Landscapes of the Pacific Northwest: Part 2." *UWSpace.* https://uwspace.uwaterloo.ca/handle/10012/13406.

11

Everything Old Is New Again: Reverential Naturalism in Cascadian Poetry

SUSANNA MORRILL

Scholars argue that residents of the Pacific Northwest engage with nature as a popular, regional alternative to participating in more traditional, institutional expressions of religion (Shibley 2004, 155–66; Silk 2009, 105–14). Data from the 2017 Pacific Northwest Social Survey (PNSS) confirm this contention about residents of the region. Sixty-two percent of respondents from British Columbia engaged in outdoor activities at least once a month, and 57 percent of them considered it a spiritual experience. Fifty-four percent of respondents from Oregon and Washington engaged in outdoor activities, and 55 percent of them considered it a spiritual experience. The statistics show even more interest in spiritually motivated efforts to protect the environment. In this case, 69 percent of respondents from British Columbia had engaged in environmental activities at least once in the past year, and 53 percent of these respondents considered this a spiritual experience. In Oregon and Washington, 68 percent of respondents engaged in environmental activities at least once in the past year, and 48 percent of them considered this a spiritual experience.

The oral-history, leader, and focus-group interviews of the Cascadia project allow us to better understand what this engagement with nature in the Northwest looks like and what it means to the region's residents.[1] These interviews give us insight into how and why some respondents considered outdoor and environmental activities to be spiritual experiences. The picture is understandably complicated, but patterns emerged. For some interviewees, nature served as either an extension of an institutional religious tradition or a central part of a self-created individual spirituality. Many interviewees who did not identify nature as a place of religious or spiritual exploration still considered it an important part of their lives and a characteristic of Cascadian identity; this seems to demonstrate what Paul Bramadat in this volume thematizes as "reverential naturalism." Furthermore, as evidenced in popular poetry and diaries from the region, these kinds of encounters with nature have long-standing roots in the

Pacific Northwest, dating back into the nineteenth century. For a critical mass of residents, nature has served and continues to serve as a place of experience – sometimes explicitly spiritual – that is rooted in the cross-section of individual and regional identities. This present-day regional expression appears to have strong connections to Euro-American settler experiences, reimagined through literary framing and driven by an economic elite eager to "sell" the economic and residential possibilities of the area to the rest of the country and themselves.

Explanation of Terms

I use different but related terms in this essay: "religion/religious," "spiritual/spirituality," "reverential naturalism," and "nature religion." As used here, the terms "religion" and "spiritual" are broadly based on Clifford Geertz's (1973, 90) definition of religion as "1) a system of symbols which acts to 2) establish powerful, pervasive, and long-lasting moods and motivations in men by 3) formulating conceptions of a general order of existence and 4) clothing these conceptions with such an aura of factuality that 5) the moods and motivations seem uniquely realistic." These systems of meaning are based on an understanding of an ultimate reality that is not exclusively confirmed by scientific or commonsense knowledge but, rather or also, experiential and faith-based. The term "religion/religious" specifies that this system is based in institutional structures such as denominations or formally organized groups. The term "spirituality/spiritual" refers to more personal systems that are not based solely in formal institutional structures but, instead, are part of individual systems of beliefs, practices, feelings, habits, ethics, and morals.

Paul Bramadat (Chapter 1 in this volume) defines reverential naturalism in the following way: "reverential naturalism favours an orientation that is both accepting of scientific approaches to nature and nonetheless inclined to perceive and imagine the natural world in ways that are redolent (from the Latin *olere*, 'to smell') of mysticism, panentheism, animism, pantheism, and inclusive forms of theism." Although residents of Cascadia may not all knowingly embrace this perspective, it has enough of a presence in the personal experiences of residents, as well as in the public discourse of the region, that it serves as a common source of communal identity and/or discussion. For Bramadat, "Reverential naturalism is an embodied perspective, a way of physically being, or being physical, in a particular geography."

Nature religion is a concept developed by Catherine Albanese. Albanese (1990, 12) writes: "Nature religion seemed to encourage the pursuit of harmony, as individuals sought proper attunement of human society to nature and this mastery over sources of pain and trouble in themselves and others." This is an elusive and unorganized form of worship and religious engagement – it is a kind of "lived religion" that, according to Albanese, is often an unconscious part of people's worldview: some North Americans have looked to nature to find spiritual truths and spiritual connection. She (1990, 199) writes: "Unorganized and unacknowledged as religion, it is – given the right places to look – everywhere apparent. But it is also a form of religion that slips between the cracks of the usual interpretive grids – or that, more slippery still, evades and circumvents even adventurous ways to name it." In individual, cultural, and institutional forms of nature religion, she suggests that there are "gradations" in the centrality of nature and the intensity of religious engagement (Albanese 2002, 66–67). I see Albanese's notion of nature religion as a spiritual or religious manifestation of reverential naturalism.

The Natural Environment Expresses Regional Exceptionalism

Even among Cascadia interviewees who did not identify nature as a place of religious or spiritual experience, nature – the beauty and the appreciation of nature – was regularly cited as an identifying feature of the Pacific Northwest. For many Cascadia project interviewees, regional nature was exceptional. This distinctive natural environment was often seen as something that drew together British Columbia, Washington, and Oregon into an identifiable and cohesive region and gave respondents a sense of pride and distinctiveness from other parts of Canada and the United States. For instance, oral-history interviewee Heather, a faithful evangelical Christian from Seattle, talked about loving the beauty of the region, along with its open cultural environment, while oral-history interviewee Thomas, from Victoria, directly connected the concept of Cascadia with the love of nature that he saw as flourishing west of the Cascades: "I like ... the idea that on this side of the mountains, on the west coast of the mountains, the Left Coast, that we think of ourselves as more in touch with nature and progressive and sort of separated from central Canadian religious hierarchies and government hierarchies." Oral-history interviewee Scott, from Portland, similarly saw the region as a cohesive, natural environment:

> When you say "Cascadia," I think Seattle, Victoria, and Vancouver. All have the same, the same natural settings, you know. We've got forested mountains around. We've got parks galore. You're never more than a fifteen-minute drive away from something, and you feel like you're in a wilderness, you know. And there's not many parts of the country where that's so available to people, to residents, to people that live in areas like that.

Oral-history interviewee Henry, from Portland, mentioned that, despite a national border, he saw that Portland, Washington, and Vancouver, British

Columbia, were more similar than Portland and San Francisco because of the similar environmentally focused "outdoorsy, riding bicycles" lifestyles. Interviewed for the Seattle millennial focus group, Fiona observed that while plenty of people in California loved nature, that it was more easily accessible in the Pacific Northwest. Daniel Mendoza, a lay Catholic leader from Vancouver described the area as being special because it was the "closest you can get to the natural state of things." For many interviewees, the beautiful natural environment – and the engagement of residents with this environment – created a continuous cultural sensibility and served as the basis of transnational regional cohesiveness.

Additionally, nature held a special place in the individual identities of many of those interviewees who did not derive a spiritual or religious experience from it. Exhibiting the reverential naturalism described by Bramadat, many interviewees expressed pride and interest in the exceptional nature of the region. Ainsley, a participant in the Vancouver millennial focus group, posited a connection between the land, culture, and identity: "It's not just that land creates a sense of culture, but I think land also creates especially [for] people that have grown up here, a sense of identity." For him, this connection created in residents a "real sense of connection to the environment." Oral-history interviewee Eugene from Victoria described himself as "passionate" about nature though not spiritual about it. Oral-history interviewee, Steve, from Vancouver, echoed this sentiment as he mused that nature around his home had a distinctive effect on him, though he rejected the idea that it was spiritual:

> I mean, I love nature. I love part of being in this particular location, and, you know, you go down the bottom of the hill here and turn right, and you go along that road, there's umpteen different beautiful parks and stuff like that. And to walk through their fields is great. I love that. Particularly in contrast to downtown Vancouver, it just, it just makes me feel different, you know. It's more intense and so on, and here it's super relaxing. So, I mean to that degree, but the whole spiritual thing? No.

Oral-history interviewee William from Portland acknowledged that some people had spiritual experiences with nature, but while he understood why people could feel special in nature, he did not feel the same way himself: "I don't[.] I understand what people see in walking in the forest and the skies and, you know, the beauty in nature. But no, nature hasn't [been an important part of faith]. I wouldn't say that it has been. To answer that question directly. No." Oral-history interviewee Roy, from Spokane, took up the idea that nature produces awe, not a spiritual feeling, noting that he felt a strong connection with nature and saw it as incredibly important:

"When I," this is something that religious people will ask me. They love con-
flating words. Like the term "awe." "Don't you ever feel awe?" They conflate
that with some kind of supernatural experience. I said, "When I take, when,
my birding binoculars are 12 × 36, and they're image stabilized, I can look on
a clear night up at Jupiter, and I can see five, sometimes six moons of Jupiter's
what, sixty-three or -four moons. But I can see several moons, and that is
amazing" ... I feel awe in all kinds of observations, from, you know, macro to
micro levels. I am in awe of this entire life. But I do not see evidence of anything
supernatural.

Oral-history interviewee Christopher, from Portland, also questioned the idea
that nature created for him a spiritual experience, though he acknowledged
that it evoked in him a positive, distinctive feeling: "I mean it's certainly peace-
ful, meditative certainly." Jamie of the Victoria millennial focus group observed
that she saw people change when they moved to the area and were exposed to
nature and Indigenous culture and forced to think about their connection to
the land. She noted that this experience could be spiritual – or not – for those
changed by the encounter.

Thus, even among the many interviewees who did not identify their experiences with nature as being religious or spiritual, nature had a special place in
their individual lives; they saw that it made their lives better and fuller, whether
it added to their daily sensory and aesthetic experience, challenged their curiosity, or gave them a sense of tranquility. In their descriptions, respondents claimed
that nature in the Pacific Northwest region was exceptional, that it helped to
create a transnational, nature-facing ethos and that it enhanced their individual
lives. Reverential naturalism thus served as a cohesive intersection between
regional and individual identities.

Finding Religion and Spirituality in Nature: Historical Trajectories

A significant number of Cascadia interviewees indicated that they sought and
found religious or spiritual solace in their encounters with nature, either seeing
it as an extension of an institutionally based religious faith or part of an individual spiritual experience. Oral-history interviewee Keith, from Victoria, for
instance, echoed many of the interviewees above, noting the beauty of the
region and comparing it to heaven: "Yeah, I just, you know, I think by and
large heaven is right here. We have heaven." He went one step further than
the above interviewees, however, and identified his encounters with nature as
having a spiritual resonance. Specifically, he talked about how he loved the
outdoor activities of crabbing, fishing, oystering, and taking care of marine
birds. He saw his care of marine birds as a kind of spiritual expression: "So

that's kind of my spirituality that I get from that, you know, and I've rehabilitated, you know, rehabilitated and then released them, a lot of times on my
own money."

Based on anecdotal evidence, scholars studying religious life in the Pacific
Northwest have long argued that the inhabitants of this region, more so than
other North Americans, engage religiously and spiritually with nature. Indeed,
these observations served as one of the motivations for the Cascadia project
and its systematic survey and interview methodology. Mark Shibley (2004, 156)
writes: "In the Northwest, where official religion does not pervade the cultural
landscape, nature religion is ubiquitous – in regional literature, in rituals of leisure, in environmental movement ethics, in Native American culture, and even
in official religious institutions." Like Albanese, Shibley views nature religion in
the Pacific Northwest as a lived religion based in "ecstatic nature experience"
(Shibley 2011, 168, 174). James Wellman (2008, 41) suggests that this religious
interest in nature is created by the stunning natural beauty of the region; evangelical megachurches compete with enticing hikes for Sunday morning attention. Patricia O'Connell Killen and Shibley argue that nature is so enticing to
those in the region because Pacific Northwesterners live in a region where there
is no dominant religious reference group. Lacking a "social mirror" of religious
respectability and assumptions, Pacific Northwesterners look to innovative, often
noninstitutional spiritual expressions (Killen and Silk 2004, 30). For those
Pacific Northwesterners who seek religious and spiritual experiences, the ever-
present, regional beauty of nature fulfills this need.

In the leader interviews, for instance, Reverend Richards, a mainline liberal
Protestant minister from Portland, observed "that the culture, that the message of the culture, is that where you find your spirituality is out in the pines,
or at the coast, right? Or up Mount Hood, or wherever your particular piece
of nature is. That's the cultural message, rather than the cultural message being
that you go to Vancouver Avenue Baptist.".

The ways that participants expressed their experiences of nature and its relation to spirituality were not new. Similar rhetoric about religious and spiritual
engagement with nature appears in popular poetry and diaries dating back to
the 1800s. As evidenced in nineteenth-century popular poetry, nature has long
been a place of regional and individual – even familial – religious identities.
Although they are only a small, literary part of the complex mosaic of Cascadian
engagements with nature, by exploring these early sources, we can re-enliven
the cultural structures early Euro-American settlers created and then inhabited.
We can isolate streams of pervasive, persuasive rhetoric and assumptions about
nature within the early settler society of the region that are echoed among
present-day Cascadia interviewees.

An early form of religiously inflected, nature-focused discourse appears in the works of nineteenth-century poets of the Pacific Northwest. In their work, poets such as Ella Higginson, Belle W. Cooke, Emily Carr, Pauline Johnson, and Frances Fuller Victor, among others, self-consciously articulate encounters with nature that they sometimes describe as viable, meaningful alternatives to institutional religious expressions, sometimes as encounters that reinforce institutional expressions of religion. Tapping into common Victorian nature-focused literary themes, riffing off Christian images and assumptions, and living in late nineteenth-century settled comfort, they describe nature as an ever-present but largely beneficent sacred reality. In their work, we see early forms of religious and spiritual engagements with nature that continued to be articulated by some respondents to the Cascadia project survey and interview questions.

It is not unusual that these poets of the Pacific Northwest went to nature to find spiritual lessons and a connection with God. Robert Bain, in his introduction to the poetry of the contemporaries of Walt Whitman and Emily Dickinson, argues that nature was a major inspiration for nineteenth-century poets, who tended to record poetic pictures of and responses to nature, use it allegorically, or employ it symbolically (Bain 1996, xxv). Many poets of this era believed poetry should "edify and inspire," should create social change, and writing about nature was an effective way to do this (Bain 1996, xxix–xxxi).

Pacific Northwest poets of the nineteenth century were part of this didactic nature-focused poetry tradition. They often wrote in a sermonic mode meant to inspire their readers with knowledge they claimed as special, prophetic. Emily Carr, an artist and poet born in 1871 in Victoria, British Columbia, expressed this sentiment as she articulated the role of creative producers:

> *Artist, Poet, Singer, tell me what is your goal?*
> *By listing, learning, expressing, to find the soul.*
>
> *Artist, Poet, Singer, what are you after today –*
> *Blindly, dimly, dumbly, trying to say?*
>
> *Aye, Artist, Poet, Singer, that is your job,*
> *Learning the soul's language, trying to express your God.* (Carr 2007, 58)

Carr makes poets and authors the mouthpieces of the soul, of God.

Further, again echoing Bain's analysis, many of these Pacific Northwest poets look to nature as a prophetic medium for their lives and work. Pauline Johnson was a well-known Canadian poet who moved to British Columbia toward the end of her life and produced a book of retellings of local Indigenous lore from the Vancouver area. In her description of Vancouver's Stanley Park, she equates the trees to a cathedral that elevates her (and everyone else's) thoughts:

> She [Nature] will never originate a more faultless design, never erect a more perfect edifice. But the divinely moulded trees and the manmade cathedral have one exquisite characteristic common. It is the atmosphere of holiness. Most of us have better impulses after viewing a stately cathedral, and none of us can stand amid the majestic forest group without experiencing some elevating thoughts, some refinement of our coarser nature. (Johnson 1926, 138)

For Johnson, the "divinely moulded trees" naturally lead one to think "elevated thoughts."

Sometimes this connection with God was articulated using explicitly Christian symbols, language, and theological assumptions. Ella Higginson was born in Kansas and crossed the Plains as an infant. She grew up in Oregon and later moved to Washington with her pharmacist husband (Powers 1935, 417, 425–26). In "The Awakening," Higginson goes to fern-clad hills smelling of hyacinth and finds in the renewal of the earth promise of a new self – a reborn, resurrected self:

> *I will go into the dim wood,*
> *And lie prone on the sod,*
> *My breast close to the warm earth-breast,*
> *Prostrate, alone with God,*
> *Of all his poor and useless ones,*
> *The poorest, useless clod;*
>
> *And I will pray ... :*
> *"Lord, Lord, let me take heart again*
> *Let my faith shine white and clear,*
> *Let me awaken with the earth*
> *And leave my old self here."* (Higginson 1907, 125–27)

Writing about a sunset over the ocean and the Columbia River, Midwest-to-Oregon transplant, teacher, and journalist Belle Cooke finds proof of a happy eternal existence (Powers 1935, 280–81):

> *How oft thy beauty to earth is given,*
> *Thou seem'st the dawn of Eternity,*
> *The radiant gates of a glorious Heaven;*

> Though 'eye hath not seen, not heart conceived,'
> The bliss of that land may be believed,
> When we look at the glory hung on high,
> In the gorgeous clouds,
> Oh! Sunset sky! (Cooke 1871, 188)

These poems by Cooke and Higginson demonstrate how key elements of nature religion can be "packaged" in different theological and genre "containers." In these texts, we begin to see the nineteenth-century cultural context of a regionally inflected version of nature religion that is theologically grounded in Christianity but not institutionally tethered to any particular Christian denomination.

These poetic visions parallel the lived experiences of some nineteenth-century residents of the Pacific Northwest, in this case, two women who tapped into their Protestant faiths to make sense of their experiences in nature. Marion Crabbe Bennett resided in the wilderness of Oregon and was overwhelmed by her experience of Christian truths in her encounters with nature. In August 1899, she described a gorgeous sunset that moved her to contemplate the second coming of Jesus Christ:

> The moonlight strip next [to] the horizon reminded me of the Riser of Life in the midst of Paradise: – the dark line of the gulf between Hades and Heaven: – the crimson and white clouds looked like a host of angles [sic]: while the golden opening seemed a fitting entrance for Christ to come. It was indeed a glorious sunset and as I looked, I could not but pray that Christ would speedily come to redeem his people who are so burdened with care sorrow and a constant struggle for an existence. (Bennett August 27, 1899)

In July of that same year, Crabbe experienced another lovely sunset that brought her to a knowledge of heaven: "It seems as though I had caught a glimpse of heaven; there is so much here that is beautiful and sublime, that I can not realize how heaven can be any more so: in such a scene, – in the delicious quiet and rest I seem to get a foretaste of the perpetual rest hereafter" (Bennett July 18, 1899).

Mattie Sleeth, who was active in the Woman's Christian Temperance Union and eventually became a Methodist preacher, had similar supernatural encounters with nature. One night, thinking that the church service had been cancelled, she took a walk with a companion to the oceanside:

> The moon was full and shining on the water made a magnificent scene. We walked clear to the end of the pier for the tide was low and it was very different

from the morning ... The moonlight on the ocean was worth missing a meeting for. Sunday morning the sun shines so magnificently. O how the ocean
calls me and today the tide is highest of the month but I must prepare for my
morning service. (Sleeth 1908, 26)

For Sleeth, a faithful woman who spent her life on missionary work, the moonlight scene on the water served as the equivalent, or substitute, of a church service.
In the last lines of the passage, it is almost as though the ocean provides her
inspiration, and her service is to translate this inspiration to her community.

These sentiments found in nineteenth-century poetry and diaries are remarkably similar to what some modern-day interviewees expressed. For a large
number of the Cascadia project interviewees, nature was a vehicle for exploring their religion or spirituality. For a subset of these interviewees, like Cooke,
Higginson, Bennett, and Sleeth, nature served to enhance their institutionally
based Christian faiths. Oral-history interviewee Jane, an evangelical Protestant
from Seattle who lived in Walla Walla, described how her outdoor experiences
as a young girl laid the groundwork for her born-again experience as a young
woman:

I was a teenager, and so, through Young Life, I was introduced to the person
of Jesus Christ, and that made sense to me, because I'd spent my life running
around in the out of doors. My grandfather and my father were pioneers and
climbed all the mountains. And we were five girls, and we lived in the, we lived
in the woods and in the mountains. And so I knew there was a God because
it was just so gorgeous, but I didn't understand anything until someone articulated to me as a teenager that you can actually know God in a personal way.

Later in the interview, she described her understanding of God as the feeling
of standing on the top of Crystal Mountain and being able to see Mount Rainier,
the surroundings, and the snow, knowing "God is there." Similarly, nature served
as a gateway back into more organized forms of liberal Protestantism for oral-
history interviewee Henry, from Portland, who had a mystical experience at
Mykonos at sunrise when he felt the "unity of all space and time."

For oral-history interviewee Linda, who left the Baptist church but still identified as faithful, nature served as a place to bolster and explore that faith: "Yeah.
Yeah, I think that's an, that's an important thing that we still take walks in the
park as often as we can, and try to do hikes, and get out in God's work, in
creation, or whatever. That's an important part of our, of helping us stay sane,
you know." Linda's sister, oral-history interviewee Barbara, who also grew up
Baptist but had eased away from active church membership, similarly experienced nature as a place of spiritual rejuvenation:

Yes. I don't get out as much as I would like, but yes. I definitely, it reaffirms my belief that there is something greater and bigger than us up there, that created all this. And it's not just happenstance that we have this beautiful world to live in. It reminds you that we do have a beautiful world to live in, rather than ... the day-to-day nit-picky stuff that makes us crazy.

For these interviewees, nature reinforced or in some way substituted for institutionally derived Christian faiths. It provided an experiential dimension to already existing (in all these cases) Protestant theological frameworks. In many ways, they are the spiritual descendants of Higginson, Cooke, Bennett, and Sleeth.

Additionally, in the leader interviews, Jewish, Muslim, and Sikh representatives articulated how nature was intersecting with their religious perspectives and those of their members.[2] Rabbi Levi of Portland noted the "grand openness" of the Pacific Northwest that he thought derived from the geography of the region. In attempting to connect with his members, he described how he tried to incorporate into his public teachings the ideas of stewardship and taking care of the land, while he also did services in front of the synagogue and even on Mount Hood. Rabbi Bauman of the greater Seattle area also held services outside and, like Rabbi Levi, tried to incorporate nature into his public, religious statements: "Just recently, in the last year or so, I gave a high holiday sermon about spirituality I found walking in the woods. That's something that I think in Pittsburgh might be a little woo-woo and out there, but for Seattle, I think it resonates." Ahmed Bashir, a Muslim leader in Victoria, observed that the younger people who attended the mosque tended to pick up the regional practice of going into nature in a way that did not happen in mosques in other areas. Meanwhile, Akal Singh, a Sikh leader from Vancouver, explained that Sikhs were pioneers in the Green movement, noting "nature is a name for God" and that it was easier to make the connection in a region with so much natural beauty.

Adding some additional texture to the historical and present-day experiences of reverential naturalism in the Pacific Northwest, some nineteenth-century poets and some interviewees critiqued institutional, traditional forms of religion by means of their spiritual experiences in nature. Nature in the Northwest, they argue, provides for them authentic encounters with their understandings of a Christian God, in the case of nineteenth-century poets, and individualized, spiritual understandings of ultimate reality, in the case of interviewees. This fits in with Nicholas O'Connell's (2015, xix) assessment of Northwest literature, more generally, when he argues that "a distinctive Northwest literature does exist, that its primary subject is the relationship between people and place, and that its most important contribution to American literature lies in articulating a more spiritual relationship with landscape."

Higginson, most strikingly, makes this move in her poem "God's Creed," in which she pities a churchgoing friend, contrasting her friend's experience in a church with her experience in the church of nature.

> *Fogive me that I cannot kneel*
> *And worship in this pew.*
> *For I have knelt in western dawns,*
> *When the stars were large and few,*
> *And the only fonts God gave me were*
> *The deep leaves filled with dew.*
>
> *And so it is I worship best with only the soft air*
> *About me, and the sun's warm gold*
> *Upon my brow and hair;*
> *For then my very heart and soul*
> *Mount upward in swift prayer.* (Higginson 1907, 3–7)

Higginson argues for a similar exceptional presence of the divine spirit in the Northwest with her poem "Yet I Am Not for Pity," writing that she has never seen all the wonders of the world but that she is the lucky one because she lives among the region's natural wonders, where she is in constant contact with God:

> *Let pity be*
> *For him who never felt the mighty lyres*
> *Of Nature shake him thro' with great desires.*
> *These pearl-topped mountains shining silently –*
> *They are God's sphinxes and God's pyramids;*
> *These dim-aisled forests His cathedrals, where*
> *The pale nun Silence tiptoes, velvet-shod,*
> *And Prayer kneels with tireless, parted lids;*
> *And thro' the incense of this holy air*
> *Trembling – I have come face to face with God.* (Higginson 1907, 139–40)

Pacific Northwest nature, these poets suggest, brings them to intense encounters with their Christian God. They are living in a special land where, by simply encountering their natural surroundings, they encounter God.

In other nature-focused compositions, Pacific Northwest poets either self-consciously reject Christian ideas of truth or look to nature for less overtly spiritual comfort and insight. Interestingly, many of the poems in this category were written by Canadian poets, perhaps illuminating differing national sensibilities about nature, but more likely because of the somewhat later development of a literary culture in British Columbia than in the US Pacific Northwest. This demonstrates, perhaps, the early twentieth-century move away from Romantic interpretations of nature in poetry and toward more realistic, even pessimistic interpretations of nature. Born in New York and later a ghostwriter for Hubert Howe Bancroft's history of the West (Powers 1935, 309–10), Oregon resident Frances Victor rejects traditional forms of Christian worship in a poem that questions the purpose of human suffering and rejects the story of the Fall as being unfair (Victor 1900, 83–84) and in another poem looks to "Mother Nature" to answer her questions about the meaning of human existence and life:

> *O thou great, mysterious mother of all mystery*
> *At thy lips imperious man entreats his history –*
> *Whence he came – and whither is his spirit fleeing:*
> *Ere it wandered hither had its other being:*
>
> *Will its subtle essence, passing through death's portal,*
> *Put on a nobler presence in life immortal?*
> *Or is man but matter, that a touch ungentle,*
> *Back again may shatter to forms elemental.* (Victor 1900, 19–23)

Similarly, the Vancouver, British Columbia, magazine *Westminster Hall* published poems that described nature as a place of comfort and solace. In one uncredited poem titled "In Memoriam: J.N. Aged 15," the unknown poet establishes the Northwest setting, opening with a description of a sunrise over mountains, mirrored in the lake, where a fifteen-year-old girl lost her life. The author writes about a vision of the girl in the trees surrounding the lake and considers it a blessing from God that her memory will linger forever in the natural setting where she lost her life:

> *O cedars by the waters, where we strayed.*
> *A joyous footstep rings amid your sighing;*
> *O waters that betrayed the trusting maid,*
> *Her joyous laughter lives beyond your crying!* (Anonymous 1912, 32)

In a second poem from the same periodical, instead of finding God in Northwest nature, the poet, identified only by the initials "J.D.S.," sees nature as a reflection, writ large, of their own religious search for truth. Addressing the sea, the poem begins:

> *What vexes thee, O Sea? Hast thou a heart*
> *Within that grey, light-shifting breast of thine:*
> *A lonely heart, in yearning like to mine?* (J.D.S. 1912, 24)

The poet then uses pine trees along the edge of the ocean to describe their own search for the truth:

> *Behold, there is no movement in the pines;*
> *For towers their shaggy grandeur toward the blue;*
> *No sable-suited zephyr murmurs through*
> *Their serried lines.*
> *Below, their purple talons grip the rock*
> *Touched by the tireless sequence of the tides,*
> *Whose waves the weary hands, forever knock*
> *Where Rest abides.* (J.D.S. 1912, 24)

While J.D.S. finds in nature a familiar search for rest, in a poem titled "The Lost Lagoon" Pauline Johnson looks to nature to recall a pleasant, comforting memory:

> *O! lure of the Lost Lagoon —*
> *I dream to-night that my paddle blurs*
> *The purple shade where the seaweed stirs —*
> *I hear the call of the singing firs*
> *In the hush of the golden moon.* (Johnson 1926, 113)

Victor, the *Westminster Hall* poets, and Johnson look to nature to find life knowledge, comfort, or solace in the form of memory. A Christian God is not at the forefront of these poems, but nature still serves as a place of experiential meaning and learning.

Similarly, for most Cascadia project interviewees (oral histories and focus groups) who had spiritual experiences in nature, nature was unconnected to an institutional base and, rather, created a focus for more personalized forms of religious expression and experience. In their descriptions, we see how interviewees make a connection between the exceptional beauty of the Northwest and their spiritual engagement by means of this exceptional nature. Oral-history interviewee Jayden, from Seattle, described regional nature as providing a continuous spiritual experience:

> I was, like, why this specific region? Why here? And my response to that would be, the involvement of nature. And if you look around us right now, there's clouds, there's plants, and, like, I visited other places and, yeah, there's nice plants and stuff, and I think it's special for us here, with nature being deeply involved and the mountains all around us.

Jayden's sister Beatrice, also an oral-history interviewee from Seattle, drew out the spiritual dimension in even greater detail, noting that she loved to go hiking, to the mountains, stargazing, or to enjoy the beach at sunrise: "I kind of use that as a space to pray or reflect on what part of my journey I'm on." She described a "frequency" that is in everything and binds everything together. For these two sisters, nature was an easily available site of encounter with their spiritual truths. It moved them along on their individual spiritual journeys.

Other interviewees specifically identified the beauty of nature as an aid to their individual spiritual journeys. Oral-history interviewee David of Portland described going to nature to be spiritual and clearly saw that the nature of the region nurtured his individual spirituality: "You know, I just think we live in the prettiest damn place in the world ... It's just, we have the trees, we have the ocean, we have rivers, we have lakes. And I think that mother nature did a damn fine job." Sunny, from Vancouver, identified the physical connection with beautiful nature as a place of spiritual fulfillment for her father (and herself):

> I think that, again, that spiritual but not religious kind of framework. And again, the role of the natural world in that is one that does resonate really strongly for him. And he's talked about camp, actually, which I mentioned, too, you know. He used that as an example of being at camp as where you want to be – outside, on the water, on the ocean, being connected to the tide.

Stephanie, of the Seattle adherent focus group, echoed similar themes in describing her spiritual engagement with nature: "I guess things like convening with nature and being in nature and playing music, to me, are my everyday spiritual practices ... I haven't felt compelled to seek some other kind of structured community that's specific to a religious creed." Lindsey from the Victoria millennial focus group said: "I think my own (kind of) religious perspective is completely integrated with a view of what nature is or what it means – completely enmeshed." Samuel, a participant in the Victoria millennial focus group, also described his experience of surfing in the ocean as spiritual: "Just like seeing the landscape from out there has a very kind of awe-inspiring effect on you. To me, when I think about describing it, it feels profound, it feels spiritual, it feels significant."

For these interviewees who found some aspect of their spirituality in nature, nature created an experiential moment, one that is not defined by institutional structures, either architectural or theological. Interviewees identified their experiences in nature as being spiritual in a way that placed these experiences in opposition to more traditional expressions of religion. Indeed, like the examples from the nineteenth-century regional poets, they seemed to find spiritual truth in nature because it is not constrained by institutional experiences and expectations. These experiences in nature seem to be quite individual and, on the surface, unmarked by communal, social, or cultural dimensions and, again, this seems, for those interviewed, to undergird the authenticity of their encounters.

This religious engagement with nature seemed to be shared horizontally among family members such as oral-history interviewees Jayden and Beatrice, or Linda and Barbara, but also vertically through families, as evidenced by someone like Sunny or Christopher, who seem to have learned to engage with nature from their parents. This connection can go back generations. Oral-history interviewee Jane of Walla Walla, Washington, who grew up in nature and saw her early experiences there as the foundation for her Christian faith, described one of her grandfathers as coming to the Pacific Northwest to have adventures in the grandeur of the region. Similarly, oral-history interviewee Penny, from Vancouver, said that her husband's father had a strong spiritual engagement with nature: "He was one of these, that the mountains were his church. Every Sunday, we went for hikes and things like that." As a critical mass of interviewees observed, spiritual engagement with nature is part of long-held family traditions – learned behaviour that originates in the natural environment of the region itself.

The Historical Origins of Reverential Naturalism

The work of nineteenth-century poets and diarists in the region may offer a small window into where reverential naturalism and nature religion originated, but it does not fully explain why they took centre-stage in the public discourses and the individual identities of twentieth- and twenty-first-century residents of the Pacific Northwest. The Pacific Northwest was and is a region where no religious tradition dominates. This is confirmed by the 2017 PNSS data, which records that 49 percent of respondents from British Columbia and 44 percent of respondents from Oregon and Washington did not identify with a particular religious tradition. Historically, no one religious denomination ever held cultural dominance in the region. As the chapters by Chelsea Horton and Suzanne Crawford O'Brien in this volume demonstrate, a patchwork of Protestant denominations, along with the Roman Catholic Church, established missions to Indigenous peoples in the mid- to late nineteenth century, but none of these groups ever had a stranglehold on the religious culture of the region.

Protestants, Catholics, and Jews banded together to create a cultural and social infrastructure of hospitals, schools, and charitable institutions. Dale E. Soden (2004, 54–58) notes that adherents of these three religious traditions, which he sees as the de facto religious establishment of the region, cooperated with each other to an unprecedented degree to accomplish their common goals. While the Protestant elements of this coalition dominated the agenda and discourse, those in the economic and cultural elite were aware that they had to promote an ecumenical language and vision to communicate effectively to a diverse population who had, nevertheless, a common goal of "civilizing" the notoriously rough region.

Absent a dominant symbolic or religious culture, Euro-American settler writers helped to create a common sense of regional identity. They took their culturally inherited religious interpretation of nature, along with the generic Christian theological assumptions that undergirded it, and interpreted the Northwest's distinctive nature around them to establish a unique regional identity. Perhaps these poets became popular partly because they found a nature-centred lingua franca with which to communicate a common regional experience to a wide swath of the reading population.

Complicating the picture, John M. Findlay (1997) argues that the regional identity of the Pacific Northwest has been a shifting target since Europeans settled the area. He suggests that internal and external forces have shaped how Pacific Northwest insiders and outsiders have perceived themselves in relation to the land. He writes:

> Historical perspective suggests that the Northwest has been characterized not by any one single meaning, but by a series of meanings or identities emerging over the years – each one suited to the cultures and concerns of its time; each one paradoxically expressed in essentialist language; each one contested by a variety of other ideas and a host of subregional divisions; each one also capable of building in part on, or even absorbing its predecessors. (Findlay 1997, 61)

Findlay argues that much of the early settler identity of the US Pacific Northwest was made in conversation with – usually identifying with – the East Coast and California. It was not until the later part of the nineteenth century that regional identity came to be focused on differentiating the region from the East Coast and California (Findlay 1997, 44). According to Findlay, this was the time that nature became a central part of the region's identity, largely fuelled by railroad companies trying to "sell" the natural resources of the region to outsiders as an exceptional part of the region that could be exploited for profit or enjoyed for personal edification (Findlay 1997, 51–54).

Further, there was a racial aspect to this power and the "selling" of the region. This economic elite was white and invested in keeping economic, social, and cultural power in the hands of Euro-Americans. David J. Jepsen and David J. Norberg (2017, 179) write about the nineteenth-century Northwest:

> It's a complex picture of a racial hierarchy with whites sitting on top and in control. Writing about the settlement of the larger American West, historian

Patricia Nelson Limerick called it a "legacy of conquest," where the power elite used all necessary means to monopolize the region's resources, preserve white superiority, and shape society and culture to match their vision of the future.

As this elite class nurtured the seeds of reverential naturalism, they also hardened the racial hierarchies and disparities within the Northwest. Public discourses on regional identity were driven by economic elites who desired to tap into the natural resources of the region, as well as the region's natural beauty, to enhance their economic and cultural power (Findlay 1997, 46).

At least a part of the Pacific Northwest's nature-focused regional and individual identities can be traced back to the settler culture's encounter with the natural environment and literary interpretations of these encounters, combined with the drive for the economic promotion of the region by economic elites. While the data do not establish that residents of the Pacific Northwest engage spiritually with nature more than residents of other parts of the country, I would argue that the language of reverential naturalism has become an integral part of regional identity in public and private discourses, even for those who do not view nature as a place of religious or spiritual edification. This is a way that many residents of the region define themselves as Pacific Northwesterners to friends, family, and colleagues in other parts of Canada and the United States. Nature religion within the broader umbrella of reverential naturalism also provides a sense of regionally inflected individual spiritual identity.

Though it is only a small piece of the puzzle, in the findings of the Cascadia project and in the work of these Pacific Northwest poets and diarists we have small windows into the origins of the nature-focused discourse, which was framed by the region's cultural elite and exhibits continuity with today's expressions of reverential naturalism. Nature-centred public discourse serves as a regional lingua franca, a source of common identity and agreement in a region where no one religion has ever dominated and in which residents are often self-consciously suspicious of institutional forms of religious expression.

NOTES

1 For archival and interview data, see https://www.uvic.ca/research/centres/csrs/.
2 For more on the place of nature in the religious lives of minority religious groups in the region, see Brown, this volume.

REFERENCES

Albanese, Catherine L. 1990. *Nature Religion in America: From the Algonkian Indians to the New Age.* Chicago: University of Chicago Press.
Anonymous. 1911. In Memoriam: J.N. Aged 15." *Westminister Hall* 1 (8): 37.
Bain, Robert, ed. 1996. *Whitman's and Dickinson's Contemporaries: An Anthology of Their Verse.* Carbondale/Edwardsville: Southern Illinois University Press.

Carr, Emily. 2007. *Hundreds and Thousands: The Journals of Emily Carr.* Vancouver: Douglas and McIntyre.

Cooke, Belle W. 1871. *Tears and Victory, and Other Poems.* Salem: E.M. Waite Book and Job Printer.

Findlay, John. 1997. "A Fishy Proposition." In *Many Wests: Place, Culture, and Regional Identity,* edited by David M. Wrobel and Michael Steiner, 37–70. Lawrence: University Press of Kansas.

Geertz, Clifford. 1973. "Religion as a Cultural System." In *The Interpretation of Cultures,* 87–125. New York: Basic Books.

Higginson, Ella. 1907. *When the Birds Go North Again.* New York: Macmillan.

J.D.S. 1912. "Kindred." *Westminster Hall* 2 (3): 24.

Jepsen, David J., and David J. Norberg. 2017. *Contested Boundaries: A New Pacific Northwest History.* Hoboken, NJ: Wiley Blackwell.

Johnson, E. Pauline. 1926. *Legends of Vancouver.* Toronto: McClelland and Stewart.

Killen, Patricia O'Connell, and Mark Silk, eds. 2004. *Religion and Public Life in the Pacific Northwest: The None Zone.* Walnut Creek, CA: AltaMira Press.

O'Connell, Nicholas. 2015. *On Sacred Ground: The Spirit of Place in Pacific Northwest Literature.* Seattle: University of Washington Press.

Powers, Alfred. 1935. *History of Oregon Literature.* Portland: Metropolitan Press.

Shibley, Mark A. 2004. "Secular, but Spiritual in the Pacific Northwest." In *Religion and Public Life in the Pacific Northwest: The None Zone,* edited by Patricia O'Connell Killen and Mark Silk, 139–67. Walnut Creek, CA: AltaMira Press.

–. 2011. "Sacred Nature: Earth-Based Spirituality as Popular Religion in the Pacific Northwest." *Journal for the Study of Religion, Nature and Culture* (5) 2: 164–85.

Silk, Mark. 2009. "Cascadian Civil Religion from a North American Perspective." In *Cascadia: The Elusive Utopia,* edited by Douglas Todd, 105–14. Vancouver: Ronsdale Press.

Soden, Dale E. 2004. "Contesting the Soul of an Unlikely Land: Mainline Protestants, Catholics, and Reform and Conservative Jews in the Pacific Northwest." In *Religion and Public Life in the Pacific Northwest: The None Zone,* edited by Patricia O'Connell Killen and Mark Silk, 51–77. Walnut Creek, CA: AltaMira Press.

Victor, Frances Fuller. 1900. *Poems.* Author's edition.

Wellman, James K. 2008. *Evangelical vs. Liberal: The Clash of Christian Cultures in the Pacific Northwest.* New York: Oxford University Press.

Conclusion: Religion at the Edge of a Continent

PAUL BRAMADAT AND PATRICIA O'CONNELL KILLEN

"If I had known what [British Columbia] was like, I wouldn't have been content with a mere visit. I'd have been born here" (Barman 1996, 3). In this quote, humourist Stephen Leacock captures not only many residents' sense of Cascadia but also the ways the region is often framed by others in North America. Indeed, the combination of a temperate climate, political and cultural openness, picturesque natural surroundings, thriving urban centres, and apparently inexhaustible natural resources makes the Pacific Northwest unusual in North America. These features have inspired a gilded narrative, evident in Seattle's "Emerald City" nickname and British Columbia's "Best Place on Earth" licence plates. This confidence can produce an arrogance that many outsiders, as well as more humble insiders, find irritating. When a colleague who lives near Toronto visits us on the West Coast, he sometimes quips that it is hard to see the sky in the summer, "because of all of the smug."

Beyond the natural wonders of the region, one of its most distinctive social features is the fact that conventional religious activities, identities, and institutions seem much less influential here than anywhere else in North America. This is not new. Historian of Catholicism Jeffrey Burns concluded that along the Pacific Coast, Catholic leaders have always faced "the difficult task of inspiring an indifferent people to devotion" (Burns 1987, 15). That the proportion of religious Nones in the Pacific Northwest is almost twice that of many other states and provinces calls out for an explanation. The story of the decline of institutional religion (especially mainstream Christianity but also conservative evangelical groups) might seem simple at first: surely the "demand" for what religion is "supplying" has shrunk faster here than elsewhere (and the shrinking may have started earlier, as is suggested by Mark Silk and Tina Block and Lynne Marks in this volume). That is not exactly untrue, and it is certainly the case that the region continues to be the None Zone (Killen and Silk 2004).

Nonetheless, it is wise to be suspicious any time a single story about any region (or, for that matter, any religion or individual) coalesces, and especially when it becomes hegemonic. We should always ask how this story emerged, when it became dominant, and what it occludes. After all, there are other less burnished facts beneath the generally positive "Cascadia consensus," including racially exclusive immigration policies until the late 1960s; the marginalization of African American, Asian, Latin American, and Indigenous communities (especially evident in parts of Cascadia South); often destructive natural-resource extraction practices; and the dispossession of the region's original inhabitants.

Here, we are reminded of the opening line of American novelist Charles Frazier's *Thirteen Moons:* "There is no scatheless rapture." However, students and scholars of the region ought to share an interest not just in ensuring that the region's dark stories are told but in offering an account of the region that interrogates the stereotypes with which it is associated. For example, the supply-and-demand metaphor above can be complicated by, among other things, the high levels of ethnoreligious diversity in Vancouver; strong traditions of religious and postreligious libertarianism outside of the main urban areas (especially in the United States); innovative articulations of Christianity; high levels of participation in activities such as yoga, acupuncture, and meditation, evident throughout the "western slope" area; and a resurgence of Indigenous cultures and spiritualities over the past five decades and recently, and quite robustly, in Canada.

Key Findings

In the project out of which this book emerged, an interdisciplinary and international team worked, first, to create a new and extensive pool of data, and second, to use this data to interpret some of the most striking aspects of Cascadia.[1] The three themes around which our initial discussions revolved – the implications of secularization, the significance of the border, and the barriers that might exist for traditional believers in an untraditional region – were supplemented by questions that arose during team discussions and as each author assessed the data independently. In the process of working through our questions, a complex picture of religion, society, spirituality, and secularization emerged. A few observations can be made about the key findings in the book.

The Differences

As a region, Cascadia is distinctive. Its difference from other regions of Canada and the United States is evident in both the quantitative and qualitative data gathered in this study. Institutional expressions of historical Christian forms never gained the traction here that they did in other parts of North

America. Through successive waves of in-migration the fates and fortunes of religious institutions and communities of all kinds have evolved rapidly, though at varying paces. The relative weakness of the larger Christian denominations contributed to creative ecumenical and interfaith collaborations aimed at translating into social and cultural life the inherited values of religious communities. For example, care for the environment is a major focus of these interfaith organizations today, a priority in common cause with many of the Nones.

Religious leaders and communities that sustain themselves in Cascadia do so through immigration and a willingness to adapt to the region's more open religious environment. That environment is part of an interwoven tapestry of weaker social institutions, caution about relationships, and tentativeness born of a desire to take advantage of the next economic opportunity. People may experience the freedom of Cascadia as a blessing or a curse; whether the region is framed as teeming with opportunities or threatening individuals with spirit-crushing isolation depends on one's circumstances and perspective. For example, Seattleite Stephanie, contrasting herself with cousins in the Midwest, lamented growing up in Cascadia without a large extended family, which could be "like padding" around her, a group of people with whom she could have "fewer boundaries."

For a spiritual experience, most Cascadians turn to nature. Seattleite Roger described seeing salmon spawn for the first time as a "conversion experience" that affected his three-plus decades in ordained ministry. Vancouverite Sophie commented that no one will say "you're totally off your rocker" if you say you believe in "Mother Earth and the beauty of nature." Kamal, a millennial Muslim from Vancouver, agreed and noted: "Just being in nature, you feel peace and serenity," whereas when he lived in Toronto, "there was a lot more social contact, people contact." As Susanna Morrill describes so well in her chapter in this volume, even in the work of the region's early poets, we can see the encounter with nature cast as an experience of the sublime that can simultaneously reinforce and replace conventional religious ideas and practices.

The None Zone

According to the 2017 Pacific Northwest Social Survey (PNSS), which was an integral part of our study (see Wilkins-Laflamme 2018), 49 percent of the population in British Columbia and 44 percent of the population of Oregon and Washington were religious Nones, making them the largest religious group in British Columbia and the second largest, behind Christians (46 percent), in Oregon and Washington. Even given variations from survey to survey, these numbers reflect the steady growth of Nones in the region, as Mark Silk observes in his chapter: from 25 percent in 2001 to 32 percent in 2014 to 44 percent for

Oregon and Washington; and from 30 percent in 2001 to 35 percent in 2011 to 49 percent for British Columbia. Cascadia's Nones are, as Sarah Wilkins-Laflamme describes in her chapter, mostly younger; more likely to have been born in the United States or Canada; and, in Washington and Oregon (but not British Columbia), university-educated. Further, they express a range of religious or spiritual positions: from holding beliefs in the supernatural with some connection to the spiritual but disconnected from formal religious institutions, to being indifferent and oblivious to anything spiritual or religious, to being adamantly antireligion.

Cascadia's sizable None population prompted many questions. For scholars of religion, the large proportion of Nones suggests the value of reflecting on the ways religion and spirituality are lived in everyday life; this "lived religion" approach complements the more conventional interest in religion as an institutionalized system of doctrines, ideas, rituals, prescribed practices, and formal norms. In particular, for the Nones who participated in the project's focus groups, especially the millennial Nones, being in nature played an outsized role in their experience and expression of what might be labelled "the spiritual."

In its large proportion of Nones, Silk argues that Cascadia has not been an outlier but rather the advance guard of the growth of this phenomenon in the rest of the United States and Canada. Indeed, it is important to underline that this is not a new development in the region. This form of (ir)religiosity has been passed down within irreligious families for generations, as Tina Block and Lynne Marks describe in their chapter. In other parts of Canada and the United States, irreligion has much shallower roots.

Reverential Naturalism

Scholars invent metaphors, methods, and theories to describe and interpret phenomena of a particular time and place. Often, in much social scientific research since Weber, Marx, Durkheim, and others, those tools "work" across time and space. Nonetheless, sometimes we need to question whether the inherited academic resources at our disposal accurately render the people, places, and experiences we encounter during our research. In Chapter 1, Paul Bramadat proposes that in Cascadia the perspectives on religion, the natural world, and spirituality one sees at the level of the individual and the group seem to be informed by a metanarrative he calls reverential naturalism. This variant of naturalism – in which spiritualized discourses are not anathema to a robust scientific approach to the world – seems to provide a common language and habitus for residents, regardless of how they might identify spiritually or religiously. This metanarrative is, or at least purports to be, radically inclusive (since almost anyone can enjoy the natural beauty of the region), and it might explain why so few of the theists, atheists, agnostics, liberals, or conservatives we encountered in our focus groups and interviews expressed animosity toward any other groups or this broad ethos. This distinctive approach is certainly well entrenched in the Pacific Northwest, although the generally increasing number of Nones and decreasing social stigma attached to spiritual eclecticism might combine with the challenges posed by climate change, pandemics, and the advent of the "Anthropocene" to create the conditions for the spread of reverential naturalism to other regions.

The Difference the Border Makes

Our research project tested the premise that shared characteristics transcend the national border between Cascadia North and South. The region's vulnerability to earthquakes, tsunamis, and volcanic eruptions is a recognized fact of life, as are emergency preparedness drills. While the power and dominance of nature cannot be ignored, it contrasts with the relative mildness of Cascadia's climate and its abundance of food, both of which are benefits of the mix of ocean currents and coastal microclimates that dominate the region from the crest of the Cascades to the Pacific Ocean. In the larger urban spaces, people tend to prize openness to difference and celebrate multiculturalism. North and south of the border, individualism is a cherished value, and libertarianism thrives. Environmental concerns are also prominent in a population profoundly attuned to nature. So, much is shared across the border.

During interviews, observations, and focus groups, differences between participants from British Columbia and from Oregon and Washington also became clear. British Columbians were more sensitive to the rights of Indigenous peoples and ethnic, racial, religious, and cultural diversity than were those from the United States, with some pastors and millennials from the United States being more sensitive to these matters than their Elders. These differences are partly attributable to the different attitudes toward and policies regarding immigration and diversity in Canada and the United States, the larger and currently more politically active Indigenous population in British Columbia, and the differing cultural narratives regarding identity and national exceptionalism of the two countries. The different histories of the two countries with regard to religious organizations and their relationship to government also come into play. Formal religious disestablishment in the United States led to a very different relationship between religion (specifically, church) and state than we see in Canada. In the latter society, certain forms of Christianity have been tacitly (and sometimes quite explicitly) privileged but never de jure established, whereas in the United States, religion and politics interacted in a much more officially constrained manner, even though Christian norms and privileges were, de facto, pervasive throughout the culture. Moreover, our impression is that, like most Canadians, the British Columbians we met expected their governments to be the primary protectors and agents of human welfare. In the United States, such government involvement is inflected with religious, political, and social positions that resist the notion of a government-enacted obligation to neighbours. The greater number of evangelical Christians in Oregon and Washington (and the greater tradition of political activism among this group in the United States), when compared to British Columbia, may help to explain the differences we observed.

Indigeneity in Cascadia North and South

As we were imagining this research project several years ago, we anticipated that there were likely to be differences between the ways Indigenous peoples' experiences would be framed by Canadians and Americans. We had not, however, imagined just how stark the differences would be until we started addressing the issues explicitly with participants. By way of an illustration, most of the Americans we interviewed – clergy as well as nonclergy – were not aware of the name of the Indigenous communities (tribes) that once lived (or still live) in the territory on which their homes, churches, and places of work were situated. In Canada, religious leaders generally knew the names of the communities in question and had often reached out to collaborate on issues of common concern (e.g., homelessness). Furthermore, the Indigenous people we met in the US did not seem at all optimistic about their current political latitude, whereas First Nations in Canada certainly felt that in some ways they were living in a time of unprecedented political and cultural opportunity.

Two facts may explain these differences. First, in 2015, the Canadian government released the Truth and Reconciliation Commission's report. This marked the end of roughly seven years of nationwide (and court-ordered) public hearings into the often brutal mistreatment of Indigenous peoples in Canada. By the time we entered the field for this project (in late 2017), the media coverage of these hearings was ubiquitous, whereas, in contrast, in the United States, political successes such as the Boldt Decision (1974) on fishing were decades old. Second, Indigenous peoples make up roughly 5 percent of the Canadian (and British Columbian) population, whereas they represent about 2 percent of the United States (and Cascadia South) population; consequently, their capacity to raise issues of concern is higher in Canada. There, Indigenous peoples have been quite prominent in the media and legal and political spheres, especially in the past two decades, which have seen a formal apology from the Conservative prime minister Stephen Harper in 2008, key victories in the Supreme Court, and the creation of the Truth and Reconciliation Commission. In the United States, tensions between liberals and conservatives and relations between the dominant (European-origin) population and African American and Latino citizens (and neighbours in Mexico) attract more attention both at the political and media levels. As well, in 2016, the election of Donald Trump initiated a series of political changes that pushed Indigenous issues even further to the periphery of the US political horizon. In Canada, by contrast, 2015 saw the election of Justin Trudeau, who made reconciliation a high priority of his Liberal government (a commitment some argue he has not honoured adequately).

New Directions for Research

In our view, good research often raises questions for future projects and generations. It is worthwhile to provide a brief account of what we are still pondering and the questions that we did not get the chance to address in detail in our study but that do merit consideration in the near future.

Cascadia East/Rural/North

Americans sometimes refer to a "Cascade curtain" separating the larger and denser urban spaces on the western slope from the rest of the region. In our view, the significance of the east-west (or rural-urban) differences in Canada or the United States is sometimes overstated. After all, although Vancouver, Seattle, and arguably Portland and Victoria are global cities, with the expansion of communication technology and the reality that the major markets for regional products are located across the Pacific, a global or cosmopolitan perspective is not limited to the large urban areas. However, beyond the PNSS and the archival sources that covered all of Cascadia, most of the qualitative data for the project focused on the mainly urban spaces on the western slope. While constraints on time, money, and personnel – and the fact that approximately four-fifths of the population resides in this relatively urban subregion – made this a reasonable research choice, it also created a lacuna in the volume. Another study could and should focus on the parts of Cascadia that we were not able to visit, primarily cities and towns east of the Cascades, farther north in British Columbia, and the smaller towns and cities along the Pacific Coast in Oregon, Washington, and British Columbia. In our view, studies that engage the real differences in the scale and character of social life, economies, cultural mores, politics, and the history and role of religious communities in less populated parts of the region would provide useful comparative data that would modulate and add nuance to, though not undercut, claims made in this volume.

Moreover, how perspectives on environmental protection and climate change differ between densely populated urban areas and expansive but sparsely populated rural regions is an important question to pursue in future research. Some of that difference may be accounted for by sources of livelihood in extractive industries and agriculture; some, in Cascadia South, might be attributed to the larger proportion of the rural population east of the Cascades that holds conservative and libertarian political positions. Some of these differences might be explained by the fact that rural populations tend to harbour less romantic views of nature than urban populations. These differences might also be influenced by the persistence of enduring ethnic-religious identity and immigration patterns in agricultural subregions.

Politics

While we were in the field, we asked about, and were attuned to, the implications of the different trajectories of formal party politics on the ways that religion is imagined and challenged in the region. Not many participants seemed to want to talk about these issues. The source of their reluctance remains unclear. Perhaps they were eager not to fray already fragile social ties, at least in Cascadia South, where political debate has become so corrosive. Perhaps some assumed that residents were not supporters of then US president Donald Trump and that the region would be likely to chart its own course, to the extent possible. The considerable respect that Washington State attorney general Bob Ferguson has garnered among state attorneys general in suing the Trump administration for violation of the Constitution and environmental protection statutes supports this possibility. Perhaps they were avoiding felt-but-not-yet-acknowledged contradictions between chosen narratives of the region and the hard facts of economic structures and policies. Additionally, some may have refrained out of concern for the cohesiveness of fragile local religious communities.

A question that might be engaged more deeply in the coming years would be the implications of the Trump presidency on the ways Cascadia South residents feel about their own national "project," as opposed to the ways that contemporary political realities have led Canadians to feel about theirs. Are the two sides of the border likely to become more distinctive? Do the formal political differences make a regional consciousness more or less difficult? How might political responses to pandemics, climate change, or economic instability impact the kinds of religious and cultural patterns we have traced in this book?

Reconciliation and Racism

Within Canadian and American societies, there are efforts to foster reconciliation with the people who were either displaced or mistreated in the process of creating the political and economic systems many of us enjoy today in the Pacific Northwest. As we mentioned above, Indigenous peoples bore the initial brunt of the forces that created these societies, but racialized (especially African American, South and East Asian) minorities were also often badly treated. Indeed, in Cascadia South, the racism directed against Asian, Black, and Latin American residents (e.g., in Oregon, laws against African American in-migration were not repealed until 1926) has been particularly virulent. We have seen efforts made to rectify historical wrongs, but it would be worthwhile to ask: Are any of these problems addressed in ways that are indicative of Cascadia as a region, or do the patterns of engagement reflect the national (or state/provincial) norms, laws, policies, and priorities? To what extent does devotion to the bright Cascadia story blind citizens to structural racism and the imaginative erasure of visible minorities, and does the border make a difference? As well, should we expect Indigenous issues to remain politically peripheral in Cascadia South, or might the high priority of these matters in Canada influence the prominence of the questions in US public discourse? In cities such as Seattle and Vancouver, where there are large cohorts of South and East Asian minorities, might these groups work together in the future to deal with issues of systemic or historical racism and religious discrimination? What might be the impact in the churches of Cascadia North of the Black Lives Matter activism that was often nested within US African American churches? As Douglas Todd (2008), Patricia O'Connell Killen and Mark Silk (2004), Chelsea Horton (this volume), and Suzanne Crawford O'Brien (this volume) suggest, there is a historical pattern of residents of the region working across the border when it comes to Indigenous rights (e.g., whether a particular group is "extinct") and many environmental campaigns (e.g., regarding a pipeline from Alberta that would massively increase tanker traffic in the Salish Sea between Seattle and Vancouver). Future research might trace and interpret the ways these political collaborations unfold.

Kids These Days

Readers will notice that the data we collected reflected a special interest in the religious, irreligious, and spiritual perspectives of younger Cascadians. After all, it is really in the lives of millennials that we see most clearly what Tina Block and Lynne Marks in this volume describe as "lived irreligion," the normalization of lives lived in what philosopher Charles Taylor (2007) calls "the immanent frame," without any reference to a metaphysical dimension or a conventional, institutionally moored sense of sacrality. Since Cascadia appears to be a decade or two ahead of changes that seem to be unfolding elsewhere in Canada and the United States, it would be interesting to follow the region's millennials (and their younger siblings and children – Generations Z and Λ) as they age to see what kinds of attitudes and practices they develop regarding environmentalism, economics, politics, race, sexuality, and religion. Additional studies of these younger Cascadians would be inherently interesting and may provide scholars with a sense of emerging social and religious trends in North America.

The View from the Edge

If the Pacific Northwest is a kind of bellwether for changes we may see elsewhere (see Silk and Wilkins-Laflamme, this volume), we might wonder what new metaphors or fully articulated metanarratives we will need to develop to understand the changes occurring in the region, especially among younger people for whom traditional categories (such as religion, of course, but also irreligion and, increasingly, spirituality) are at least sometimes, as Paul Bramadat puts it, inert or radically polysemic. As well, is Cascadia undergoing an advanced form of secularization that is comprehensible within existing analytical frameworks, or would it also be fruitful to pay closer attention to the sometimes idiosyncratic or counterintuitive local articulations of religion, irreligion, and spirituality one observes? Is it possible that in Cascadia we can observe reverential naturalism, but also something akin to lived secularism, lived irreligion, or strategic secularism, in which some aspects of experience (e.g., personal-wellness regimes and engagement with the natural world) are nonetheless framed in ways that seem to echo recognizable expressions of religion and spirituality?

Implications

In addition to the key findings outlined above, by the end of the project, several of us noticed consensus developing around normative political considerations that are worth sharing.

Choosing a life in which identifying with or participating in organized religious communities plays no role in the process of creating meaning for oneself is not only quite unusual in human history since the medieval period but has wider implications for the future. Interviewees from our project described fluid, loose connections, a stance of searching. Some described loneliness, isolation, and a reluctance to commit. Cumulatively, most of the interviewees, especially millennial interviewees, were aware of and concerned about weaker bonds of social connection. In the "immanent frame," what might these patterns mean for larger social and political life? Will a region that tilts toward leaving individuals on their own commit over the long haul to a viable social safety net? Can the population care as much for people as it cares for orcas, salmon, trees, and pets? Is a progressive and viable environmental policy sustainable over the long term? Given the tenuousness of social bonds in a region characterized by successive waves of in-migration, weaker social institutions, and a privileging of individual rights and freedoms, it is worthwhile to wonder whether sufficient will and imagination can coalesce in Cascadia to make sustained progress on these issues.

Rivers, oceans, flora, and fauna are not respecters of the border. Concern over the consequences of oil spills, tanker traffic, and destructive extraction of lumber and minerals are shared by populations on both sides of the forty-ninth parallel. Yet Washington State has not succeeded in instituting a carbon tax as British Columbia did in 2008. Furthermore, Vancouver, Seattle–Tacoma, and Portland are the spine of a technology corridor that runs from Eugene, Oregon, northwards. As we see most clearly in the Seattle and Vancouver areas, high tech brings with it housing pressure, transportation challenges, cost-of-living concerns, and income disparity, all of which could benefit from regional cooperation in the creation of solutions.

We wrote this conclusion during the COVID-19 pandemic, a crisis that has underlined global interconnectedness and fragility. It is also worth noting that "Cascadia Day" is May 18, to mark the day in 1980 that Mount St. Helens erupted and reminded us that Cascadia North and South share a vulnerability to global events and natural disasters. Indeed, the region is part of the "ring of fire," the system of active volcanoes that surrounds the Pacific Ocean; residents also sometimes talk of "the big one," the earthquake that is anticipated to occur any time in the next 150 years and will have a devastating impact on life in and adjacent to the "Cascadia subduction zone." While our research underlines the attitudinal differences between Canada and the United States, we wonder whether cross-border Cascadian approaches – those that exist or might be brought into being – will enable us to respond to challenges such as social dislocation, pandemics, climate change, and natural disasters.

***

There is an elusive, fluid, some might say even contradictory quality to Cascadia. Our research revealed what we describe as the Cascadia consensus, which is accompanied by the rapturous "Best Place on Earth" narrative that many of the region's residents and others choose to tell. The narrative accents promise and possibility in a place where, we heard, abundant natural resources and beauty mirror what is possible for human beings. This is a place of new beginnings, of imagining what has not yet been imagined.

Nevertheless, for all its promise, there is a dark subtext to the story of Cascadia. From the beginning, both economically and socially, the region has been built on conquest and exploitation. For example, the "Oregon Country" was the only territory in the United States where Congress authorized settlement before negotiating treaties with the Indigenous populations whose land was being taken; in Canada, most of British Columbia remains "unceded" territory. In many ways, Cascadia is unique in North America economically and culturally. The flow of capital between itself and the continent in which it is situated distinguishes it from other regions, even though it shares with other regions a similar pattern of erasure of thousands of years of Indigenous inhabitation and the contributions of residents of Hispanic, Oceanic, African American, and Asian descent. In particular, disparities of wealth within Cascadia are extreme, and entities far beyond its borders garner most of the profit from resource extraction and agriculture.

The pollution of the Salish Sea. The decline in species. The melting of glaciers on active volcanoes. Economic disparity between migrant agricultural workers, mostly from Latin America, and more recent and often Asian in-migrants working in technology, health care, and education. Family stories of both success and disappointment, told by many who migrated to the region from points north, south, east, and west, during and after initial colonization. All of these speak to a more complicated, less innocent story.

Against this backdrop of powerful nature, human possibility, and convenient historical amnesia, it is clear that religion and spirituality continue to evolve and that Cascadia is an increasingly secular place. That very secularity allows space for religious ventures, be they the preservation of historical forms of belief and practice or the exploration and testing of new practices and ideas. Behind and beneath all of these, however, is Cascadia as a place that situates humans in a distinct manner not just in relation to one another, but in relation to flora, fauna, cityscape, and landscape. In Cascadia, it is arguably nature that leaves the most indelible mark on residents' lives. Our bodies, our minds, and the stories we tell to make sense of social and personal change are all disciplined by institutions, discourses, and – especially in this region – our physical locations on maps both literal and symbolic. In Cascadia, we may observe 1) the emergence of a powerful story that frames the region not just as the best but as the most secular place on earth; 2) the relegation of certain forms of Christianity to the periphery of the public arena; 3) the romanticization of certain kinds of spirituality (Indigenous, Buddhist, Hindu) by an individualistic consumer culture; 4) the ongoing evolution and creativity of certain forms of religion and spirituality (yoga, mindfulness, evangelical Protestantism); and 5) a pervasive, distinctive, and reverential approach to the natural world.

Other regions in North America and the rest of the world may or may not be blessed by Cascadia's natural amenities, but there are similar political and social dynamics at work elsewhere on the continent that might nonetheless propel those regions, both religiously and socially, in a westward direction. In this sense, Cascadia is an excellent laboratory for seeing some of the deeper forces at work in the religious, spiritual, and secular spheres of North America.

NOTE

1 For archival and interview data, see https://www.uvic.ca/research/centres/csrs/.

REFERENCES

Barman, Jean. 1996. *The West beyond the West: A History of British Columbia*. Rev. ed. Toronto: University of Toronto Press.
Burns, Jeffrey M. 1987. "Building the Best: A History of Catholic Parish Life in the Pacific States." In *The American Catholic Parish: A History from 1850 to the Present*. Vol. 2, *The*

Pacific States, Intermountain West, and Midwest States, edited by Jay P. Dolan, 7–135. New York: Paulist Press.

Killen, Patricia O'Connell, and Mark Silk, eds. 2004. *Religion and Public Life in the Pacific Northwest: The None Zone.* Walnut Creek, CA: AltaMira Press.

Taylor, Charles. 2007. *A Secular Age.* Cambridge, MA: Belknap Press/Harvard University Press.

Todd, Douglas, ed. 2008. *Cascadia: The Elusive Utopia – Exploring the Spirit of the Pacific Northwest.* Vancouver: Ronsdale Press.

Wilkins-Laflamme, Sarah. 2018. "The Religious, Spiritual, Secular and Social Landscapes of the Pacific Northwest: Part 2." *UWSpace.* https://uwspace.uwaterloo.ca/handle/10012/13406.

Contributors

Tina Block is an associate professor in the Department of Philosophy, History, and Politics at Thompson Rivers University in Kamloops, British Columbia. Her research and teaching focus on religion, irreligion, gender, and the family in postwar North America. She is the author of *The Secular Northwest: Religion and Irreligion in Everyday Postwar Life* (UBC Press, 2016).

Paul Bramadat is a professor and director of the Centre for Studies in Religion and Society at the University of Victoria. He is interested in religion, spirituality, and secularity in contemporary liberal democracies. He is the author of *The Church on the World's Turf: An Evangelical Christian Student Group at a Secular University* (Oxford University Press, 2000) and coeditor of *International Migration and the Governance of Religious Diversity* (McGill-Queen's University Press, 2009), *Radicalization and Securitization in Canada and Beyond* (University of Toronto Press, 2014), *Religion and Ethnicity in Canada* (University of Toronto Press, 2009), *Christianity and Ethnicity in Canada* (University of Toronto Press, 2008), *Public Health in the Age of Anxiety: Religious and Cultural Reasons for Vaccine Hesitancy* (University of Toronto Press, 2017), *Spirituality in Hospice Palliative Care* (State University of New York Press, 2013), and *Urban Religious Events: Public Spirituality in Contested Spaces* (Bloomsbury Press, 2021). He has published numerous chapters in books as well as articles in *Religion, State and Society; Journal of the American Academy of Religion; Studies in Religion; Ethnicities; Ethnologies;* and the *Journal of International Migration and Integration.*

Rachel D. Brown is the program coordinator and religious studies teaching fellow at the Centre for Studies in Religion and Society at the University of Victoria. She holds a PhD in religious diversity in North America from Wilfrid Laurier University and specializes in religion and migration, food practice, contemporary Islam, and lived religion. Her recent publications include articles and book chapters on the food practices of Muslim migrants and researcher positionality and knowledge production, an article titled "Muslim Integration and French Society" for Oxford University Press's *Encyclopedia of Politics and Religion,* and a coedited book titled *Prayer as Transgression? The Social Relations of Prayer in Healthcare Settings* (McGill-Queen's University Press, 2020).

Katie E. Corcoran received a PhD from the University of Washington and is currently an associate professor of sociology at West Virginia University. Her areas of expertise are congregations, religious beliefs and emotions, organizations, criminology, culture, and social networks. She is the author of *High on God: How Megachurches Won the Heart of America,* coauthored with James K. Wellman and Kate Stockly (Oxford University Press, 2020).

Suzanne Crawford O'Brien is a professor of religion and culture and chair of the Native American and Indigenous Studies Program at Pacific Lutheran University (PLU) in Tacoma, Washington. At PLU, she teaches courses in Indigenous American religious traditions and religious diversity in North America. A fourth-generation Oregonian, her scholarship focuses on Chinook and Coast Salish religious and cultural traditions, religion and healing, religion and ecology, and the intersections of social and environmental justice. Her introductory textbook, *Religion and Culture in Native America* (Rowman and Littlefield, 2020), was written in collaboration with her mentor, Inés Talamantez. She is also the author of *Coming Full Circle: Spirituality and Wellness among Native Communities in the Pacific Northwest* (University of Nebraska, 2014) and *Native American Religious Traditions* (Routledge, 2006) and editor of *Religion and Healing in Native America: Pathways for Renewal* (Praeger, 2008).

Chelsea Horton is a historian and educator of settler heritage, with a PhD in Indigenous history from the University of British Columbia, who works at the intersection of academic and applied histories. Based in Snaw-Naw-As Territory on Vancouver Island, her primary areas of practice are research and teaching related to Indigenous rights and title; Indigenous knowledge, land use, and occupancy; Indigenous religious encounters; and settler-colonial histories and their cumulative effects in Canada. The coeditor, with Tolly Bradford, of the interdisciplinary volume *Mixed Blessings: Indigenous Encounters with Christianity in Canada* (UBC Press, 2016), she served as research coordinator for the "Religion, Spirituality, and Secularity in the Pacific Northwest" project from 2017 to 2019. She is an associate fellow at the Centre for Studies in Religion and Society at the University of Victoria.

Patricia O'Connell Killen is a professor of religion emerita and Humanities Division Faculty Research Fellow at Pacific Lutheran University. She earned a PhD in religious studies from Stanford University. Her research interests include how cultural wisdom traditions are (and are not) employed as resources for addressing novel challenges; the history of Catholicism in North America; and religion and spirituality in western North America, especially in the Pacific Northwest. Among her publications, she is the primary editor, with Mark Silk, of *Religion and Public Life in the Pacific Northwest: The None Zone* (AltaMira Press, 2004); coeditor, with Roberta Stringham Brown, of *Selected Letters of A.M.A. Blanchet, Bishop of Walla Walla and Nesqualy, 1846–1879* (University of Washington Press, 2013); and coeditor, with Mark Silk, of *The Future of Catholicism in America* (Columbia University Press, 2019). In 2001, she received the Paul Bator Memorial Award from the Canadian Catholic Historical Association for "Writing the Pacific Northwest Back into Canadian and U.S. Catholic History: Geography, Demographics, and Regional Religion," CCHA, *Historical Studies* 66 (2000): 74–91.

Lynne Marks is a professor in the Department of History at the University of Victoria, in Victoria, British Columbia. She is the author of *Revivals and Roller Rinks: Religion, Leisure and Identity in Late-Nineteenth-Century Small-Town Ontario* (University of Toronto Press, 1996) and *Infidels and the Damn Churches: Irreligion and Religion in Settler British Columbia* (UBC Press, 2017), as well as a range of articles and book chapters on topics related to the history of religion, irreligion, ethnicity, social welfare, gender, class, and feminism in Canada.

Susanna Morrill is an associate professor of religious studies at Lewis and Clark College in Portland, Oregon. Her work in the recent past has focused on how early Mormon women used popular literature to argue for the theological importance of their roles in the home, community, and church. She is the author of *White Roses on the Floor of Heaven: Nature and Flower Imagery in Latter-Day Saints Women's Literature, 1880–1920* (Routledge, 2006). Her chapters and articles have appeared in the *Journal of Mormon Studies, The Blackwell Companion to Religion in America* (Blackwell, 2010), *The Religious History of American Women* (University of North Carolina Press, 2007), and *Historicizing Tradition in the Study of Religion* (De Gruyter, 2005).

Mark Silk is the director of the Leonard E. Greenberg Center for the Study of Religion in Public Life and a professor of religion in public life at Trinity College in Hartford. He is the author of *Spiritual Politics: Religion and America since World War II* (Simon & Schuster, 1988); *Unsecular Media: Making News of Religion in America* (University of Illinois Press, 1995); and, with Andrew Walsh, *One Nation,*

Divisible: How Regional Religious Differences Shape American Politics (Rowman and Littlefield, 2008). He writes a weekly column for the Religion News Service.

James K. Wellman Jr. is a professor and chair of the Comparative Religion Program in the Jackson School of International Studies at the University of Washington. In 2017, he received a Five-Year Term Professorship in Global Christianity, which supports his recent initiative to create a Center for Global Christian Studies at the Jackson School. His areas of expertise are in American religious culture, history, and politics. He also works on and teaches in religion and international issues, particularly related to religious nationalism, human security, and US foreign policy. He has received numerous nominations for the Distinguished Teaching Award. His publications include an award-winning book, *The Gold Coast Church and the Ghetto: Christ and Culture in Mainline Protestantism* (University of Illinois Press, 1999), and the edited volumes *Belief and Bloodshed: Religion and Violence across Time and Tradition* (Rowman and Littlefield, 2007) and *Religion and Human Security: A Global Perspective* (Oxford University Press, 2012). His monograph *Evangelical vs. Liberal: The Clash of Christian Cultures in the Pacific Northwest* (Oxford University Press, 2008) received a Honorable Mention for the Distinguished Book Award by the Society for the Scientific Study of Religion. In 2012, he published *Rob Bell and the New American Christianity* (Abingdon, 2012). His newest book, coauthored with Katie Corcoran and Kate Stockly, is *High on God: How Megachurches Won the Heart of America* (Oxford University Press, 2020).

Sarah Wilkins-Laflamme is an associate professor in the Department of Sociology and Legal Studies at the University of Waterloo, in Ontario, Canada. She completed a DPhil in sociology at the University of Oxford in 2015. Her research interests include quantitative methods, sociology of religion, immigration and ethnicity, and political sociology. She has published articles in top Canadian and international peer-reviewed journals in the fields of sociology of religion, religious studies, and political science, including the *Journal for the Scientific Study of Religion; Canadian Review of Political Science; Sociology of Religion; Canadian Review of Sociology; Studies in Religion;* and the *British Journal of Sociology.* She is coauthor of *None of the Above: Nonreligious Identity in the U.S. and Canada* (New York University Press, 2020).

Michael Wilkinson is a professor of sociology at Trinity Western University. His research interests include evangelicalism, Pentecostalism, globalization, and religious diversity. His publications include *After the Revival: Pentecostalism and the Making of a Canadian Church* (McGill-Queen's University Press, 2020), *A Culture of Faith: Evangelical Congregations in Canada* (McGill-Queen's University Press, 2015), *Catch the Fire: Soaking Prayer and Charismatic Renewal* (Northern Illinois University Press,

2014), and *The Spirit Said Go: Pentecostal Immigrants in Canada* (Peter Lang, 2006). He is the editor of *Encyclopedia of Global Pentecostalism* (Brill, 2021), *Winds from the North: Canadian Contributions to the Pentecostal Movement* (Brill, 2010), *Canadian Pentecostalism: Transition and Transformation* (McGill-Queen's University Press, 2009), *Global Pentecostal Movements: Migration, Mission, and Public Religion* (Brill, 2012), *Pentecostals and the Body* (Brill, 2017), and *A Liberating Spirit: Pentecostals and Social Action in North America* (Wipf and Stock, 2010). He is currently working on *Pentecostal World,* to be published in the Routledge World Series.

Index